MW00331517

Robin Gaines

DAGNABIT!

A Sequel and Anthology

by Mike Gordon

DAGNABIT!

DAGNABIT! ©2021 Mike Gordon. All Rights Reserved.
This book may not be reproduced in whole or in part, by any means, mechanical
or digital, without the written permission from the author or publisher.

ISBN: 978-1-57833-853-5 (Soft)
978-1-57833-852-8 (Hard)
Library of Congress Control Number: 2021909000

First printing June 2021

Book Design: Carmen Maldonado, 𝕿𝖔𝖉𝖉 𝕮𝖔𝖒𝖒𝖚𝖓𝖎𝖈𝖆𝖙𝖎𝖔𝖓𝖘
The body typeface for this book was set in ITC Clearface.

Published by:
Miracle Mile Publishing Co.
611 E. 12th Ave., Anchorage, AK 99501

Distributed by:

𝕿𝖔𝖉𝖉 𝕮𝖔𝖒𝖒𝖚𝖓𝖎𝖈𝖆𝖙𝖎𝖔𝖓𝖘
611 E. 12th Ave. • Anchorage, Alaska 99501-4603
(907) 274-8633 (TODD) • Fax: (907) 929-5550
with other offices in Juneau and Fairbanks, Alaska
sales@toddcom.com • **WWW.ALASKABOOKSANDCALENDARS.COM**

Printed in China through **Alaska Print Brokers**, Anchorage, Alaska

Dust jacket cover art by Ken Kennell.

Dedication

for Shelli

What others say about
DAGNABIT!

Open **DAGNABIT!** *to any chapter to reveal a gem of a story alive with vivid characterization and portrayal of life in Alaska told with laugh-at-life humor and brutal honesty. The reader's bonus is insight into two of Alaska's most colorful characters: Ruben Gaines and Mike Gordon.*

Tony Lewkowski
Close friend and confidant

....

I am exceedingly grateful to Mike Gordon for having penned this exceptional work, which transports me back to the Anchorage and the Alaska I grew up in. His deeply personal narrative is moving and so well written that moments into this work I am transported back to a history that only those of us fortunate enough to have lived it can recall. DAGNABIT! is so well told that even those who have never visited Alaska can and will come to know it through this work, which I consider a quintessential coming of age story for Mr. Gordon, Anchorage and Alaska.

I have never read a book in my entire life that has moved me as deeply as DAGNABIT!. Perhaps it's because of my personal relationship to the times and places so well described or perhaps it's just Mike's writing and gift of storytelling. Either way, I would encourage anyone to sit back and enjoy this book. Just don't be surprised when you find yourself taken away by it and completely immersed in the tales and writing within.

Lastly, if you are also fortunate enough to remember Ruben Gaines' voice, hear it as you read. If fate should shine upon us and we meet "a little further up the creek" you can thank me then.

Russell Polsky
Discerning reader,
displaced Alaskan hockey puck

I've known Mike Gordon since I stuck my head inside Chilkoot Charlie's (the namesake club after my dad Ruben's fictional character) in the early '70s and was treated to Mr. Whitekeys' version of Alaska's Flag, done in the style of Jimi Hendrix's Star Spangled Banner. Classic stuff. I played in bands at the club throughout the '80s, giving credence to the notion that anything you live through only makes you stronger! Guess you could say Mike and Ruben had a "bromance" before the concept even existed...

John Gaines
Ruben Gaines' son

I would like to offer a personal thank you to Mike Gordon for bringing our dad back to life in his no-holds-barred memoir. I've laughed, cried, rolled my eyes and enjoyed another glass of wine reading DAGNABIT!.

I still have an envelope addressed to "Ruben Gaines, Alaska" which arrived in our mail one day. That kind of fame is certainly not what dad set out to achieve; he just wanted people to "dig it." Homes throughout Alaska were tuned in and attentive to the radio at 5:30 p.m. for Conversation Unlimited. Dinners, phone calls and many other activities were planned around that half hour.

My dad was a world-class story teller and I know he was proud of Mike's ability to do justice to the art. When my dad arrived in Alaska, the territory didn't know it needed a story-teller, poet, cartoonist, humorist, and a radio raconteur who came with several personalities!

Dad didn't attempt to tame the Last Frontier and wasn't fond of those who did. He loved it the way it was—full of colorful and interesting characters—men, women, children, dogs, ducks, seagulls, moose, bears, fish, etc. Mike does justice to all Alaskans, the raw and rowdy as well as the sophisticated.

Mike certainly doesn't live in a small world and he's shared much of it with readers who are in for a real adventure.

Christine Burkett
Ruben Gaines' daughter

DAGNABIT!

Tell-all tales, history, travel, and Ruben Gaines lore and poetry all conversationally delivered and captivating from start to finish. A satisfying sequel to a popular prequel.

Svaja Worthington
Honorary Consul from the State of Alaska to the Republic of Lithuania

....

Alaska has managed to pack a lot of color into its short history, and few Alaskans have added to that color more than Mike Gordon. Mike spends much of DAGNABIT! reflecting on his adventures with long-time friend and radio legend Ruben Gaines, who created the character Chilkoot Charlie, the namesake of Mike's iconic Anchorage watering hole. For old-time Alaskans like me, this was a funny and often poignant trip down memory lane. And as a radio personality, I especially enjoyed remembering one of the true Alaskan pioneers of the business. But even if you've never touched Alaskan soil or listened to an Alaskan radio station (and I'm sorry if you've never had either pleasure), DAGNABIT! will offer you a thrilling look into what makes this place and its people unlike anything you will find anywhere else on earth. Mike Gordon has set himself apart as one of the premier chroniclers of the Alaska experience.

Mike Pocaro
650 KENI, Anchorage

....

Learning the Ropes and DAGNABIT! are voyages of adventure, friendship, struggle, success and personal reflection. These are the stories of an exceptional man in a debauched city during a wild era. Where Learning the Ropes explored the depths of Mike's heart, DAGNABIT! explores the depths of his character.

Matt Kissinger
Senior Principal Business Developer
Qatar Petroleum
Hiker, skier, savant, will do yard work for Guinness

....

DAGNABIT! should interest students of Alaska letters and history for two important reasons. Foremost is Mike Gordon's highly personal portrait of Ruben Gaines, an entertainer of towering talent for whom a serious evaluation has long been overdue. Then you have the author's pertinent observations about a range of other characters who gave Alas-

6

*ka a unique flavor — for lack of a more discreet word — in the last half of the 20th century. People better known by their nicknames than their legal signatures: Mafia Mike, Wicked Wanda, Sealskin Charlie, Tiny Tim. (Yeah, the "Tiptoe through the Tulips" singer, who Gordon once presented in Anchorage on a bill that included a female contortionist.) Plus the inside scoops on brawls, court cases, and once-popular establishments like Bobby McGee's and Hogg Brothers. You won't find these details in academic histories, which is why so many of them make splendid soporifics. But adventurous souls of the future will read this and Gordon's first book, **Learning The Ropes**, and curse that they were not present in Alaska during the era of big oil and wild money.*

Mike Dunham
Retired Alaska broadcaster, journalist, and author

....

Mike Gordon's new book DAGNABIT! is a colorful and enjoyable read. The book, Gordon's second about his life is part travelogue and part tribute to his dear friend and inspiration, Ruben Gaines, one of Alaska's grand characters of many talents revolving around the smooth use of words that the younger generation missed out on appreciating.

Gordon offers up an inside look on a variety of topics, including a bygone era of Anchorage from his childhood years and the decades preceding pipeline-building days. Gordon's stories offer a reminder of what a unique place Alaska was and is, its own fledgling society with its own traditions and world outlook and how it became a refuge for those needing a fresh start or a last chance, a reminder, too of how in Alaska you received the benefit of the doubt.

There are nuggets of marvelous pleasures included, such as the story behind the Spenard windmill, and tales from inside Chilkoot Charlie's, operated by Gordon for decades as the biggest, and possibly, the loudest bar in Alaska.

Gordon names names in certain incidents, sometimes telling stories that are not especially flattering, even his own mea culpas, but often leave the reader wide-eyed.

A segment delving into Mike's art collecting habits is educational, but also nostalgic, with names popping up of dearly departed artists whose works help define the Last Frontier for those who are enticed by the wilderness, who wish to remember it a certain way, or who don't have the ability to explore it as much as they would like.

While this is very much an Alaska story, it is also very much Mike Gordon's story and that means he reports on his many journeys to far-off lands, not only to climb the highest mountains on each continent, but the adventures experienced in the flatlands, too.

The vibrancy of the inside workings of Chilkoot's, often tied to the roller-coaster ride of Alaska's boom-and-bust economy, are equaled by some of the fine lifestyle experiences offered in foreign countries.

This is a several-hundred-page toast to friends past and present. A time when no one locked their car or house doors is a time that has passed in Anchorage, betraying a touch of wistfulness of when the city was less like others Outside.

Lew Freedman
Author, sportswriter and longtime Anchorage Daily News journalist

....

*The adventure put forth in **Learning the Ropes** was brash, compelling and sometimes almost unbelievable.*

*In **DAGNABIT!**, Gordon gives flesh and palate to the people and places that made **Learning the Ropes** a reality. To read **DAGNABIT!** is to understand the who and what Alaska really was and still, at its core, truly is.*

Tom Laret
Sommelier, guide, adventurer:
"dudeness" personified

....

*Mike Gordon's first book, **Learning the Ropes**, is a great read and his second book, **DAGNABIT!**, shows that he is not a one-trick pony. Alaska has a world class writer in Mike Gordon who makes the reader feel present in the story being told. DAGNABIT is not only another great read but it introduces readers to the little remembered giant Alaskan character, artist, author and radio personality, Ruben Gaines.*

Art Hackney
Media and political consultant
Hackney Communications

....

I had the good fortune to perform for Mike Gordon at World Famous Chilkoot Charlie's in Anchorage, Alaska for over a decade, through boom and bust. I thought I knew Mike pretty well until I read (and loved) his first book, **Learning the Ropes**, which gives a glimpse of his fascinating and action-packed mountain climbing story. Now comes the newest effort, *DAGNABIT!, the essential companion to "Ropes" and a treasure trove of uniquely Alaskan characters, history, bare-knuckle battles, the nightclub business, outdoor adventures, world travel and much, much more.*

You'll be taken on a rough and tumble thrill ride through Mike's incredible and heart-warming life story. His razor sharp memory paints a detailed picture in every chapter.

As importantly, DAGNABIT! is a timeless and loving tribute to legendary Alaskan writer, artist, broadcaster and humorist, Ruben Gaines.

Bon voyage!
Tommy Rocker
Las Vegas entertainer and club owner

TABLE OF CONTENTS

Foreword

Following on the heels of *Learning the Ropes, DAGNABIT!* focuses less on my personal life and climbing adventures and more on my close relationship with Ruben Gaines and my life in general, including travels far and wide. This sequel also covers in greater detail my lengthy Chilkoot Charlie's and Alaskan historical journeys. Writing *DAGNABIT!* I stood back, used a larger canvas and a broader brush.

I trust my readers will enjoy the broad array of Ruben's wonderful prose and poetry as well as his uniquely Alaskan cartoons. It is an honor to present them and I am indebted to Ruben's sons, Phil and John and his daughter, Christine for allowing me to do so. I'd also like to thank those gifted offspring for taking the time to read my rough manuscript and for their comments and contributions.

In this rapidly changing sound bite world and our cancel culture, disposable society we Alaskans need to cling tightly to our past—our uniqueness—those many small things that differentiate us from the rest of the world, and much of it a gift from one man. Alaska can ill afford to forget Ruben Gaines, dagnabit!

******

A number of people have been kind enough to read my evolving manuscript, made thoughtful suggestions and assisted with editing and/or written a blurb, namely: Lisa Maloney, Reidun (Lilla) Paxton, Matt Kissinger, Svaja Worthington, Art Hackney, Charlene Albertson, Tom Laret, Jack Kent (Toman), Tommy Rocker (Greenough), Ken Kennell, Sharon Richards, Walter John, Dr. David Beale, Joe and Gena Columbus, Nate and Colleen Baer, Russell Polsky, Tony Lewkowski, Norman Rokeberg, Mike Pocaro, Mike Dunham, Lew Freedman, and my daughter, Michele Ritter. I would also like to thank my publisher, Flip Todd of Todd Communications for his professional assistance and steadfast support. Last but not least, my wife Shelli has once again been of invaluable assistance in editing, proofreading, formatting, Photoshopping, and whipping this sequel into presentable condition. I am grateful for her remarkable memory which helped me recall many interesting twists and turns in our shared adventures.

Introduction

How much less enriched our Alaskan lives would be without Ruben Gaines. By entertaining us all those years (fifty give or take) he also helped to define us. Alaskans have a sense of unique identity that is to a large degree the gift of one man—a wonderful, supremely talented man who loved both Alaska and Alaskans, and who fit perfectly into the time and space he occupied.

I was even more enriched than most owing to the fact that I had a very close twenty-five-year relationship with Ruben. We had a business relationship due to him allowing me to use the name Chilkoot Charlie's for my bar business, but mostly we were like father and son. He was my mentor. He was old enough to be my father given the fact that my own father was born in 1910, only two years before Ruben. Dad died in 1977, but Ruben lived on for another seventeen years.

The first short stories I wrote while at Advance Base Camp on the north side of Mt. Everest in 1989 were inspired by Ruben. They included original versions of *Max and the Axe, Johnny Tegstrom, The Entrepreneur, Shame, I'll 'Fo It On You!, Central Junior High,* and *The Wild Duck.* When I got back to Anchorage I tried to give copies of them to Ruben after a sushi dinner one night. We were sharing some drinks in my condo on Sorbus Way with my wife, Shelli.

Ruben said, "Just read them to me," so I did.

Afterwards he said, "Those are pretty good, kid. Keep it up."

Sometimes I can hear Ruben's voice in my head when I'm writing, so if you don't like my writing, blame it on Ruben, dagnabit!

******

"Dagnabit" is a word Ruben used frequently, both personally and through his radio character, the crusty sourdough, Pop. It can be spelled with either one "b" or two, though one seems to be the "alternative" choice. I started out spelling it with two, then I discovered that Ruben used only one. Don't ask me why he chose only one; perhaps for succinctness? I could not determine that two is more correct and since I didn't have any other reason for using two, I changed it back to one. After all, I'm not Alaska's poet laureate.

The word is a slang contraction, a bowdlerization of "goddammit." Linguists refer to words like "dagnabit" as taboo deformations. It's a piece of pseudo-profanity—a word purposefully evolved in order to say it when we don't want to say the other word. In this case it expresses the same frustration or emphasis in a less profane way than that other word. And it needs to be spoken forcefully with heavy emphasis on the middle syllable.

******

The stories herein are primarily about Alaska. I'm an Alaskan. About that there is no question; however, I have been fortunate enough, partly by virtue of my mountain climbing adventures, to stand on all seven continents, as described in my memoir, *Learning the Ropes*. And my life has been flavored and scented like wine blended from the grapes of vines grown in various soils by my travels and the people I have met while on them. I have, toward the end of this book, detailed a few of my travels because they had an impact on me and I thought they would interest my readers. Ruben was an Alaskan also. Though a lot of people don't know it, he lived on the South Island of New Zealand for a year, and he loved it.

If you've traveled much you already know that being an Alaskan abroad makes you of more immediate interest to most people. It's a door-opener, at least in locations where the average person actually knows of it.

My nightclub, Chilkoot Charlie's, opened its doors in Anchorage, Alaska on January 1, 1970. It had been in operation for over 12 years and was prospering when Ruben Gaines and I signed our second hand-written business agreement on August 12, 1982, in the Corsair Restaurant across from the Captain Cook Hotel on Fifth Avenue.

Our original agreement had been hand-written by me and had been signed over lunch at the Black Angus Restaurant on Fireweed Lane before Chilkoot Charlie's opened. That original agreement, which has been lost to the ages, had basically stated that for services rendered and the ability to sell his products in the bar, Ruben would allow me the exclusive right to use the Chilkoot Charlie's name in the bar and restaurant business. Since Ruben was known to imbibe he was also given the right to drink free in the club for the rest of his life. Over the dozen years between my nightclub operation beginning and that second agreement with Ruben, the local landscape had changed dramatically.

Not only had the business grown exponentially, but construction of the Alyeska Pipeline from Prudhoe Bay to Valdez—which prompted a stretch of wild boom years throughout Alaska—had been completed at the end of May 1977. Anchorage was flush and so was I, which called for a readjustment in my business arrangement with Ruben.

Here is a copy of the second letter on Chilkoot Charlie's stationery:

2435 Spenard Rd. — Anchorage, Alaska 99503 — Ph. 272-1010

Ruben Gaines   Aug. 12, 1982
2205 Boniface Pkwy.
Anchorage, AK.

Dear Ruben,

In 1969 you ellowed Jadon. Inc. exclusive
use of the name Chilkoot Charlie's in the
bar and restaurant business. You also
designed our logo and produced some clever
wording for the backs of our cocktail napkins and
our match covers. In return you were to
be able to sell your wares at the bar and
drink for free on our premises.

Although no one can argue that the success
of the business today is not due to my
attentions and perseverance there is also
no doubt of the lasting value of your
original contribution.

Our original arrangement was equitable
when we made it; less so as time went

Chilkoot Charlie's

Rustic Alaskan Bar

2435 Spenard Rd. — Anchorage, Alaska 99503 — Ph. 272-1010

on, but for many years the business was in very serious financial straights with its actual survival in jeopardy.

Today things are different. The business is healthy and doing far more than anyone's expectations. It can afford to be more generous to you in return for those very important contributions so long ago.

Starting with August, 1982, for as long as Jedon can afford it; for as long as I am president of Jedon, Inc. and for as long as you live, you will receive $500.00 per month between the 1st and the 10th of each month, to be mailed to:
2205 Boniface #45 99504

Since there is no obligation on the part of the corporation and the payments are considered to be gifts they are not a deductible business expense to the

Chilkoot Charlie's

Rustic Alaskan Bar

2435 Spenard Rd. — Anchorage, Alaska 99503 — Ph. 272-1010

corporation and hence, are not taxable income to you.

Have a nice day and I, for one, hope you live a long, long time.

Your admirer &
friend,
Mike Dodon, Pres.
Jedon, Inc.

Accepted _Ruben Gaines_
Dated _8/12/82_

✳ My CPA tells me this morning that the IRS might decide that these pymts. are taxable income to you. You should get your own professional advice on the matter.

Chilkoot Charlie's

Rustic Alaskan Bar

Ruby Rokeberg

Ruben Gaines played an important role in my life as a business relation, writing inspiration, creative counselor, friend and mentor, but his
was not my only formative relationship. Almost two decades earlier I had
the great fortune of having Ruby Rokeberg as a doting surrogate mother.

Glancing out the living room window of our duplex on Illiamna Ave.
one day in 1954, I couldn't have missed seeing Ruby on her hands and
knees furiously yanking my newly transplanted flowers from the flower
bed. It was the summer before I entered Central Junior High School as
a 7th grader.

My family had previously lived on Government Hill in Richardson
Vista, a large complex of apartment buildings where there had been no
place for gardening. So we were new to the neighborhood, Susitna View
Park, just west of Turnagain-By-the-Sea Subdivision where Ruby and
Mel lived. Their son, Norman, and I had become friends.

Though we had raised chickens and rabbits and had planted a vegetable garden in Florida, there were no horticulturists in my family, and
no knowledge of Alaskan flora. Nonetheless, my dad and I had hauled
shale rocks from along the Seward Highway, surrounded one end of a
small stand of birch in our front yard with them, and backfilled the en-
closure with topsoil. I was assigned the task of providing the plants for
the new flower garden, so I dutifully went into the woods across the
street and dug up a number of fireweed, blue bells, columbine and lu-
pine. Unbeknownst to me those were practically weeds by any Alaskan's
definition, regardless of their beauty in the wild.

As I crossed the yard, Ruby was vigorously replacing my transplants
with domesticated perennial flowering plants interspersed with pansies
and other annuals. It was a kindly gesture in spite of its abrupt execu-
tion, and we took it at face value—a seasoned Alaskan's introduction to
Alaskan Gardening 101.

Noticeably in a dither, Ruby asked me, "What are you trying to do,
kid, ruin the neighborhood?"

As a friend of Norman, I had plenty of occasions to visit the Rokeberg
home. In fact, we neighborhood kids found any occasion an opportunity

not to be missed because Ruby, of Danish descent, made excellent Danish pastries.

In those days, before our local bureaucrats set up shop and began to force-feed us a mind-boggling array of regulations—all of course for our own good—a person could prepare food in one's own kitchen for commercial purposes. The Danish pastries and cookies Ruby made in her kitchen were served to none other than passengers on Pacific Northern Airlines flights.

Ruby's baking efforts also produced a small percentage of rejects, and though they might not have been pretty enough to sell to the airline, they far exceeded the culinary and artistic standards of Norm, Johnny Tegstrom, Vaughn Cartwright, and yours truly. We were regular visitors, like Pavlov's dogs, responding to the smell of pastries rather than the sound of a bell. Of course, we liked Norm too.

Ruby also baked the dessert trays of French and Danish pastries for the Garden of Eatin', Anchorage's leading restaurant in the 1950s and 1960s. The fact that the city's finest restaurant was located in a Quonset hut in Spenard speaks volumes about the era. After World War II, the Navy was overstocked with those long, half-domed, steel buildings that required so little in the way of foundations and could be easily assembled with unskilled labor. They were sold as surplus and set up all over town to accommodate the needs of the steadily expanding city.

Incidentally, my first wife, Lilla, and I lived in a Quonset hut on Duben Avenue in Muldoon for a year after returning to Alaska in 1967. We had moved from an air-conditioned suburban home with a two-car garage and large fenced backyard in Sacramento for $135 per month into the Quonset hut with no yard for $175 per month. That first winter back in Anchorage the hut's fuel oil furnace erupted and covered what little we owned with soot—twice.

In the 1950s, Ruby used to take us boys on an occasional adventure. One summer, when I was probably still attending the old Central Junior High which was later razed to accommodate construction of the Alaska Center for the Performing Arts, Ruby took Norm, me, and Roger Harman—who lived across the street from my family—on a fishing trip to the small town of Hope. We drove there in the Rokeberg's burgundy-colored 1950 Mercury.

Before the earthquake of 1964, there was a general store in Hope run by an elderly gentleman who sold everything under the sun, with the goods stacked from floor to ceiling on either side of several aisles. It is one of the many missing uniqueties (I'm coining that word) that helps to define pre-earthquake Alaska from post-earthquake Alaska. I can still walk its aisles in my mind every time I think back to the summers my family and I used to spend in Hope camped along Resurrection Creek, my mother determinedly bent over the creek panning for tiny flakes of gold by the hour while my dad, my friends and I snagged humpy and dog salmon from the crystal clear stream.

Those were halcyon days. We would set up camp and spend weeks there. My sister, Pat, was of the age that she was dating GIs from Elmendorf and Fort Richardson. My dad would befriend them, especially the ones that worked in "Supply," and after my sister had moved on they would still come around to visit my dad with gifts of military surplus items: ten-man tents, sleeping bags, air mattresses, cots, lanterns, entrenching tools (shovels), and all sorts of useful equipment. Our crawl space was full of the stuff and our camp was comfortably appointed, despite the fact that Pat was not always thrilled with the extended presence of her ex-boyfriends.

Of course the Hope General Store sold the ubiquitous red-and-white Daredevil fishing lure, but I had little need for it. I made my own lures, i.e. snag hooks. Growing up in territorial Alaska in the 1950s, though they were probably out there, I didn't know a single person who fly-fished or practiced catch-and-release. We were harvesters. My idea of a fly was a chunk of lead with a big treble hook attached. I would haul a Coleman burner down to the crawl space under our house, melt lead in a pan and pour it into the molds I had punched into the dampened sand with a hoe handle.

As soon as the lead was poured into the mould I inserted twisted pieces of coat hanger, sinking them in up to the eye with a pair of pliers. After my lead weights had cooled I would tie the eyes to the underside of treble hooks and I was good to go. I then attached a piece of bright red, orange, or chartreuse plastic or felt to the base of the treble hooks so I could see the juxtaposition of the "lure" to the fish. I'd cast it hopefully up-stream and beyond them, then jerk smartly on the line at the proper time to impale the hapless critters.

We had a grand time camping and snagging salmon with Ruby, but the return trip turned into a real adventure when heavy rains and a flash flood washed out the Seward Highway just north of Indian. We were stuck on the wrong side of the torrent of rubble and debris, and there was nothing we could do but improvise until the road crews were able to make emergency repairs.

Fortunately, there was a log cabin nearby owned by a friend of Ruby and Mel's who worked for the Alaska Railroad, so we didn't have to sleep in the car. We had plenty of fresh-caught fish to eat, a roof over our heads and a deck of cards, so it became a delightful sojourn. The fish we couldn't eat did not fare so well due to a shortage of ice. They became fertilizer for the Rokeberg's backyard garden, resulting in a bumper crop of spuds later that season.

Ruby looked after our small group of kids like we were her little ducklings, not only taking an interest in what we were doing but doing things *with* us. She was fun to be around, always making the best of things—even those rotten salmon. Years later my mother admitted to me that Ruby was the only person in her life of whom she had ever been jealous.

I said, "But why, Mom?" She replied, "Because *my son* regularly came home carrying on about *Ruby this and Ruby that!*"

Of course I was just being an adolescent and had no idea what my enthusiasm about Ruby had meant to my mother. There is no doubt Ruby was tough competition though, and she was home all day—Mel frequently working out of town—while my mom taught school five days a week. Mom also didn't have those requisite Danish baking skills.

Though Ruby was a sweetheart, she was a little hard on Norman, who never seemed to be able to live up to her expectations. Ruby and Mel had lost their first son "Donnie" to polio. He was a senior in high school at the time of his death, seven years older than Norm, and a fine young man by virtually everyone's measure. He was among the last polio deaths in Alaska, tragically succumbing to the disease only a year before the Salk vaccine was released.

Ruby was never the same after the loss. Donnie had been exemplary—the perfect son. He hung up his clothes. Norman was intransigent—a bit of a challenge—and left his room a mess. Ruby couldn't help spoiling him because of the loss of her eldest son, but she also couldn't help nagging at him and would refuse to wash his clothes until some were hung up and others found their way to the hamper.

It is a shame neither Ruby nor Mel lived long enough to see Norman serve as Rules Committee Chairman in the Alaska State House of Representatives. They would have been so proud of him. I was. Norman was an exemplary legislator: smart, effective, and well-grounded philosophically. People would razz him about being "Gordon's personal legislator," which could not have been further from the truth. Norman is and always has been his own man. He does listen to others but he keeps his own counsel.

Our Boy Scout Troop 673 was sponsored by the Spenard Lions Club and we met in the North Star Elementary School until homesteader Chet Lampert allowed the club to put one of those ubiquitous Quonset huts on his property on the north shoreline of Blueberry Lake—now the northeast corner of Northern Lights Boulevard and A Street. Edwin Ellsworth Peabody (1902- 1970), aka Eddie Peabody or "King of the Banjo," played his banjo for us in that Quonset hut, and clever boys that we were, we made up a little "ditty" about how Eddie "Playbody" had peed for us.

Another highlight of my scouting years is that the Black Panther Patrol, of which I was the patrol leader, was awarded the coveted Presidential Award for having the best campsite throughout the course of a Summer Camporee held near Campbell Airstrip. Ruby had made our patrol flag—a prowling black panther sewn on a field of red. Just so there's no misunderstanding this was more than ten years before Marxist college students Bobby Seale and Huey Newton formed their revolutionary socialist political organization in Oakland, California.

Norm, Johnny and I all became Eagle Scouts. Norm even got to attend a Boy Scout Jamboree in Valley Forge, Pennsylvania. That was the most incredible trip I could imagine at the time and was I ever envious.

Ruby loved to dance and was known to drag unsuspecting males of all ages onto the dance floor. In the 1920s, after returning to Denmark to spend her teenage years in Copenhagen working as a housemaid, she took great pleasure in taking center stage at a dance exhibition and introducing the most popular dance of the roaring '20s, the Charleston, to Denmark. She even coerced the members of the Black Panther Patrol into taking dancing lessons.

When the dreaded day arrived she dragged us to a dance studio on Spenard Road where the Tiki Lounge was in later years and introduced us to two beautiful, statuesque blonde twin sisters, in their late twenties or early thirties, from Vienna. We were instantly transformed from adolescent Black Panthers, without the least interest in learning to dance, into Eager Beavers.

Over the course of several months we learned to tango, waltz, foxtrot, and rumba. I was pretty height-challenged at the time, being only an inch or two over five feet tall, and as such spent much of those sessions in a dancing embrace with my face smothered by one or another pair of humongous breasts. It was hard to keep my mind on my feet.

Ruby's husband Mel was a mild-mannered, intelligent man with a slight Norwegian accent who also took an interest in us kids. He was an electrical foreman who worked on large construction projects all over

Alaska. Mel was born in Minnesota, grew up in Norway, and worked hard to Americanize his speech, but like most Norwegians he had a problem with pronouncing the letter "J."

Until I was middle-aged, the only time I had been fishing on the Kenai River was when Mel took Norm and me to Bing's Landing to fish for rainbow trout with the world famous Bing Brown, one of the early guides who helped transform the river into the international fishing destination it is today. Of course, I left my humpy-snagging gear at home on that occasion.

One day when I was maybe a sophomore in high school and Norm and Vaughn were freshmen, we were all practicing throwing a discus in the Rokebergs' front yard. I somehow managed to throw it right through their large living room window. I felt terrible about the incident and promised Mel and Ruby I would pay for the damages. It was a lot of money for a kid and I'm sure they thought I would probably never keep my promise, but I squirreled away money from my paper route and paid back every cent.

I know that meant a lot to both of them, Mel in particular, and it was no doubt part of the reason I was included when, in 1967, Mel put up $8,000 at 8% for Norm, Johnny, and me to invest in a business that ended up being the Bird House Bar, twenty-nine miles south of Anchorage on the Seward Highway.

Once in the early 1980s, when Norman and I were all grown up, and Mel and Ruby were elderly, they all—along with Norm's wife, Gayle—came to visit my wife Shelli and me in Halibut Cove. They rode from Homer across Kachemak Bay on the *Danny J* ferry.

At that point the now-famous Saltry Restaurant had only been open for a year or two. Because of the small size of the restaurant then and the large size of the group, we had dinner upstairs and Marian Beck, the proprietress, waited on us herself. There was a very limited menu, most of the items caught by Marian's husband, Dave, a commercial fisherman, and either "sushied," "pokied," or pickled.

There was no alternative menu. Sushi had not become popular in America yet, especially in the Alaskan outback, and it wouldn't have mattered to Ruby if it had. She threw a fit, demanding of Marian, "Do you know about Pearl Harbor? Don't you know who won the war?!"

All the while, Mel was kicking her under the table and the rest of us sat staring in stunned silence. It was a button on Ruby I had never witnessed being pushed. I know Marian has a temper too, but she kept her cool, smiling and carrying on admirably. It was quite a show, and Shelli and I and Norm and Gayle—and Marian—have laughed about it many times since.

Ruby not only made pastries, she also made cakes for weddings, birthdays and other occasions. She had not been able to make a wedding cake for my first marriage, which occurred in San Francisco, or my second, which had taken place unremarkably in my log cabin on Sixth Avenue in Anchorage, but she was determined to make the cake for my marriage to Shelli. She called me several times and I kept mentioning it to Shelli. The cake wasn't a big issue for Shelli, but it was for Ruby, who felt we needed a proper one.

She did make the cake, which was at my request a carrot cake, requiring cream cheese on it instead of frosting. The little sugar rosettes which Ruby spent days patiently forming with her arthritic fingers and freezing in Tupperware containers would not adhere properly to the cream cheese like they would have to regular butter cream frosting.

The cream cheese was so soft the flowers tended to sag and fall off, so Ruby had to stand guard over the cake, butter knife in hand, surreptitiously slapping those rosettes back in place. There was never a more focused wedding cake attendant until it was time for it to be served, but it was a beautiful cake and a big hit at the reception. Ruby had outdone herself, and I was pleased that she was so pleased to have been involved.

Looking back, Ruby stands out as one of a few parents that gave generously of their hearts and time to us kids when I was growing up. Another was Mr. Snipes, the father of Larry, a schoolmate and fellow Boy Scout. I always addressed him respectfully as Mr. Snipes, even into adulthood. And Mel certainly deserves honorable mention.

I took the time to visit Ruby after Mel had died and she was living alone in the Pioneer Home in downtown Anchorage. I also attended her funeral so I could say a final goodbye. While expressing my farewell to her peaceful but inanimate countenance, I thought about the other Ruby—the oh-so-animated Ruby, diligently tending the wedding cake, yanking those feral plants from our newly-planted garden, and giving Marian Beck the upbraiding of her life about her menu at the Saltry's insensitivity to those still angry over Japanese atrocities in WWII—and couldn't suppress an adoring smile behind my tears.

Ruben Gaines was born in Portland, Oregon in 1912. He had a successful career in Hollywood during World War II and knew a lot of the Hollywood celebrities of the day. He worked for five years at the Hollywood Mutual Studios of KJS, Los Angeles, writing most of the network's continuity for their musical productions. He also wrote much of the drama for shows like "California Melodies," the music version of "Music Depreciation," and "This is the Hour." Ruben wrote and directed musical productions with Frank DeVol, Buddy Cole, and Henry Zimmerman—all enormously talented and successful men.

Ruben told me how he and Ed Stevens, another talented radio guy and sportscaster, deep in their cups and one or the other of them blindfolded, threw a dart at a wall map. The dart landed on Alaska—which I suppose is as good an explanation as any for why they headed north.

Ruben spent a long rainy first winter as a radio announcer in Ketchikan. He said 206 inches of rain fell that year. That's when he created Chilkoot Charlie and his nemesis, Six-Toed Mordecai. Ruben claimed the wind and rain blew right through the shack that housed him and his equipment, and when the snow melted, the grounds outside were littered with liquor bottles. Later, he was to entertain the whole state of Alaska with his tales of the exploits of these two titanic ne'er-do-well sourdough reprobates.

Before settling in Anchorage, Ruben also worked a spell in Fairbanks, where he and Ed Stevens would brilliantly broadcast "live" Major League Baseball games. Of course, there were no satellites back then, so Alaskans had to wait perhaps a couple of weeks for tape recordings to arrive by air, and calling the States was expensive, if not impossible for most people. Ruben and Ed would receive the basic game information via the coded "line score" from the Teletype machine, fill in between the lines from their fertile imaginations, and then preemptively "broadcast" the game as if it were live, including the excitement one would expect from the announcer, the sound of the ball being smacked, (a pencil whacked against the microphone) the roaring crowd and all. People in the Bush never knew the difference between Ruben and Ed's broadcasts and the real thing. The two would saunter into a "Two Street" bar afterwards and patrons would wonder out loud, "What are you doing here? You're supposed to be Outside!"

"Outside" was how Alaskans referred to the rest of the country. Many still do. Our late Senator Ted Stevens was famous for his remark, "We don't care how they do it Outside."

Coop and the Cop

While attending Anchorage High School from 1954 to 1960, one of my best buddies was Clarence Boudreaux, our class valedictorian. (I just had to use spell check.) The relationship did not reflect as well upon Clarence as it did upon me. Another pal, one of my closest for most of my life, was Glenn Cooper (Coop), and the academic disparity between Clarence and Glenn was even greater than the one between Clarence and me. But boys will be boys, regardless of their IQs or academic standing.

In those days if we had a six-pack of Country Club malt liquor for the night, we were in heaven, and I remember one particular evening that began as one of those nights.

Early on that Friday night, Coop, Clarence and I were all working on our courage before going to a dance in the Anchorage High School auditorium. We were doing this with a couple of six-packs of our favored malt liquor, purchased at the drive-in window of the Sabre Jet Liquor Store near Fifth Avenue and Gambell Street. As I recall, there was an actual mock-up of a Sabre jet mounted to a pole in the air over the store.

"Anyone in there got an ID?" asked the clerk.

"Yep. I do!"

"Okay," and the beer was passed through the car window without further ado.

We were parked on a turnout on Clay Products Road, which ran through the woods to Point Woronzof beyond KFQD radio station at the east end of what was then the two lane dirt KFQD Road, which later became Northern Lights Boulevard. We were imbibing and planning our evening in the near-darkness when a police car unexpectedly pulled into the turnout in front of us, headlights on, blocking our exit and putting us into an immediate state of hysteria. Country Club cans and six-pack holders went flying into the bushes and under the car as if this activity would go unnoticed by the officer in the approaching vehicle.

Mr. Policeman got out of his car, flashlight in hand, and began shining the light under our vehicle and into the bushes. By now Coop, who was driving, had the window down and I believe the officer was the first to speak.

"Having a party, are we boys?"

Long pause.

"Well, I'll tell you what I'm gonna do," he said as he picked up and inspected a can of Country Club with one hand, up-ending it so the remnants flowed out onto the ground.

"I want each of you to give me your driver's license and your phone number, and you had better be home in a half-hour. Because that's when I'm going to call each of your parents and tell them about your little soirée."

So much for our evening of gamboling in the school gymnasium with those mysterious creatures of the opposite sex.

I had already been caught drinking by my parents, who were both very disappointed and upset with me but who never once acknowledged what poor role models they were. They were more worried about how their son's behavior reflected on them, both teachers in the Anchorage School District. So this was not our first incident with alcohol. I went home, told my parents what had happened, and though they weren't happy about it, it didn't feel like a lifetime crisis to me.

Poor Clarence. His parents had no idea he drank alcohol. He was the model child. His dad was a "bird" colonel at Elmendorf Air Force Base, and the reputation of the family was at stake. He went home and mustered the courage to tell his parents what he had been caught doing. It was a very big moment in his life and his dad was certain that I had been the one who had led his son astray.

Cooper might not have been class valedictorian, but he was nobody's fool. He didn't go home and spill the beans to his mother. He sat next to her (*and the phone*) watching television all night waiting for the phone to ring so he could put on his deep voice, and act like the man of the house, his step-father temporarily working out of town. Fortunately for Glenn, his acting skill was never put to the test because the policeman never called and his mother thought he was a sweet boy for visiting with her all night instead of carousing with his friends. Score one for the Coop Chute.

Who knows? Maybe the cop got busy and just didn't have time to make the calls, but I've always preferred to think that he never intended to make them in the first place. Hell, with his creative sense of humor he could have auditioned to go on air with Ruben and Ed Stevens. We no doubt made his night, and I pray there are others like him out there today.

Of course, I'm talking about Alaska before statehood, and before construction of the Alyeska Pipeline. It was different back then. The people were different. It was as if we were all in it together—a unique fledgling society with our own traditions, vernacular and world outlook. If you had car trouble on the road, everyone would stop to offer assistance. Alaska was a last chance, a refuge for many who had failed or messed up elsewhere. In Alaska you received the benefit of the doubt.

It was a small population, though, and if you messed up again you knew there was nowhere else to go. Almost everyone lived a quasi-subsistence lifestyle. Produce was expensive to buy, so we grew our own vegetables. Salmon and the yearly moose and caribou were stowed away for the winter. People didn't lock their car doors or even their house doors. All that changed practically overnight—and forever—when Alaska, like a third-world country, was overrun by big oil, big money, and a tsunami of people from Outside.

At age twenty-five and still casting about for a long-term career, I thought I would try my hand at radio broadcasting. I drove downtown to the old Federal Building on Fourth Avenue, took the required Federal Communications Commission test, and applied for a job at KHAR radio station.

Ken Flynn was the station manager. He placed me in a booth and had me read some radio commercials. One, I recall, was for Volkswagen, the German car maker.

Afterward he said, "I hate it when some kid walks in straight off the street and sounds better than I do." Then he hired me.

Ken, a few years later, opened and successfully operated his own namesake advertising firm in Anchorage after asking my advice over lunch about the matter, and Chilkoot Charlie's became his first client. He did very well, selling his business and retiring before I did.

So now I was selling life insurance for New York Life, looking for a bar location in Anchorage and going weekdays in the mornings to KHAR to learn how to work "the board," a big commercial radio station soundboard. My instructor was none other than Ruben Gaines. This chance meeting was one of the most important in either of our lives, though neither of us could possibly have imagined it at the time.

I showed up early each morning and sat next to Ruben as he masterfully told his stories and acted out his characters over the air. It was truly something to behold. One of his characters I loved was Pop, a cantankerous old fart who would interrupt, criticize, and annoy the announcer—Ruben. Like Elmer Fudd, first credited with using it, one of Pop's favorite words was "dagnabit!" Pop used the word for emphasis and to express frustration. Elmer expressed frustration with it when once again outwitted by that clever "wabbit." To make the proper voice for Pop, Ruben would thrust out his lower lip until it was greatly protruded. It was riveting to be in the presence of such protean talent.

In the middle of this activity each morning, Herb Shaindlin, an intense guy with a pock-marked face, mustache, goatee, big bushy eyebrows, and a balding gray pate, would walk through the room in front of us, address his morning salutations to Ruben, pull his sheets of network news from the Teletype machine, and depart. Finally, on the last day of my first week he asked, glancing at me then addressing Ruben, "Who is that strange man?"

Hazing

I could be wrong about this, but my recollection is that it was in 1959, my junior year at Anchorage High School, the school was ranked as one of the best in the country academically. It was also simultaneously ranked as one of the more prominent drinking schools, the latter credential being the one that received the most applause from me and my classmates. And my extracurricular activities certainly contributed more to that latter achievement than my scholastic achievements did to the former.

Many high schools and universities in America have had to deal with unacceptable hazing practices in athletic letter clubs, fraternities and sororities. Anchorage High School, which became West High in 1961 the year after my graduation, was no exception. To the best of my knowledge Anchorage High School, or West High's, last issue with hazing occurred in 1958, the year I was initiated into the Athletic Club after having lettered in hockey. I remember parts of the hazing well, and not just because it created a scandal and was the last year athletic hazing was allowed at the school.

The most personally humiliating event in the initiation was what is sometimes referred to as the "elephant walk," but which we referred to as the "Choo-Choo Train." If I'm not mistaken, it was overseen by our coaches. We were forced to crawl naked, through an obstacle course of benches, chairs, netting, and various other obstructions with one thumb up the rear end of the guy in front of us and the other one in our mouth.

When a whistle was blown, we were ordered to reverse the position of our thumbs, in the process yelling "Choo-Choo!" My thumb was folded into my hand and never got into the rear of the guy in front of me. Fortunately, the guy behind me was employing the same subterfuge. Under such circumstances one does the best one can.

Another ritual I remember having to perform was wandering around the lobby of the still-functioning 4th Avenue Theatre on a crowded weekend night eating popcorn out of a Kotex box. Given the choice of looking silly at the movies or playing "Choo-Choo Train," I'll take the former every time.

There was also a car wash in the school's rear parking lot in which we initiates were required to wash the cars of letter club members, all wearing their letter jackets. Most of the lettermen came with various solids and liquids, as well as individual preparations for us to ingest upon command. The solids consisted generally of red peppers, the liquids being Liquid Smoke, Tabasco sauce and the like, while the individual preparations were usually some vile green concoction. One of my fellow initiates was forced to drink and eat too many of the proffered delights for his system to manage and ended up hospitalized in a coma, creating the scandal that ended the whole affair.

During my freshman year at the University of Alaska Fairbanks (1960–1961) I lived on campus in Stevens Hall, and there wasn't a lot to do socially. Since an enthusiastic counselor had signed me up for nineteen credits my first semester—in spite of my never having cracked a book in high school—it was just as well. It was time to apply myself.

In addition to that academic load I was a starting defenseman for the school's hockey team, the Nanooks. I also became proficient at table tennis and even better at playing pool, tutored by a fellow freshman exiled by his parents straight from the mean streets of Baltimore. For an outdoor diversion from our normal activities, including drinking liquor or beer whenever we could locate either, we would go rabbit and ptarmigan hunting on weekends.

Since UAF was a land grant college, my male classmates and I were required to participate in the ROTC program, and I even found myself on the drill team pledging for the Pershing Rifles, the only collegiate level military fraternity. The University of Alaska, in College, just outside of Fairbanks, was listed as Company A-11. I was a very committed trooper and I loved studying military tactics and military history, especially from the Civil War era, one of my favorite subjects to this day.

As I recall, the initiation, which was totally proper, took about a week during which we had to paint a brick blue on one side and white on the other with "PR" painted on each side in the opposite color. This brick had to be with us at all times and I still have it in my home at age seventy-eight. If we encountered an officer we were required to come to attention, salute and have ready from memory any one of a number of ditties to deliver upon demand. I remember them well.

Q. How's a cow? A. Sir. She walks, she talks, she's full of chalk—the lactic fluid extracted from the female member of the bovine species, highly prolific to the Nth degree, Sir.

Q. What time is it? A. Sir. I apologize for the fact that my chronometer is in such inaccord with the great sidereal movement by which time is commonly reckoned that I cannot with complete accuracy state the exact time, however, without fear of being too far wrong, I will state that it is approximately (look at watch and state the time), Sir.

Q. What is leather? A. Sir. When the fresh skin of an animal, cleaned and divested of all hair, fat and other extraneous material is immersed in a dilute solution of tannic acid, a chemical combination ensues. The gelatinous tissue of the skin is converted into a non-putrescible substance, impervious to and insoluble in water. This, Sir, is leather, Sir.

If you got any little detail wrong, especially forgetting Sir where required, you were in for further grilling on the spot and perhaps some pushups.

The ROTC program was well run, producing an excellent drill team. I found myself at the University of San Francisco, also a land grant college, for my sophomore year, and though everything else was more to my liking, their ROTC program was not. It was slipshod and chock full of favoritism. Toward the end of my sophomore year, when we had to decide whether we would participate in upper division ROTC or not, I chose not to. I had taken and already passed the written and oral tests and had been accepted. All I had to do was put my signature on the dotted line, but I got so pissed off at an inspection when I saw one of the favored, ass-kisser officers brush-polishing his shoes before the inspection, then receiving a higher inspection score than I did, that I marched into the colonel's office and told him he could take his "chicken-shit" program and "shove it."

It was happenstance. I was lucky not to have gone into upper division ROTC because it kept me out of Vietnam. I already had a scholastic deferment and, as fate would have it, I fell in love and got married during my junior year. The military didn't start drafting married men until things got pretty heated over in Southeast Asia, and by then I had a child. When the military started drafting even men with children, they didn't make it retroactive to men who already had a child.

My battles were fought in the corporate world, being seventeen credits short of a college degree, trying to provide for my growing family by doing sales work, first for New York Life Insurance Company, then for Hallmark Cards, and finally for Gillette Safety Razor Company, Toiletries Division. But it was better than getting shot at.

I was annoyed when the practice of hazing was eliminated by the Anchorage School District because I was never going to be able to be the hazer. I had been required to go through it and felt that I was being cheated out of "getting even." I know it was an immature reaction, but I was a sophomore in high school. The word sophomoric, according to

Webster's Dictionary, is derived from the thinking of a sophomore in school, meaning someone who acts self-assured and opinionated, but is in reality inexperienced and immature. My sort of immature reaction is what, unchecked, helps perpetuate these degrading and potentially harmful practices.

The reality is that I was lucky the hazing ended since I have never had to deal with the moral predicament of having participated in the role of hazer. However, in retrospect I certainly was not as lucky missing out on being a hazer as I was not having to participate in our divisive and disastrous activities in Vietnam.

Despite sometimes getting it totally wrong, I have never been afraid of making big decisions, even on the spur of the moment. For the most part I believe it is better to do so than to be frozen with indecision and procrastination. Taking action exposes opportunities; indecision dispels them.

Not long after my introduction to Ruben and "the board," oil was discovered on the North Slope and a state auction raised $900 million from the sale of leases at Prudhoe Bay. That was a colossal amount of money in 1969. I figured that considering the changing landscape I would contact Skip Fuller, who I had talked to a year earlier about the Alibi Club in Spenard, to see if it was still for sale. It was, but the price, which I had thought was too high, was now even higher. The price of everything was higher.

Not wanting to miss out on the potential bonanza of owning a bar during a boom period, lawyer friend Bill Jacobs and I bit the bullet, borrowed the pre-arranged $20,000 from his mother for a down payment and closed the deal.

Over lunch at the Black Angus Restaurant, Ruben without hesitation, said, "Chilkoot Charlie's! That's a great name for a bar!" and signed my hand-written agreement.

It was full speed ahead. I had a bar, a name and a theme, though I was a little worried about the location on Spenard Road near Fireweed Lane. It turns out that I should not have worried. The eponymous neighborhood around Spenard Road, advertised by local merchants as the "Miracle Mile," was full of watering holes and local character already. It also sported Caribou Wards, a department store whose spokesman, Caribou Pete, boasted the first escalator in town.

I had also struggled with the name of our new Alaska-themed bar. I had been torn between Chilkoot Charlie's and that much-maligned local variety of salmon—the pink, or humpy. I kept a pad on my nightstand, waking up throughout the night to write down ideas. I had larger-than-life images and ideas about the titanic fictional sourdough reprobate, Chilkoot Charlie and his nemesis, Six-Toed Mordecai, along with schools of ideas about Mr. and Mrs. Humpy. Chilkoot Charlie won out because he was an established character with a wealth of ready-made, high-quality material already available due to Ruben's radio broadcasts, cartoons, pamphlets and LPs.

After a fifty-year run and a gradual expansion to ten times its original size, who could argue that it was the wrong decision?

Max and the Axe

The first U.S. soldiers were killed in South Vietnam in July 1959 when their living quarters near Saigon were raided by guerillas. Those were not "shots heard 'round the world," though they should have been. I was a junior at Anchorage High School, and it was around this time I went on a memorable moose hunting trip with Bill Peters and Max Pierce, both friends of my parents.

Max, an Internal Revenue Service investigator, had a kind of face you never forgot. Not because it was characteristic in any way—just the opposite. It was a face devoid of anything remotely resembling personality. He had a saturnine countenance that ran straight through. You could have given Max a million dollars or stuck a hot poker up his ass and his reaction would have been equally unremarkable.

As an adolescent I never could understand what his wife Ruth saw in Max or what my parents saw in the company of either of them.

Much later my older sister Pat told me, "It had a lot to do with drinking."

How I became involved in the moose hunting trip with Max and Bill remains a childhood mystery.

Bill Peters was the consummate Alaskan character. Before the Great Alaska Earthquake of 1964 he reigned over the Portage Garage fifty miles south of Anchorage. The garage sank roughly six feet during the earthquake, along with the rest of Portage. Due to its close proximity to the end of Turnagain Arm, its abruptly reduced elevation, and the height of the tides in the Arm, the site of that fledgling community became, and remains, an uninhabitable saltwater slough. The remains of the Portage Garage can barely be seen today.

But at the time of this story Portage was thriving. It was the gateway to the ice-free port of Whittier, via railroad and a couple of tunnels through the mountains, which was still occupied by the United States Army. You could not drive to Whittier and there was no reason to put your vehicle on a railroad car destined for Whittier because there was not any place to drive it once you got there. Nearly everyone in Whittier lived in the same fourteen-story building, the Hodge Building, due to the heavy snowfalls—241 inches a year on average. That's over twenty feet, in case you're calculating.

That single building, years later converted into a condominium development and renamed Begich Towers, housed practically everything in the community, including a bowling alley, a cafeteria, a movie theater, and a barber shop. During winters the locals dug tunnels in the deep snow between the Hodge Building and other buildings in town.

The Hodge Building opened for business in November 1956 to much fanfare and was referred to as the "wilderness skyscraper." It was named after a remarkable but little-known man, Walter Hodge, a West Point graduate with a civil engineering degree from Cornell University. In 1930 Hodge was assigned to the Alaska Road Commission and he designed and built roads and bridges all over the territory. A few days before Pearl Harbor was bombed by the Japanese, he was appointed Executive Officer of the 18th Engineer Brigade tasked with working on the construction of the Alaska-Canada, or Alcan Highway. The highway, originally 1,700 miles long, was completed in 1942 and took only nine months to construct. A soldier working on it described it as being "miles and miles of miles and miles."

In 1972 the building received its new moniker in honor of U.S Representative Nick Begich, who served as Alaska's sole congressman for a little over a year and a half before disappearing, along with his aide, Russell Brown; the pilot, Don Jonz and House Majority Leader, Hale Boggs, in a Cessna 310 on a flight from Anchorage to Juneau for a campaign fundraiser. I managed to purchase two side-by-side apartments on the top floor of the building at a state auction during the late '70s that I eventually sold to real estate developer Pete Zamarello to help finance my second divorce.

But I digress. Bill Peters attended to all the cars that were left in Portage by people coming and going from Whittier. They were stored in a big parking lot across the Seward Highway from his garage. He parked them, removed the snow from them, got them started after long stretches of disuse, and repaired them in his shop if they were in need. He had a thriving business. So did Dick and Mary Lou Redmond who owned Diamond Jim's bar, located right next door to the garage until the bar was moved to Indian after the 1964 earthquake and subsequent littoral encroachment.

Bill was a brilliantly self-sufficient man who feared nothing and could do most anything. He ran a trap line for beaver and muskrat along the railroad tracks, their stretched and drying pelts hanging in circular metal rings all around the place. He could make "corned beef" out of his seasonal moose or repair your transmission. The last time I saw him was along the Hope Road years after the quake. He had built a cabin just off the roadway and was digging a water well the hard way—by hand—shoring it up with hand-cut logs and removing dirt with a rope and bucket as he descended.

Bill also had an impressive menagerie at the garage. He could have charged admission and perhaps did to the stray tourist of the time. He raised peacocks, pheasants, pigeons, quail, rabbits, ducks, geese, chickens and two young calves, just for starters. In addition to overseeing the garage operation, he managed to feed and water all the critters every day and tend his vegetable garden during the summer months.

Bill was a brawler and a boozer, and when he drove to Anchorage for that rare weekend of fun, he would stay at our home, clean up, and head for the Forest Park Country Club. My mom said he was a womanizer. Bill would get shit-faced drunk, come back to the house loud and obnoxious, and he and my dad would stay up all night long. Drunk and disorderly, he literally destroyed one Christmas Eve at our home on Illiamna Avenue.

I was a sophomore or junior in high school at the time and I loved Bill Peters for all his incivilities.

He taught me how to "Drive the car. Don't let it drive you."

He would take me on the trap line with him and we'd shoot ducks along the railroad tracks. He gave me a deal on an old, ugly Cushman motorcycle, the engine of which he had re-bored. It wasn't much to look at, but because it had been re-bored, it would keep up with the brand-new flashy Cushman Eagles of the day. I'm lucky I didn't kill myself on it.

Bill was a man's man and a woman's man all wrapped in one and I'd have followed him to the end of the earth, so it doesn't really matter to me how I ended up on that moose hunt with him and Max. I still remember the peculiar look on my mother's face when, at age 12, I innocently blurted to her after having seen Bill naked in our shower, "Mom, his balls hang all the way down to here!" my right hand reaching almost to the floor.

Bill had previously hunted for moose near the lake at the head of Twenty Mile River, a glacial stream that flows into Turnagain Arm just north of Portage, also a great spot to dip-net for hooligan, aka smelt or candlefish, around the second week in May. He arranged for himself and Max and me to be flown in by float plane and to be picked up in three days. My parents were to watch the Portage Garage during that time–no small undertaking.

Unbeknownst to us or anyone else but him, our pilot crashed his plane while returning from taking another hunter into the Bush a couple of days later, and though surviving the crash, had to walk back to civilization. Bill and Max and I were comfortable enough in a small log cabin by the lake, though we never saw hide nor hair of a moose. We had enough provisions for the three days we were to be there, and when the fourth rolled around, we took advantage of a package of powdered eggs that had been left in the cabin. We fashioned fishing poles from alder saplings and used some salmon eggs, also left in the cabin, to catch Dolly Varden trout.

It wasn't unusual for a pilot to be a day or so late to pick you up in those days. You just dealt with it. The guides generally had only one plane and depending on weather and circumstances might or might not be on time. But when the fifth day rolled around, we decided we'd better start taking things into our own hands. The plan was to build a raft and float ourselves and our gear down the river to the Seward Highway.

This is when I witnessed Max begin the most amazing transformation. He had been his usual dull self until then, but it seems when Max was young and before he had become a mindless bureaucratic cog, he had worked in a government CCC (Civilian Conservation Corps) Camp during the Great Depression. He grabbed the double-bladed axe from the cabin, which like most cabins in those days was stocked and equipped for people in circumstances such as ours, and suggested that he cut the logs for the raft because he was "pretty good" with an axe. Bill and I readily but dubiously agreed and then stood in awe as Max cut and trimmed log after log. He was a virtuoso. Envious beavers took a work break to witness the performance.

Another couple of days rolled by and the raft began to take shape. The character and humanity in Max's face grew in direct proportion to the size of the blisters on those pencil-pushing hands.

In my spare time, I read and reread the copy of *The Life of Billy the Kid*, also left in the cabin. If you want to know *anything* about Billy the Kid or Pat Garrett just ask me. I can even tell you what pages the mustard stains were on: 36 and 39. One scene sticks out in my memory. The Kid was drinking in a bar when a guy walked in with matching pearl-handled revolvers strapped to his waist. The Kid had already spotted those revolvers and considered how nice they would look on him when the fellow wearing them, who had had too much to drink, began to berate the Kid. "The Kid's an egg sucker," he said. "The Kid's a goddamn egg sucker!"

The guy with the pearl-handled revolvers, too drunk to be scared, was challenging a real, flesh-and-blood sociopath who was fixated on his pretty guns. When I set down the book and left Billy, now wearing brand new matching pearl-handled revolvers, to check on the raft progress Max was working on his umpteenth blister.

Now on day seven in the woods the Dolly Varden and powdered eggs, though heaven sent, were wearing pretty thin but the raft was ready and appeared seaworthy. We piled all of our gear onto it, tied a long rope to one end, and Max and Bill pulled it along the shore while I, on board with a pole, steadied the load and kept the raft from intersecting with the shore. It took a couple of hours for us to get to the other end of the lake from which the creek drained and just as we were preparing to embark on our down-river journey, our pilot circled the lake and landed. It was no doubt a good thing for us and our gear because, though I understood the circumstances and felt I was in capable hands, Twenty Mile River is not exactly the lazy Mississippi and there were no nautical engineers in our group. Nor did I fancy being the only one on board that vessel.

My parents, junior high school teachers, neither mechanically inclined, were happy to see us for reasons aside from our survival. In addition to taking care of the garage business, the garden, the animals and birds all those days, they had to feed the two calves by mixing up their meal and letting them lick and suck it off their fingers, which were practically raw, twice a day.

It was rumored that a few days later Max chased Ruth around their small L Street apartment naked as a jay bird, with a plum in his mouth. I've often wondered if that bureaucratic cog hadn't permanently slipped its gear.

Ruben was not only a world-class raconteur; he was a skilled cartoonist. He ripped off pieces from a roll of wrapping paper, cranking out cartoons to entertain friends in bars and restaurants. He employed his cartoon skills in making the transition from radio to television, utilizing a stylized cartoon duck to portray weather conditions while announcing them. If the forecast called for rain DUCK would be holding an umbrella; if sunshine was forthcoming DUCK would be wearing sunglasses. DUCK thenceforth became a staple in the cartoons Ruben created.

Ruben was a creative genius, not a marketing genius. He manufactured and framed far more cartoons than he or I could sell, but he loved crafting them, so I told him I would purchase all that he produced. I even suggested that he employ different kinds of animals like beavers and porcupines, which he did. Ruben made me promise not to hoard his cartoons, so I've given them away over the years as special gifts and for charity auctions. But I'll admit I still have a pile of them.

Summer on the Kvichak

There was a "Help Wanted" poster from the State of Alaska taped on the wall outside the University of Alaska Fairbanks cafeteria. They were looking to hire a deckhand for a test fishing boat during the upcoming 1961 salmon season. It was one of those nights we were served liver and onions, so I had plenty of time to peruse the poster. I would rather eat a bad oyster, oatmeal at altitude, or remarry my second wife than even be in the same room with liver and onions.

I had spent the previous summer working in Lower Cook Inlet as a deckhand on the *Wild Duck*, a 32-foot gill netter belonging to my parents' teacher friend, Terry Klingel, so I had recent experience. I applied for the job and was hired, but this summer, though essentially performing the same tasks, I would be a state employee working under the direction of a game biologist on the Kvichak River in Bristol Bay.

There were four to six weeks of open time between the end of my spring semester at UAF and when I was due in Bristol Bay. My parents were visiting my sister and brother-in-law, who were living in a little house in Willow Glen, a quaint old neighborhood in San Jose, California, so I flew south to join everyone.

I loved my first brother-in-law, Carl Norwood. Everyone loved Carl. He was good looking, charming and fun. Carl worked at a men's fine clothing store nearby and he was a walking advertisement for traditional men's clothing. Of course, he got a discount on his purchases at the store, but my guess is there was not a lot left of his paycheck to bring home by the time he got decked out. All of us were broke, but we were having fun. Instead of going out, we ate in and played marathon games of Hearts each night.

We were all pretty evenly talented at playing Hearts—except for my mother. Dad loved socking it to you with the queen of spades whether you had the lowest score or not. My sister was a fence-sitter who took few chances, and I was known to try to "shoot the moon" given half a chance. Carl liked to "shoot the moon" too. In Hearts there are 26 points; each heart is worth a point and the queen of spades is worth 13 points all by herself. You cannot lead with her. The aim is to get no points, but if you can manage to get all 26 points, or "shoot the moon," you get zero points and everyone else gets 26. You have to follow suit if you can; if you cannot, you can play any card you want. High card in the suit played takes the hand. The game is over when someone goes over a predetermined number of points—often 100—and the winner is the one with the fewest points. We all took a turn at winning except for my mother, who never won.

Perhaps it was because she tried too hard to give the queen of spades to the person with the lowest score instead of pushing the highest person out. Perhaps it was because it was hotter than all get out that summer in Willow Glen, and there was no air conditioning. Or maybe it was because Carl's mother, a lousy drinker, was in the house simultaneously for a while and openly didn't take a liking to mom. Whatever the case, one night after mom had lost yet again she blew up, screaming at the top of her lungs, "I'm tired of losing all the time!" and threw the deck of cards into the air, scattering them all over the living room. The rest of us were simultaneously aghast and amused. And we were quiet for the rest of the evening—even Carl's mom.

One night we pooled our money and I was elected to drive to a neighborhood restaurant to purchase a pizza. The selections were hand-written on a blackboard with multi-colored chalk, and one of them was anchovy pizza.

Don't ask me why I did it. I'm not sure to this day. I've always been a risk-taker. I was raised in Spenard on TV dinners, goulash, leftovers, white bread sandwiches and cheese spread-filled celery sticks my mom made me for school lunch. I had never seen, much less eaten, sophisticated dishes like escargot, goose liver paté, vegetables like artichokes or anchovies. I hardly knew what an anchovy was.

Suffice it to say the pizza, purchased with the last of our dollar bills and pocket change, was as inedible as a flattened cardboard box plastered with fish-flavored salt. My standing in the family that night was lower than anchovy doo-doo, and you know where that is.

Since we were broke and consuming a fair amount of beer, Carl and I decided to become brew masters. We initially brewed a fairly tasty batch, bottling it in used quart-size beer bottles with the aid of equipment we'd mostly scrounged from the surrounding neighborhood. Ah, but in our eagerness to produce, the next batch was another story. We bottled it too soon.

We stacked the bottles neatly in the basement for aging and before a week was out they began to explode—twenty-four hours a day. Boom! Boom! It was like grenades were going off under the house. The floor shook. The china rattled. Carl and I, the butt of jokes, were told we'd have made better demolition experts than brew masters.

The explosions went on for days (and nights), but we were afraid to enter the basement for fear one of those bottles would explode while we were down there. Finally, when there were only a few bottles remaining (we had been counting) and there was more time between explosions, Carl and I ventured down there holding flattened cardboard boxes (*sans* anchovies) in front of us and lobbed rocks at the remaining bottles until we had burst the last of them.

In spite of the heat that summer, Carl and I were tasked with re-painting the house. The side with southern exposure was badly blistered and peeling, so we had to scrape the old paint off with wire brushes and sandpaper before we could re-paint the wooden siding. That project instilled in me a lifelong appreciation and respect for house painters. It was too hot to be outside painting. Hell, it was too hot to be stretched out by a pool with ice-cold lemonade.

Each day after struggling mightily in that outdoor furnace for a couple of hours we would decide that we required supplies of some sort, like new hats or stir sticks—any excuse to get out of the heat. Our "shopping trips" consisted of jumping in the car and heading for the nearest bar to have a beer. My recollection is that we hadn't finished even the scraping of the siding by the time I had to return to Alaska for my summer job. Carl might have finished the job on his own, but I have a hard time believing that.

Before flying back to Alaska, my dad and I drove to the city to visit the campus of the University of San Francisco and met with the Jesuit in charge of admissions.

He said, "You've proven you can do the work at a four-year institution. We'd be glad to have you."

It wasn't the last time USF went to bat for me. The full story is told in *Learning the Ropes*. I was thrilled to be accepted and would return to the city in the fall to complete my college education without the icicles that had decorated the inside of my dorm windows in Alaska.

The Kvichak River, navigable along its entire length, flows southwest from Lake Iliamna, Alaska's largest freshwater lake, to Kvichak Bay, an arm of Bristol Bay. The river is about 50 miles long and accommodates the largest sockeye salmon run in the world. The name of the river means *from—or up to—great water*, that being Lake Iliamna. Nakeen Cannery, where I was located, sat on a slough on the west side of the river about fifteen miles north of Naknek as the crow flies, that town located on the east side of Kvichak Bay. The cannery was abandoned years ago when the slough silted over.

Nakeen Cannery was an imposing facility during its day, sitting on the edge of the slough, the river's edge held in place by a sweeping row of pilings rising maybe forty feet in the air above low tide, and packed with fifty or more fishing boats when they weren't out on the river or bay.

I recall once seeing a 32-foot fishing boat hanging thirty feet in the air: It had been tied to the pilings at high tide but whoever secured it didn't allow for the bow and stern lines to properly slip up and down the pilings and accommodate the extreme difference between high and low tides. Whoever tied that boat up like that probably never lived it down. Jokes about the guy are no doubt still echoing around what's left of the old cannery.

There were huge processing and storage facilities, administrative buildings, executive living quarters, a couple of bunk houses—in one of which my boss and I were ensconced along with the company fishermen—a cafeteria, and an airstrip with a large wooden water tank on four legs high in the air next to it.

My boss turned out to be a humorless bible-thumper to whom any kind of fun was a four-letter word. Not long out of college, he was a decent enough guy, just boring as hell and prone to proselytizing and lecturing others on his personal brand of morality. His mind was one of absolute certainty about absolutely everything. It must have been a real comfort to him. To the rest of us it was a burden.

The summer turned out to be the most profitable ever for everyone involved except for my boss and yours truly since we were both on salaries. Mine was $500 per month with room and board. The run of sockeye salmon was so large the state extended the fishing period indefinitely and opened up the entire river to fishing to help control the escapement. Most boats still used cedar floats which were not as buoyant as the later foam floats. Fishermen would stretch out three shackles of gear right in front of the cannery at high tide and the float line would boil with frantic, splashing sockeyes. As soon as the net was out it had to be immediately pulled in or it would sink from the weight of the fish caught in it. Once in the boat, the hold would be so full of salmon there might be only an inch or two of freeboard left, the captain motoring gingerly up to the dock to unload before the boat took a rogue wave and capsized.

Fishing periods were determined by escapement as they are today. But the techniques used then were archaic, just like the use of pues—a tool I'll explain in just a moment. One part of the formula for calculating escapement was laying colored fabric on the bottom of a stream and having state employees count the salmon that passed over it, using hand-counters. Another component was aerial observation from small aircraft.

A third was my boss and me. In our small test-fishing boat, we would use a gill net to fish each low tide and our catch was somehow combined with the information acquired by the other means to determine the amount of escapement. There were fish galore. My boss tried to talk the state into letting us use the boat to fish for ourselves when not fishing for the state, but the state, not unreasonably, said no.

In the early '60s, all the fish were canned after being pued from the boats into the tenders. A pue was like a pitchfork with a single slightly curved tine. As deck hand I tried to stab the fish either in the head or toward the tail fin so as not to damage the meat any more than necessary. Accuracy depended upon the number of fish and the amount of time available. As far as I know, back then there simply wasn't the sort of local or international market for fresh and fresh-frozen salmon, nor the demand for troll-caught salmon treated with tender loving care that exists today.

Something else that doesn't exist even now, so far as I've been able to determine, is any reference to pues or pueing either on Google or in any written history I've researched. I tried every kind of spelling I could think of and finally called my Halibut Cove neighbor and friend, Clem Tillion, who confirmed the pue spelling. If Clem "Cod Father" Tillion doesn't know how to spell it, who would?

I had a lot of spare time on my hands between fishing low tides every twelve hours and I used most of it to read the library of paperback classics I had brought with me. I read *Les Miserables* by Victor Hugo, *Of Human Bondage* by W. Somerset Maugham, *Silas Marner* by George Eliot, *Moby Dick* by Herman Melville, *The Hunchback of Notre Dame* by Victor Hugo, *Animal Farm* and *1984* by George Orwell, and *The Way of All Flesh* by Samuel Butler, among others. I soon discovered the best way to enjoy the outdoors while avoiding those pesky mosquitoes, as well as my proselytizing boss, was to climb up on the water tower behind the cannery to read. That water tower was my reading room—my sanctuary.

When the fishing season finally ended and I had completed my self-imposed unofficial semester of classical literature there was a lull in activity before the fishermen from Astoria, Oregon and elsewhere on the West Coast returned, financially enriched, to their home states. The nets were stowed away, the aluminum company boats they operated were cleaned up and pulled from the river, and the marathon poker game began. It was a table-stakes game that went on twenty-four hours a day with a lot of hard-earned money flowing to and fro. There was a fair amount of alcohol flowing as well. When the supply ran low—God forbid—everyone pitched in and paid a pilot to fly to Naknek for a whole plane-load more.

There was a young guy from Oregon we knick-named "The Gopher" because a lot of money was flowing in his direction that he stuffed into any pocket or opening he could find in his shirt or pants. He for damn sure wasn't going to quit and leave the table because he was on a lifetime winning streak. I won some money too—almost a month's salary. Proud of myself, I later reported my winnings to my roommate and boss who said, "Yeah, but look how you got it." I should have known better than to even mention it. Poker was just another sinful endeavor to him.

Returning to the University of San Francisco campus I began my sophomore year inside the beautiful Saint Ignatius Cathedral listening to the welcoming speech of President John F. X. Connolly, S. J., who said among other things, "the city of San Francisco is your campus." I was in far different waters than I had just left. Castroville, "The Artichoke Center of the World," was only a hundred miles south near Monterey Bay, which was swarming with record numbers of anchovies destined for Caesar salads in The City by the Bay.

Altogether, that was a pretty exciting set of prospects for a kid from Alaska who had never lived in a big city and had yet to eat either an artichoke or an anchovy—except the cardboard pizza variety of the latter.

"Death of a Companion"

One misses the presence of dead cars along Anchorage thoroughfares, anymore. Back in the times before boroughs and municipalities, lone vehicles, having belched their last, sat in desuetude at various highway checkpoints and, crumbling into spare parts with the help of passing scroungers, disintegrated. Public abandonment was the eventual fate of many Alaskan wheels, for salient reasons: they died earlier, and most often in the dead of winter.

Alaskans were pioneers—the relationship of a northern driver and his car was rather like a dogmusher and team—until the invention of the headbolt heater. That device, a revolution in the arctic vehicular process, warmed the car through umbilical union with energy sources. Before then, dealings between man and driving machine were on a primitive survival level. A driver scraped a hole the size of a silver dollar through the windshield frost—the thought of this, in today's traffic, raises goosepimples the size of pickle warts—and peered through, like a submarine commander at his periscope. This assumes of course that the frigid car even *started* that morning. They were fellow adventurers who developed such tolerances for each other as bind shipwreck survivors and common victims of earthquakes, famine, etc., together. But the winter solstice, no respecter of sentiment, inevitably blew its boreal breath between them and in time chilled the protective relationship of man and machine. What the hell, the heap stopped starting. This time it gave out on Dowling Road, South Anchorage. The driver emerged, slammed the door in its frozen face, and thumbed his way home.

When the human part of the relationship departed the scene, the mechanical remains soon became that: remains. But it was the nature of their disintegration over the winter months that occupies memory.

Despite the inanimate status of the abandoned car, something strongly personal was connected with its passing, something more than soulless wreckage, certainly more than plain junk. After the car sat for a day, then two, a week, a month, at the roadside—one wondered if the ex-driver didn't visit the site sometimes to reflect on their longtime history together—it began visibly to retreat into its metal shell and lose identity. Most abandonments occurred in January, and swiftly a layer of frost claimed the chassis and reduced the separate features—lights, bumpers, trunk—into a single formlessness. Succeeding layers of frost erased signs of shape, and finally the hulk, though unrelated to surrounding scenery, gradually faded into, and was reclaimed by, the frozen north.

Once, when an abandoned car was still identifiable, a certain incident brought a moving aspect of the man-and-machine relationship to mind. One dim twilight on Northern Lights Boulevard I saw a couple of ravens sitting on the hood of a dead pickup; they reminded me of buzzards perched atop the skeleton of a buffalo, whitening and wasting away on the winter prairie: slowly fading signs that pioneers once passed this way.

Collected Ruben Gaines IV ©1989 Ruben Gaines

Augustus Chidley

"Guess what?" I asked.

"What?"

"I got into a bar fight, chipped my front tooth, and have to wear this ugly white temporary for a while."

"Guess what?"

"What?"

"I have to have my tonsils removed"

"Guess what?"

"What?"

"I bought a new poppy red Mustang convertible with wire wheels."

The year was 1964. Bob Seale, my New York Life personal manager at Number One Montgomery Street in San Francisco, never grew tired of the "Guess what?" game. Bob was always very animated and melodramatic and loved to retell my adventures.

My first wife Lilla, daughter Michele, and I lived on the second floor of an old apartment building under the freeway on Octavia Street managed by the Lonergans, a young couple who were friends of ours from my years at the University of San Francisco. Below us lived Old Lady Fogel and her beautiful daughter. When we would party on weekends with the Lonergans, Old Lady Fogel would bang her broomstick on the metal garbage chute that ran down the middle of the building and shout up at me, "Go home, you stupid from Alaska!" As you might imagine, I had a couple of appropriate responses. One time a drunken vagrant crawled in Old Lady Fogel's downstairs window and was taking a nap on her couch. Lucky for him, it was the daughter who came home first and found him.

That Mustang was the coolest car on the road at the time. When I'd drive down Fillmore Street kids would chant from the sidewalks, "Mustang! Mustang!" With its white convertible top, it was a show-stopper. My friend, Pat Lonergan, was so jealous and covetous of that car he wouldn't talk to me for a week after I drove it home.

The general manager at New York Life, a dignified, grey-haired gentleman named Jack Cullen, called me into his office after my purchase and said among other things, "Whatever you end up doing, young man, you had better make a lot of money." At twenty years of age, I was at the time the youngest New York Life salesman in America.

There were no parking spaces in our building on Octavia Street, so I had to rent a very cramped one-car space in a building about half a block away to park my car. When backing out I had to go very slowly because I couldn't see worth a damn and there were only a couple of inches on either side of the car at the garage door opening. One morning on my way to work, wearing a three-piece suit, button-down shirt and wing-tipped shoes, I was backing ever-so-slowly across the sidewalk when suddenly I felt an unusual bump and heard a low, groaning sound. I leaned out my open door, looked back toward the street, and saw two legs with shoes and rumpled socks sticking out from under my car.

I thought, "Oh, my God! I've almost run over someone!" As a matter of fact, I had backed over the legs of an old man, and when I put the car in forward and drove part way back into the garage I ran over them again, though I didn't realize it at the time. Fortunately for the old guy he had fallen lengthwise into the sunken area where the sidewalk curb met the street. I really can't explain to this day how it happened, but believe me, I was scared shitless. Later, I surmised there had been some alcohol involved on his side of the equation. But at the moment, not only was I afraid I might have killed someone, we were also a struggling young family, and I was late on my car insurance payment to State Farm.

After giving what assistance I could and procuring an ambulance, I immediately began the task of communicating with the State Farm people and canvassing the neighborhood for any eye-witnesses. Though I was almost certain the incident had been witnessed, no one would admit to having seen it.

The State Farm representative I dealt with wasn't much older than I. He was helpful, but not entirely reassuring. He told me my coverage should be in place while leaving the matter open to a decision from higher up the chain of command. Over the next couple of days and sleepless nights we learned the name of the old-timer I'd run over was Augustus Chidley, that he was a veteran, and had been taken to Marine Hospital for treatment.

Another college friend of mine from the University of San Francisco, John Sellai, was managing Pinelli's Flower Shop out in the Avenues. I called John and ordered a twenty-five dollar flower arrangement to be sent to Mr. Chidley. That was a lot of money for me at the time.

The State Farm guy had been in contact with the hospital and learned that Mr. Chidley was okay and able to receive visitors, so we arranged a mutually convenient time to meet at Marine Hospital. My understanding was that it was nothing but a goodwill visit, but it turned out my new insurance friend had other plans.

At the appointed time we were at the reception desk of the hospital asking the whereabouts of Mr. Chidley. The nurse at the counter told us rather unceremoniously that Mr. Chidley was not in a good mood.

"Did you send him flowers?" she asked. "He just now refused to accept them."

Giving me a quizzical look, she said, "See how they spelled his name on the Get Well card."

I stared in horror at the card on the flower arrangement my good buddy John had sent on my behalf to soften up the old guy. It was addressed to Augustus "Shitley."

After a momentary discussion the nurse agreed to take us in to see Mr. Chidley. We sucked it up and followed her. He was in a large ward and appeared to be well taken care of, but he was definitely not in a good mood. We made our introductions. I made my apology interrupted by, "You not only ran over me once; you ran over me twice!"

There were a few light moments provided by the nurses who had nicknamed him "Old Rubber Legs," because, amazingly, neither of his legs had been fractured by the incident, but I thought it best not to bring up the flowers and the unfortunate misspelling of his name. Mr. Chidley, who was more upset about his glasses being broken than anything else, began to calm down—a perfect time for my friendly insurance agent to make his lowball offer of $1,500 to settle all present and future claims. To say the offer was not well received would be the understatement of the mid-1960s in the entire Bay Area.

World War II broke out again in all its fury (numerous expletives deleted).

"You scoundrels! Get the hell out of here! I've been in two world wars! I've been gassed! I've been run over by tanks! No goddamn, punk kid is going to kill me by running over me with a fancy new car!"

It turned out I did have coverage with State Farm, and fortunately everyone survived the incident. In the meantime I had to go to Number One Montgomery Street and report to my personal manager, Bob Seale.

"Guess what?"

"What?"

"I ran over an old man. Twice."

In the letter that began this tale, I acknowledged that Ruben drew the Chilkoot Charlie's logo for me. It is a splendid logo, perfect in every respect. It is simple but profound, and readily recognizable; it stands out anywhere. It is an ideal cartoon image of the titan figure it represents.

During my mountain climbing years, at my wife Shelli's suggestion, I borrowed an idea from the Iditarod dog racers who postmark decorative cachets, carry them the roughly 1,000 miles to Nome, postmark them again, and then give them to supporters as collectibles or sell them to raise money. Ruben drew cartoons for each of my Seven Summits climbs with Chilkoot Charlie in an outfit appropriate for each mountain.

The Denali cachet saw him dressed as a sourdough with mittens and a hat with ear flaps; for Kilimanjaro he wore the uniform of a French Legionnaire; for Elbrus he had on a big Russian-style fur hat; for Aconcagua he wore a big straw hat and a serape; for Vinson he was shaking hands with a penguin on the summit; for Kosciusko he wore an Australian Outback hat; and for Everest he was a sourdough again.

Carrying over a hundred cachets on each climb, I would have them postmarked at a location near the base of the mountain, haul them to the summit in my backpack and have a photo taken with them. Then I would have them postmarked again somewhere near the base. Upon returning home, Ruben hand-colored each of the cachets—a job he dreaded but performed with kind-hearted tolerance—and signed them. I then numbered and signed them. They made great gifts and I was proud that people collected them, some framing them and hanging them in their homes or offices.

Chilkoot Charlie in Girdwood

It was the second of three simultaneous Chilkoot Charlie's operations in different Alaskan cities. Locals called it Chuck's. Plenty of people preferred it to the original operation in Anchorage. It featured the same basic décor: spruce slabs, fish nets on the ceiling, copies of floor-to-ceiling Betty Park paintings of Chilkoot Charlie and Six-Toed Mordecai, keg seats, wire spool tables, and peanut shells. But it was more capacious than the original at the time and it was sort of out in the woods. The bar, dance floor, live entertainment and games were all in one big room. It was a fun place, as was the community it was rooted in, Girdwood, aka Girdweed.

I purchased the business from Doug Lewsader in the early '70s. He and his wife, Thea, had operated the place for a few years as the Crow Creek Mountain Lodge. Lewsader, also known as, "Lewsader the Crusader" because of his penchant for religious ranting, was in fact an unscrupulous character who took me aside and let me in on the secret of how he made a substantial profit from the sale of his draft beer. He bought frozen kegs from The Odom Corporation at a heavy discount and melded them half-and-half with healthy, fresh kegs. I wouldn't be a bit surprised if he put MacNaughton Canadian Whiskey in his Seagram's Crown Royal bottles too.

Before moving to Girdwood Lewsader was the personal pilot of Billie Sol Estes. As such he probably knew way too much about the fertilizer quota scandals and a string of a half-dozen or more murders and cover-ups, all linked in some way to then-vice president Lyndon Johnson, Estes, and a slew of Johnson cronies. Papers reported that after the mysterious plane crash that killed Coleman Wade, the builder of most of Estes' grain storage facilities, the normally talkative Lewsader showed up in court represented by the very expensive lawyer, John Cofer, a longtime associate of LBJ, and with nothing more to say. Word was that Doug was told to "get lost" or else have his name added to that long list of unfortunates. So, he kept his head down in Girdwood and flew helicopters for the oil companies for a while.

In his book, *A Texan Looks at Lyndon, A Study in Illegitimate Power,* J. Evetts Haley reports,

> *As the civil litigation precipitated by the collapse spread, the testimony of scores of men was searchingly sought, among*

these that of Douglas Lewsader, Billie Sol's loquacious pilot, who at first could not even afford a jack-leg lawyer. But when the testimony of Lewsader—the pilot who had flown so many political notables for Estes—came to be taken his counsel was one of the most able and expensive in Texas—John D. Cofer.

In each case the public wonders: Who paid Cofer? The bankrupt Billie Sol? Then how? If not, who? And why?

Before Cofer took over and tied a knot in Lewsader's tongue, that knowledgeable gentleman had spilled a lot of loose and indiscriminate information. He told of a 'command call' he had one night to come to Estes' home. When he got there a big, burly man with Billie introduced himself as an agent for the Teamsters union, Hoffa's outfit that was having its trouble with Bobby Kennedy, who had lost no love on Lyndon, but who still in his capacity as Attorney General, the arbiter of federal justice and boss of the FBI—might lower the boom on Billie Sol. All of which was in the realm of political reason.

In view of the well-known fact that gangsters think and operate in terms of blackmail and payoffs, his suggestion was logical and from the point of view of all involved, if not prudent, at least reasonable. One thing about gangsters, they come to the point. His proposal was that 'for a million dollars we will deliver the dope on Lyndon Johnson.' It was a waste of words to elaborate upon its possible use among men of parts and imagination. Bargained into the hands of Bobby, it might slow the sometimes rusty wheels of justice from grinding down on Billie Sol. In the hands of Estes it might mean that Lyndon would have to go all the way to keep Billie out of trouble. At least these were the sordid implications.

His proposition made, the gentleman rose to his feet, flipped out his card with the address of a Chicago Club and, suggesting they check his credentials, said: 'Here's my card and here's the Club. I'll be back in two weeks to get your answer. Whoever lets this news get out will be dead!'

According to Lewsader, on April 21, 1963, two weeks later to a day, he was back for an answer. Estes had checked the Club and confirmed his identity. Aside from the other imponderables in such dealings, however, was the uncertain question of whom he really might represent. Puzzled investigators have wondered if it might have been Lyndon, or even the Kennedys, applying the ancient materialistic test as to whether Billie Sol himself was amenable to blackmail and hence politically exceedingly dangerous.

Billy Sol, the paragon of Pecos virtue who 'never took a drink, smoked, or cursed,' turned the proffered professional services down. After all there is a limit to which decent men can go.

Lewsader had gotten about as far from south Texas as he could without leaving the United States and it certainly appears he had good reason.

The manager I put in charge of the Girdwood Chilkoot Charlie's was Dale Vaughn (1942-2010), aka DV or my nickname for him, Orv, who had been the manager of my Anchorage operation. Dale's nickname for me was Harv or Councilman Cocksucker when he really got going. He had been an army sergeant in Vietnam, put in some time on the Cook Inlet oil rigs, and developed a distinctive look of horn-rimmed glasses, closely cropped hair, and white socks. He was a redneck.

He and his wife, Darlene, lived upstairs over the bar for a while, like Doug and Thea had. It was dark, cramped, and lacked privacy. Darlene was so unhappy with the arrangement that I bought a double-wide trailer and set it up next to the club for them. They never thanked me, and as far as I could tell the upgraded living arrangement failed to make her any happier.

Dale was not the sort of guy who would normally have taken up skiing. I had to insist on it. We were operating adjacent to a ski resort, after all, and competing with the hotel for skiing customers. He took up skiing and actually enjoyed it. It might have been the only time in Dale's life that he didn't wear white socks with his black horn-rimmed glasses, but I doubt it. It was well understood by those in the know that you could always make money with someone willing to bet Dale was wearing other than white socks, no matter what else he might be wearing.

We used to joke that Dale was an asshole, but that he was a perfect asshole. He and I used to get into huge arguments like I have never gotten into with anyone else in my life. It's still a mystery to me why I allowed myself to get drawn into so many shouting matches with him. When he was running Chilkoot's in Spenard and I was running Gordo's, which I'd converted to a gay clientele, we would get into shouting matches in the latter, then move upstairs so as not to be so disruptive, only to return to the bar to find we'd scared off all the customers.

Girdwood presented some of the usual problems of the era. There were a few locals who had themselves convinced that they were going to run the club, not me or Dale. After receiving a call for help one night from Dale, I drove down the highway with a few heavily armed friends and came to the very brink of a shootout with these loons. Fortunately, they backed down. In the '70s, just because you had your name on the liquor license didn't mean you were going to be readily accepted as the boss by your patrons. You sometimes had to establish your bona fides by use of force.

"What do you mean you're not going to accept tabs anymore?" "Bullshit!" "You can't raise the price of draft beer." It's no wonder Lewsader watered it down.

I never did manage to make any money operating that club. I was paying for live bands and management in a small, seasonal community with generally only weekend nights to prosper. To make matters worse, Dale, who liked to shout at me, "You never pounded a single nail!" at the top of his lungs, without ever acknowledging that he had never invested a single cent for his significant share of the corporation, started hanging out all the time with fellow bar owner Eddie at Eddie's Hayloft on the Old Seward Highway in Anchorage instead of looking after our business.

After returning from a mid-life crisis runaway to Belize I was able to sell the Girdwood business to someone who wanted to move the license to downtown Anchorage, which was then becoming an attractive location. Dale went to work for Eddie, where he had been spending all of his time anyway.

During the time I owned Girdwood Chilkoot's I also owned, with a couple of friends, a chalet on Brighton Drive, just down the hill from the Alyeska Resort's Day Lodge parking lot. We had a clear view of the ski slopes out our side window, so when we got up in the mornings we could see what the weather was like on the mountain. When there was ample snow we could ski from the lodge right to our front door. I spent a lot of time in Girdwood with my kids, my nephew Curt, and my second wife, Tiffany, skiing and just relaxing. Driving forty miles out of town was like leaving the state since there were no cell phones at the time. When I decided to sell the Girdwood bar operation in the early '80s, I told my teenage daughter, Michele, about it and she started crying.

I asked, "Why are you crying?"

It was because she thought I was going to sell the chalet where we had spent so much quality time together. She was immediately okay once I explained I was talking about the bar.

I hired a manager named Pat Osborne, the son of an old pal of mine named Stan Osborne, aka Stanley Steamer, from when I sold life insurance out of New York Life's Anchorage office. Pat had recently graduated from UAF and had a good appreciation for music. He and I arranged a going-away party for Dale, and I showed up with a white suitcase so we could all write rude going away comments on it with a marking pen for fun.

Dale, drunk and sitting at the bar next to me—I was also drunk—began berating me with his "You never pounded a single nail!" bullshit. When drunk, he would shout the same epithet over, and over and over. Eventually, I told him to shut up or step outside with me. He didn't, so we did. It was no match and if several people including Pat Osborne hadn't pulled me off of him, my years of pent-up rage might have been his quietus.

Later, on duck-hunting trips across Cook Inlet with our cronies, Dale would grouse about it over and over, shouting, "He put the *'booots'* to me!" He was right. I did. And I'd do it again.

"Beyond Laughter"

I once heard laughter

  that resounded from

  the carpeting of flowers

  to the ceilings of the heavens

   and, unbounded, mingled with the wind,

  ringed earth and met its echo,

  and their answerings

  made giant tides

  that drew me

  after them,

  seduced;

  their rhythm

  was my everything

  until I awoke alone

  one somber dawn:

  they'd dashed

  against the

  silence and

subsided, and

since then

are only

faintly heard

from bounded

distances.

A Chugach Album and On Youth ©1979 Ruben Gaines

Following Felix

The Interior Alaska city of Fairbanks has more than a century-long history of boom-and-bust economics, starting with the discovery of gold in 1902 by Felice Pedroni, aka Felix Pedro (1858-1910). Next came the military build-up before and during WWII, then the DEW Line or Distant Early Warning Line construction during the Cold War that operated from 1957 to the late '80s, and finally the $8 billion, 800-mile trans-Alaska Pipeline construction that began in April 1974 and was completed in June 1977. I got in on the last one, though it was a pyrrhic experience in many ways.

Felix Pedro Hispanicized his name upon arrival in New York City in 1881, but he was actually Italian, born in the small village of Trignano in the Apennine Mountains in the Province of Modena. He worked his way westward to Alaska taking jobs in different cities along the way and began searching for gold in the Fortymile area. When he finally discovered it in the Tanana Hills northeast of Fairbanks in 1902, on a small unnamed stream now known as Pedro Creek, he created a full-blown gold rush with his comment, "There's gold in them thar hills!"

When Pedro died of a supposed heart attack in 1910, at the age of 52, his business partner, Vincenzo Gambiani insisted, even on his own death bed, that Pedro had no heart problems and had, in fact, been poisoned by his wife. His body was shipped off to San Francisco and buried in nearby Colma, but in 1972 the body was exhumed and returned to Italy, where an autopsy was performed. Testing of hair samples supported Gambiani's insistence that Pedro had indeed been poisoned. He was reinterred in Fanano, Italy.

During the Egan administration, Alaska's political boss ensconced behind the unlabeled door right next to the Governor's office in the capitol building in Juneau was Alex Miller, aka "Big Juice." My mentor, Skip Fuller, agreed to accompany me to Juneau, introduce me to Alex, and solicit the resolution of an issue I had with the Department of Labor on condition that I become a Democrat. It was an eye-opening experience, done more easily than I might have imagined. A man of my word, I became an Egan Democrat.

Skip and I were present when Alex ordered the commissioner to his office, had me explain my problem to him and told him what he wanted him to do. It was obvious the commissioner didn't like being told what to do, but when the hearing was held in downtown Anchorage, a dismayed young state attorney whispered to me outside the commissioner's office, "It appears the commissioner has his mind already made up on this matter." Of course, I didn't say a word.

Palling around with Alex and other power broker friends of Skip's for a few days and nights, playing all-night table-stakes poker in a legislator's room in the Baranof Hotel—and winning—I heard some amusing stories. Alex told me about when he was young, naïve and first delving into politics in Fairbanks. Back then he did what he was told.

As an election approached he was ordered to go out and procure names from tomb stones to register their ghosts as Democrat voters. He said he dutifully brought back a list of names, but when they got to Felix Pedro's name, his political overseer said, "Oh, we can't use that one!" and crossed it off the list. It sounded true enough to me at the time and I laughed out loud, though obviously it was only an amusing story since Felix was by then buried in his home country of Italy. The remainder of the story probably did have more than a grain of truth in it.

My Chilkoot Charlie's location was on First Street in Fairbanks right across from the Chamber of Commerce building which sat on the bank of the Chena River. I had in mind a chain of Chilkoot Charlie's nightclubs and thought it would be best to establish a few locations in Alaska before venturing "Outside."

I opened the operation in Fairbanks more than a year before the pipeline construction began only to discover everyone in town was chasing the same dollar. It was an expensive foray. When the boom finally did hit, there was plenty of money to go around—but Fairbanks was even more out of control than Anchorage, which is saying a lot. Prices were sky high. I seem to remember a cup of coffee and a doughnut costing something like $2.50—in 1973.

I had purchased the Wonder Bar from Larry Wike who also owned the Riverside Bar and two or three others. The Riverside faced onto "Two Street" and the two bars backed smack up against one another because there was no alley between First Street and Second Street. You literally walked through a doorway out the back of one bar and into the other. Both bars catered primarily to an Alaska Native clientele.

My manager, Dan Wright—aka God Dan Wright—and I decorated the place with spruce slabs, netting, and all the other appropriate accoutrements. These of course included wire spool tables, padded kegs for seats, Chilkoot Charlie and Six-Toed Mordecai paintings—copied from the originals painted by noted Alaskan artist Betty Park for the Anchorage operation. We encouraged our new customers to cover the floor with peanut shells, just like in Spenard and Girdwood.

I bought a little home in a neighborhood between downtown and the airport for Dan to live in and for me to stay in when I was in town, which was frequently. I was as familiar with the new Parks Highway drive then—roughly 350 miles between Anchorage and Fairbanks as I am with the 221-mile drive between Anchorage and Homer today. I taught Danny how to do daily reports of income and expenses and how to make the daily bank deposits of net proceeds.

Arriving in Fairbanks on my regular visits, I would find a drawer or two of a dresser in Dan's bedroom with weeks of envelopes stacked neatly by date—no daily reports and no deposit slips—with the money having been pulled out and replaced by receipts as he needed cash to pay bills. Who needs a bank? So, the first thing I'd have to do was fill out the daily reports, deposit what money was left, if there was any, and take the paperwork to our bookkeeper.

In addition to the usual rowdiness prevailing at the time, there was a rather large group of U.S. Army draftees from the mean streets of Baltimore who were stationed at Fort Wainwright, just outside Fairbanks. They were not thrilled to be there, to put it mildly. My guess is the Army didn't know what to do with them, so they sent them to the most remote outpost they could think of.

These miscreants hung out in a nearby parking lot and all along First Street, between the parking lot and our front door. Dan, to get to and from the club each day, had to wend his way through a virtual gauntlet of guys wearing unfriendly, aggressive dispositions, making threatening comments, and openly displaying walking sticks, knives, and other weapons. He soon made friends with some bikers who escorted him and his girlfriend through the crowd and started wearing a Colt .45 semi-automatic openly on his hip. Fortunately, he never had to use it. There was an actual riot in downtown Fairbanks at one point with bricks being thrown through retail store and bank windows.

My competition in Fairbanks was most unwelcoming also. In fact, I came to the conclusion that locals would have preferred to have someone from Texas—or anywhere other than Anchorage—competing with them for business. A lot of people in Fairbanks simply had nothing but disdain for Anchorage or people from Anchorage. In their eyes, "Los Anchorage" was that big, callous, superficial, pushy upstart intent upon controlling the whole state financially and politically.

I cannot recall the number of times I heard, "I've been here (Alaska) for forty (or fifty, or sixty) years and I've never been there (Anchorage)," said proudly, loudly and dismissively.

I discovered the Chilkoot Charlie's theme was easily and effectively transportable and attracted the same sort of welcome clientele. But then there was the problem of entertainment that worked well in one location not working in another as exemplified by the disappointing attraction of Mr. Whitekeys, who drew large, enthusiastic crowds in Anchorage. But Fairbanks and Mr. Whitekeys were like oil and water.

One night soon after his arrival, after having said something about the American flag—I don't remember what—Whitekeys took a break, stepped off the stage and was cold-cocked by a guy that had taken offense at his comment. I could never convince him to venture north to that interior city again.

The undeniable proof of my unwelcome status was when I got burned down. It was an obvious case of arson, but there wasn't even the pretense of an investigation. I thought I knew who the culprit was, but I couldn't prove it. Suffice it to say it was in all likelihood a nearby competitor.

Now I'm stubborn, and here's proof of that. Instead of leaving town, like I should have, I stood in knee-deep water in the basement of my burned-out bar and negotiated a deal with Larry Wike for the purchase of the Howling Dog Saloon in Ester, a little old gold mining town a few miles outside of Fairbanks.

It was a nice little town, but it had the hardest water I have ever encountered and there was arsenic in it to boot. Today it's still a nice little town populated by artists, a lot of University of Alaska Fairbanks faculty, and it still sports the world's hardest water with arsenic in it to boot.

The Howling Dog Saloon guys moved to another nearby small town, Fox, where the operation remains to this day. My manager, Dan Wright, left town in the middle of the night in a nice new motor home with his little blonde girlfriend and a bag of my money, of course leaving me to complete the last of the daily reports.

The new location in Ester was already a rustic Alaskan saloon, which made it easy enough to convert to a Chilkoot Charlie's. This was readily accomplished by Jim Ables, my new manager imported from my Spenard operation. I bought a little house on the main street that was once the post office and was only a few doors down from the bar. There was a very nice older couple living directly across the street and, just beyond them, in a beautiful log cabin, lived none other than Magnus Colcord "Rusty" Heurlin (1895-1986), a noted Alaska painter.

At the time, I was serving my second term on the Anchorage City Council and the Anchorage Borough Assembly. My marriage to my second wife wasn't going well and neither was the business in Ester or at the second Chilkoot Charlie's in Girdwood. If I could have run either operation myself I think I could have made a go of it, but having them located in distant communities, managed by others, even though I had made them part owners, was not proving to be a successful formula.

I was in Ester when I got a call from my mother, then living in Honolulu, telling me my dad was hospitalized on his death bed with cancer. I remember discussing my predicament over the phone with my manager in Anchorage, Howard Pumpelly (1941-1991), aka "How Weird." I told him, "Howard, I just can't drop everything and go over there," to which he responded, "I had to make the same decision once and I made the wrong one. Go!" So I did. Thank you, Howard.

Going to Hawaii for a week, where I sat for long hours with my mostly unconscious dad in the hospital was actually just the break I needed. It gave me a chance to achieve a sort of closing with dad and ponder my immediate circumstances objectively. When I returned to Alaska, I parted with politics by not running for a seat on the assembly of the newly unified Anchorage city/borough. I unloaded the Ester Chilkoot's by selling it back to Larry Wike and soon ran off to Belize in a mid-life crisis that is fully covered in *Learning the Ropes*.

I mentioned that Mr. Whitekeys would never return to Fairbanks, but he did write a song about it for his Anchorage audience in which he said, "It's not the end of the world, but you can see it from there!" He also described the puke on the street-side walls of the Polaris Hotel in the fall that you could bet your last dollar would still be there in the spring.

The song was hilarious to Anchorage audiences, but I'm sure he has better sense than to sing it in Fairbanks, in the unlikely event he ever does return.

Before I started traveling all over the country to find entertainment for the club in Anchorage, I spent a lot of time visiting my locations in Girdwood, Fairbanks, and then Ester.

As mentioned previously, Rusty Heurlin lived in Ester. Rusty is universally recognized as an Alaskan master artist. His original paintings are highly sought after and very expensive. He is in the same lofty realm as Sydney Laurence, Eustice Ziegler, Ted Lambert, and Fred Machetanz. Rusty is not as well known outside of Interior Alaska as the others, but he is very well known in the Interior or to anyone knowledgeable about Alaskan art. Large paintings of his used to adorn the walls of the Fairbanks Airport, though on a recent overnight visit I didn't see them.

Rusty's paintings portray wondrous pastel hues of the Arctic, and his depictions of the Interior and far north—the coldness, the alpenglow, the winter skies, and the lifestyles of Native Alaskans—are unsurpassed. Rusty was also a world-class character and an expert at the shell game. He prided himself on knowing the capital of every country in the world and loved winning bets at it. But I beat him once, when I turned up with my future wife, Shelli, to close on the sale of my little house in Ester. I'd come prepared with the name of an African country and capital that had been recently renamed due to a *coup d'état*. The stakes were a case of beer, so my win didn't further endear me to him.

Rusty's best pal was my friend and creator of the Chilkoot Charlie character, Ruben Gaines. Ruben was in the habit of traveling to Ester to "cook a buzzard" with Rusty for Thanksgiving, as he explained.

The first time Ruben made his annual sojourn after the opening of the Ester Chilkoot Charlie's, he sauntered in with station manager Ken Flynn from KHAR and Rusty in tow. Ruben announced to Jim Ables, recently appointed Ester manager, that I had made a deal with him that among other things allowed him to drink free at Chilkoot Charlie's for the rest of his life.

Ables, a character in his own right replied, "Oh, he did, did he?" and proceeded to "six-pack" the three of them with screwdrivers. I showed up not long afterwards—the bar now literally covered with screwdrivers— and the bullshit was so deep within an hour that the handful of other patrons in the place had to dash to their cars for hip-waders.

By way of explanation, it used to be legal to buy someone as many drinks as you wished; never mind whether they wanted them. Better that they didn't. "Six-packing" was commonplace in the '70s and '80s. The recipient was either supposed to drink the purchase on his behalf or wear it. David Asplund, the son of the first Municipality of Anchorage mayor, who also owned Asplund Supply Company, used to like to set new records with the number of drinks he bought me in Spenard. He kept upping the ante until one day he 164-packed me with scotch and sodas, pouring the contents of a dozen large, 64-ounce pitchers over my head. I happily rang up the purchase, went home, changed my clothes, and returned to my business. You might be guessing that money was easier to come by at the time. It was.

What's in a Name?

A major airline, later absorbed by Delta Airlines, used to proudly proclaim: "Western Airlines; the *oooonly* way to fly!" Well, it certainly was the only way to fly from Anchorage to London and back in 1980. They had just inaugurated the service with a $500 round trip fare.

Back in Anchorage, as I jogged through the snow in a neighboring subdivision, the Western Airlines radio ad played over and over in my head. I had never been to Europe and was trying to think of some way of taking advantage of that deal and being able to write it off as a business expense.

Let's see... British bands... Chilkoot Charlie's... hum... British bands were really a big item in the 1980s. London was a hotbed of musical talent. The "British Invasion," as it was called, was in full swing. It occurred to me that there had to be some great bands in that city that weren't yet recording stars and might be interested in traveling to the States for a gig. Bingo.

It was late March when Don Fritz, my manager at the time, and I flew to London. I remember the month because when we got through looking for bands in London, I decided we might as well go to Paris while we were in the neighborhood. We were two single guys in Paris in springtime, and both very much in love with women back in Anchorage, but more on that later.

We did not contact any entertainment agencies to help us with our London entertainment search. We just collected the local alternative papers from the newsstands and followed our instincts. We were in London for a week, visiting requisite tourist destinations during the day like the Tower of London, Big Ben, and the Tate Museum, then hitting the clubs and pubs all night.

Toward the end of the week, we walked into the 101 Club in Clapham—a dingy little pub that presented original bands. The smoke was so thick you could have cut it with a knife, and a band named The Fix was setting up to play. We had a couple of beers, spent a little time talking to the band's manager, Frank Sansom, and settled in to listen to some original music.

When they started playing, we were mesmerized. What an original sound they had. The lead singer, Cy, wearing a white tank top, had loads of charisma, a great voice, and a uniquely captivating stage presence. Jamie, the guitar player was excellent, but I was particularly taken by the creative use of the keyboards by Rupert. Finally, there was Adam, the drummer, who banged away so energetically with his tongue out I thought he might bite it off.

We spent the entire evening talking to Frank, listening to the band, and visiting with them after they had finished playing. We were full-fledged fans. I proposed setting up a West Coast tour of the United States including a gig at Chilkoot Charlie's en route. Frank the manager was interested. So was the band.

At some point in the evening, I told Frank that I thought the band should consider changing their name, stating that they would never make it with a name like The Fix.

"The name has too many negative, unsavory connotations and it doesn't comport with the band's sound," I said.

The next day we met Frank at his office, discussed the proposed tour in detail, got some cassettes and promotional material, and were soon off to Paris. We had tentative agreements in hand with a couple of other bands we had seen as well.

No disrespect, but I had been struck by the paucity of pretty women in London. Perhaps it was the high standard I carried with me in my heart and mind—the woman I loved in Anchorage—my future wife, Shelli Shannon. Conversely, I had scarcely gotten through the Paris Charles de Gaulle Airport and had a stiff neck from turning my head so often. Talk about night and day.

It's pretty hard to beat springtime in Paris, though it was hardly a hotbed of rock and roll. We would visit sites like the Jeu de Paume, the Louvre, and Napoleon's Tomb during the days, then have a nice meal, and go to the Folies Bergère. But mostly we spent our evenings hanging out in the sidewalk cafés on the Left Bank. Particularly entertaining were the clowns who would stealthily parade behind clueless passers-by, cleverly mimicking their mannerisms for tips from us as we sipped our Dubonnet apéritifs *avec soda et citron*.

During our last afternoon in Paris, after sightseeing and buying some nice presents for our loved ones back home, we decided to stop at a delicatessen for food, then just stay in our hotel near the Arc de Triomphe for the evening. We walked out with a couple of very large paper bags full of pâté, French bread, cheeses, sliced meats, fruit, and several bottles of wine, then hopped into the back seat of a Mercedes Benz taxi-cab driven by a middle-aged blonde woman with a big, beautiful boxer dog in the front seat. In Paris people take their dogs everywhere with them, including to fine restaurants.

Of course, the dog jumped to the immediate conclusion that we were all now in the same pack and we were all going somewhere for a world-class feast. He was the happiest dog I had ever seen. He was pressing so hard against the front seat, and leaning so far over it, that he was nearly in the back seat with us. He looked back and forth between Don and me and the bags of food, taking in the odors, grinning from ear to ear, and licking his chops in anticipation of the finest meal ever. He was in doggie heaven.

It wasn't far to the hotel, and when we had paid our fare, unloaded our bags of goodies, and started walking away I thought that dog was going to have a heart attack. He went from doggie heaven to doggie hell in record time. The taxi window on the passenger side was halfway down, so the only thing he could get through it was his head, out of which came the most pitiful barking sounds in canine history. There was an unmistakable look of betrayal in those big brown eyes. It was gut-wrenching for all three of us as the taxi pulled away and those sad eyes and painful sounds faded away into traffic.

We soon had the feast the poor dog had anticipated, *sans le chien*, accompanied by some very nice French wines. We got perfectly ploughed in the process to the point of photographing each other brushing our teeth in the bidet. Most of the evening conversation revolved around The Fix, the ladies waiting for us in Anchorage, and that hapless boxer.

The next day we flew back to Anchorage via London. Shelli had been on my mind during the whole trip. She met me at the airport and had accepted my proposal of marriage within hours. Poor Don was not so lucky. He had an armload of presents that were never delivered because when he called his girlfriend from the airport, she told him she did not want to see him anymore.

Within days I was in touch with Doug Boad, an entertainment agent friend of mine in Portland who, after hearing recordings of the Fix, was as enthusiastic as we were. He immediately began working on a tour of the West Coast with a stop-over in Anchorage to play Chilkoot Charlie's. Unfortunately, the band fired Frank Sansom, replacing him with some-one who thought the band should stay in London and continue working on a recording contract. There went our plans. We had another band from London play the club with only minimal success, but this story does have a happy ending.

One day, less than a year after our trip to London, I was driving down Fireweed Lane when one of the band's unmistakable songs, "Red Skies," began to play. It was the third single on their debut album, *Shuttered Room* that ultimately reached number thirteen on the Billboard Album Rock Tracks chart.

A lot of big-name bands played the Sullivan Arena before the advent of long-range jets and the opening of Russian air space, and fortuitously within another year or so the band was in town for a concert in that venue. Chilkoot Charlie's co-sponsored the show with George Lichter of Northern Stage Company, as we usually did, and the boys visited Chilkoot's afterward. Unfortunately, I was out of town.

Fast-forward to November 2002. The band was still together, and they were available to play Chilkoot Charlie's itself. We presented them for two nights running. We took the band out for dinner before the second concert, at which time I reminded them of the first time I saw them in London and my comment about their name.

Frank Sansom had been relieved of his position because he was not the person they needed to take them to the top, and we had been unable to pull off that original tour he'd helped plan. But they had taken my advice and changed their name from The Fix to The Fixx, this being at least nominally, in my opinion, the reason for their success. That's my story anyway, and I'm sticking to it.

"Baranof"

This verse is part of a visual-audio project, to be presented under later auspices, done in collaboration with the dean of Alaskan artists, Rusty Heurlin. It is called "The Great Land" and consists of 16 canvases in oil with commentary in sound. Some of the verbal accompaniment to the paintings is poetry. The following is heard while the beholders see Heurlin's impressions of Alexander Baranof and his fleet approaching Sitka. He has been commanded by his government and the Russian American company to establish a home base for fur-hunting operations. The verse intends to tell the rest:

The ghostly shapes of half a thousand craft

Converge on Sitka under Baranof

The bluff and lordly, swift *bidarkas* staffed

With Aleuts and Russians, men who scoff

At seas like mountains shaped by tyrant gales,

While Baranof himself beneath his sails

Stands chief of all about him, fore and aft.

Invincible, unchallenged now, they ride

Through dawning mist of history to found

A fortress from which, ranging far and wide,

They'll claim the fabled north as Russian ground.

Through quest and conquest, courage, cruelty,

Imposing will, inflicting slavery,

The plan of empire shall not be denied.

Yet Baranof, no man of childlike trust,

Is well aware of nature's raging force,

For once she rose in wrath. A single gust

Drove many of his argonauts off course,

Delivering them helpless to the sea.

He's well inured to swift calamity:

And to ignore it. Carry on, he must.

There's more to come. The island straight ahead

On which he'll build his fort will be the scene

Of rebel carnage, and the host of dead

Will be his own. But this will only mean

Yet more resolve, though other forts will fall.

He will destroy the totem pole, and tall

Will fly the flag of Baranof instead.

Already half a century has seen

The decimation of a native race,

The Aleut, by trickery, rapine

And brutal greed for fur; soon but a trace

Of otter, seaborne sable, will remain

Along the coast and the Aleutian Chain.

The red of blood stains waters one-time green.

But time restores, And history, again,

Though shaped by human conquest and desires,

Its pages written by the swords of men,

Outlives them. As the conqueror aspires

Toward West he knows, while setting down his page,

He's but the instrument of changing age.

Forever this is true, both now...and then.

Conversations Unlimited 5 ©[no year noted] Ruben Gaines

Band Trips

Historically, fellow employees at Chilkoot Charlie's complained that I and my managers—mostly Don Fritz in the earlier years and Doran Powell in later ones—flew on band trips to the Lower 48, to Hawaii, and even to Europe, stayed in luxurious hotels, went out to extravagant dinners each night, and generally had a great time at the expense of the company.

What we actually did was raise the entertainment bar in Anchorage. Though we might have stayed in nice hotels and had some nice dinners, we flew and drove long distances to see a lot of mediocre acts proffered to us by unscrupulous agents, hanging out in dingy, smoky bars when we would rather have been in bed. But we did ultimately bring home some gems.

Shelli, fully believing the employee myth, came on one trip with Doran Powell and me to southern California. The drive between venues was typically more than an hour, and that was the only trip in which she actually participated in the hunt. She attended another one or two trips, but stayed in the hotel watching movies and getting on a first-name basis with the room service staff. We had told everyone for years that it was more work than play and we now finally had confirmation from a credible first-hand witness.

Incidentally, the rule was that we would never, ever, hire a band that Shelli liked because her musical tastes were so divergent from that of our clientele though she did miraculously, and on her own, discover a band once called Sonya for us in Hawaii that we used multiple times.

From the start, I had never planned on having live professional entertainment in Chilkoot Charlie's. The entertainment was the bar itself, me, and my staff. It all started with a piano and banjo duo called the Rinky Dinks, accompanied by shaker cans and sing-along sheets to encourage customer participation. When it was time to replace the Rinky Dinks I placed a blind box advertisement in the *Anchorage Times* for entertaining acts.

I received several responses, but only followed up on one—a guy named Doug Haggar who billed himself as Mr. Whitekeys. The application he used was a medical claims form on which he filled in "None" in the space provided for "Total Cost of This Illness." That got my attention.

He didn't have a phone, so he drew a map of where I could locate him near Fish Creek, halfway between Spenard Road and the Turnagain-by-the-Sea subdivision.

I brought Doug to the club one evening to audition and I had as many of my regulars on hand as possible to judge his act. The results were mixed. About half of my customers liked him a lot and the other half didn't like him at all. I tilted the balance in favor of Mr. Whitekeys because I recognized his talent. The rest is local legend. Doug worked for me steadily and exclusively for four and a half years and proved himself to be not only quite the talented showman, but a self-motivated, reliable, and professional entertainer. He put together a zany ensemble of guitar, bass and drums with him at center-stage as the pianist and lead vocalist.

At first the band had no name so Doug experimented with several including The Spamtones, Rudy Palm Tree and the Exotic Fruits, the Oosik Music Company, Bitchin' Ernie and the Grunts and even Jimmy Spenard and His Combo of Lard. Patrons would show up and demand to hear the band that had played the previous week. We even ran a public contest to name the band. I don't remember what name won. I coyly suggested the Chilkooties, but unsurprisingly, Doug didn't like that name. It seems to me the one that lasted the longest was the Whale Fat Follies—You'll Laugh, You'll Weep, You'll Fall Asleep.

Doug would take a month or six weeks off and return with a whole new set or two that would have tears running down our cheeks, especially the first night. And he always called the shots. "Hava Nagila," the traditional Jewish folk song sung in Hebrew, was a very popular sing-along song at the time, but Whitekeys would never play it no matter how many times it was requested. Nor did he like being badgered to play other favorites of the day, such as "Great Balls of Fire," by Jerry Lee Lewis. He would say, "I'm not going to play that song, but I'll play one with some of the same notes in it."

Doug was also our promotions manager for a time. He created a clever ad campaign titled, "So You'll Know Who to Blame," which featured each of our quirky employees. I was presented as Julius Caesar Dithers, the founder of J.C. Dithers Construction Company and Dagwood Bumstead's boss in the long-running comic strip, "Blondie."

All good things come to an end, though, and Doug eventually moved down the street to occupy a portion of the Fancy Moose, a large nightclub on Lake Spenard. Doug had his own performing space inside the Fancy Moose. He named that space the Fly By Night Club. The fuselage and wing of an airplane jutted out of the front of the building. A few years later he moved back toward Chilkoot Charlie's and opened his very own Fly by Night Club in a free-standing building where he performed until his retirement.

Over the years a lot of people have asked me what it was like working with Doug Haggar, aka Mr. Whitekeys. On a strictly business level Doug was generally fun to work with, but he had an impenetrable wall around him at least a foot thick. I would not call Doug a misanthrope, but aside from his family relations he was not exactly a warm and fuzzy guy, and if you got beyond business as usual and into the weeds a little with him he was unpredictable and often difficult. My intent is not to diminish Doug in any way, but I guess this is about as good a place as any to relate an interesting political tale. You can draw your own conclusions.

By the early '80s there had, for a number of years, been a large black cloud floating over bars like mine and Doug's that hired professional entertainers. It had been a member of Doug's band who had filed for unemployment benefits while on leave from Chilkoot Charlie's that had required me to travel to Juneau with Skip Fuller, resulting in my becoming an Egan Democrat. Now I found myself facing a serious insurance problem that affected both Doug and me as night club owners.

In particular, Ron Courtney, the owner of a sizable club called the Green Dragon, was being sued by his own insurance company for back payments of worker's compensation insurance on band members that performed at his club. The insurance company's position was that band members were not independent entertainers but employees and that company wanted to be made whole retroactively.

There was a lot of money at stake and Courtney fought the claim. My recollection is that he wound up settling with the insurance company for a rather large chunk of change. Not long after that Doug's insurance company went after him. I was nervously observing all this activity from the sidelines and decided to take the initiative.

First, I spoke with Senator Patrick Rodey, a friend of mine from Anchorage High School. It so happened there was an insurance bill on its way through the Senate and in then-current law there was already a short list of exemptions from worker's compensation coverage, such as housekeepers, so Pat just added two words to the list: contracted entertainers. A mutual friend, Representative Mike Szymanski, dropped a similar bill into the State House. The bills made it through both houses of the legislature without comment by anyone, catching the insurance industry and their lawyers flat-footed.

Governor Bill Sheffield called me up one morning and said, "Hey, Mike. I've got this worker's compensation bill sitting on my desk here in Juneau. Do you think I ought to sign it?"

I laughed out loud and assured him I was absolutely certain he should sign it, which he did.

That was the end of the big dark cloud. I believe Courtney got his money back and Doug, who had demand letters on his desk amounting to thousands of dollars and was talking settlement arrangements with his insurance company, got to dump the whole mess in his trash can.

A few months later Governor Sheffield was campaigning for re-election and I agreed to host a fundraiser for him at Chilkoot Charlie's. The price of admission was a $100 ticket. Of course I called Doug Haggar and he refused to buy one.

Flabbergasted, I asked, "Why?"

Doug said, "I can't afford it."

Giving credit where credit is due, it was Mr. Whitekeys who came up with the Chilkoot Charlie's slogan, "We cheat the other guy and pass the savings on to you!" He couldn't very well take it down the street with him, so he came up with another one for his Fly By Night Club: "We lose money on every drink, but we make it up in volume." He might also have coined the phrase, "No good deed goes unpunished."

After Whitekeys, the next regular performer at Koot's was Jack Toman, whose stage name was Jack Kent. He was the most talented musician I ever worked with. Jack might not have been as zany as Whitekeys, but he was good-looking, a fabulous vocalist and musician, and an extraordinary entertainer. Like Whitekeys, Jack played piano with bass and drums backing him up, but he also played guitar, bass, drums, trumpet, trombone, and flugelhorn himself. Whereas Whitekeys had wit, Jack had class. Both played at piano bars. During Jack's reign of several years the piano bar was laconically referred to as the "Meat Rack," it being lined from one end to the other with infatuated young female customers.

Jack has remained one of my very closest friends. He flew to Anchorage to host my 70th birthday bash and for my retirement party. Shelli and I have also spent time with Jack and his significant other, Jan, in St. Louis, where they reside, as well as in Las Vegas. Jack is not just a friend. He's a brother.

In 1985 I completed the addition of the Spenard Bingo building to the north side of the business, doubling our square footage. We now had competing entertainment on two sides of the club. We started by filling the new stage with local acts, but I also began scouring the rest of the country for quality groups. One of my discoveries was a great musical comedy duo from California named Bird and McDonald that we used off and on for years. Bird and McDonald coined the phrase, "In Alaska you don't lose your girl, you just lose your place in line."

I will never forget the off-night Bird and McDonald were in the bar partying and thought they had cornered the market on pull tabs. On faulty information they figured if they bought the entire remaining pull tabs in one of the open games they would walk away with a quick $1,000. They sat at the Horseshoe Bar for hours opening pull tabs and in the end wound up losing $1,000 instead. That performance was funnier than anything they ever did on stage, and they were very funny on stage.

A local musician, Tom Greenough, aka Tommy Rocker had been playing around town at Harry's and other venues but wanted badly to play at Chilkoot Charlie's. He approached Don Fritz more than once, but I was not convinced a solo entertainer could handle the large stage on the North Side of the club.

In desperation, Tommy Rocker told Fritz that he would play for nothing just to get on our stage. I agreed, but I did not have high hopes. Boy was I wrong.

Tommy played for me for so long and I ended up paying him so much money, that he bought his own club in Las Vegas and now has two—the second in Henderson, Nevada.

Tommy would get on stage with just his guitar and a rhythm machine. He was extremely entertaining—very funny—and he brought in a great crowd. He also had different personas. Everyone's favorite was Daryl Green, a cowboy redneck asshole. He would play the "Rodeo Song," and flip off the crowd, which would then throw balled-up napkins at him. He could be a surfer dude or a Rasta man, and he played a lot of Jimmy Buffett material.

One of the reasons Tommy was so successful at attracting and retaining large crowds and keeping the dance floor packed was that he never took a break; he wasn't about to let his crowd leave and have to rebuild it again. He would play right through from start to close. I was never able to convince another single entertainer or group to try it, and of that lot Tommy's the only one I know of who has two of his own clubs now.

Tommy had a fictitious agent named Irving Levine. I hated that guy. Tommy, acting embarrassed, would say, "Mike, Irving says I need a raise," when I was already paying Tommy lots of money. Of course, unbeknownst to most people, Tommy had a law degree and he really did not need an agent. The fictitious agent was simply Tommy's way of letting me hate someone else for the squeezing I got. But Tommy was worth the money. He would outdraw excellent four-piece bands on the competing stage while getting paid as much as the other four together—or more. But then, of course, the bands took breaks.

We tried our best to hire only "A" caliber bands though sometimes we would get in a pinch and hire a "B" caliber one, typically not as good but perhaps a party band that would create a fun atmosphere. That's generally not a good idea. We provided transportation to and from Anchorage, housing near the club, and a vehicle for the bands to drive but the "B" bands were, let's just say, a little harder on the furniture. A significant draw for quality bands was that they could rehearse during off hours on the main north side stage, which was not open to the public during the day.

The longest-lasting entertainer at Chilkoot Charlie's after Tommy Rocker was Pete Ettinger (1961-2020). Doran Powell and I discovered Pete playing out in the "boonies" in Canada. We were aware of Pete and had wanted to hire him previously, but he had been too expensive. Now we found him on hard times, fronting a mediocre band in a small bar in a small town, a two to three hour drive from Vancouver, British Columbia. He looked very unhappy on stage and when he took a break we managed to convince him that we had some good musicians that he could work with in Anchorage. Pete formed his own band from our local talent and played successfully at the club for more than fifteen years.

I have rarely witnessed talent that seemed more natural. Pete made it look easy. He was a flawless performer and he could sing anything. He was reliable, he took care of business, he was easy to work with, he was loyal, and he wasn't hard on the furniture.

Pete was also a perfectionist. He stayed current by keeping up to date on popular songs, and he required his band members to rehearse regularly. All the musicians, with the exception of one—Bart Boggan—had to be replaced because they didn't want to work that hard. So Pete wound up bringing his band members with him from Canada. Bart, the one local who stayed on, is now one of the owners of the club.

Pete, a Canadian from Nova Scotia by birth, was also a "hockey puck," as am I. Though he was gracious, charming and genuinely liked people, he could be provoked and would actually jump down off of the stage to physically confront a patron who was disrespectful to him or his band.

Pete was tragically killed one morning while crossing Tudor Road in the crosswalk—but against the light—when he was struck by a pickup truck. He was rushed to the hospital where he was pronounced dead on arrival.

Markets for bands are hot for a while and cool off for various reasons. Some are better for finding original bands, while others are better for finding cover bands. I always preferred bands that had their own original songs and dreamed of a recording contract but were willing to play mostly cover material to pay the bills. I enjoyed the bands playing their original material as long as they mixed it in with cover songs to keep the dance floor full of shaking booties. Our first long-running market was the San Diego area. We had a good agent there who did not waste our time showing us bands that were not good enough or would not travel to Alaska for four to six weeks and play from 9 p.m. to 5 a.m. five nights a week—the grueling schedule of the time. A couple of bands I remember bringing to Anchorage from San Diego were The Automatics and Last Call. Greg Chaille, lead singer of Last Call, became our promotions manager.

Back in the '90s there was a successful club in Honolulu called The Wave that hired the same type and caliber of bands we did, and neither Don Fritz nor I minded going to Hawaii to check out bands at The Wave.

This is where it gets ugly though: One time we flew from Hawaii to Las Vegas to meet our Argentina-born agent, David Sailon, having only enough time to drop our bags off at Caesar's Palace and crawl into David's cramped Camaro. We drove four hours to Barstow, where we saw the last set of a terrible band, then drove four hours back to Las Vegas.

We tried to deal directly with bands when we could in order to avoid the 10% to 15% agent commission. David would find out where we were going next, contact bands in that area, get promotional material and/or CDs, and attempt to represent them to us even though he had never seen or heard them. He was sneaky like that and frustrating to deal with because he was so anal about everything, but somehow he managed to be charming on top of all that due mostly to his old-world Argentine style and underlying sincerity.

We brought David's son's band, Sailon, to Anchorage for a couple of successful gigs. His son was a masterful violinist, adding some musical spice and versatility to the band's sound. His presence allowed them to play music by Kansas, a band Doran and I lost our tails on during a foray into the promotions business. We brought them to Anchorage to play at the Performing Arts Center in partnership with Kim Jones's Sourdough Productions, but the turnout was abysmal.

We found a band or two in the Seattle area, notably The Beatniks and Cherry Popping Daddies and a few in Portland. Though both cities are mostly original band markets, we could find good cover bands by driving to their outskirts.

Our sound man, Ron Stevens, and I went to Minneapolis, referred to as the "Third Coast," where there was a vibrant musical scene due to the efforts of Prince and his state-of-the art recording studio. Minneapolis was where we found one of our better bands, Pretty Boy. I remember we arrived in town early on a Sunday night, picked up a local entertainment paper from a newsstand, and saw that the band was playing a club near our hotel. I called our agent and asked about them. He said, "They're a great band and you'll love them, but they'll never go to Alaska."

On stage in the small club were four good looking guys with long hair. The lead singer sported long bleached blonde hair, tight pink Levis, no shirt and no shoes. The dance floor was crowded with beautiful young women mostly dancing with each other. Ron and I were thunderstruck. When the band's set ended I walked quickly up to the stage, handed the lead singer my card, and asked him if the band would consider coming to Alaska. He smiled brightly and replied, "Why not?" Thus began a years-long relationship. When they eventually broke up the lead singer, Dennis Lind, stayed in Anchorage and played all over town for years as a solo act.

On band trips, I've not only learned more about people I have traveled with but have also made some notable acquaintances. Don Fritz and I began going on band trips in 1980 concentrating originally on Seattle, Las Vegas, Los Angeles, and San Diego. It is true that I enjoy fine dining, including fine wines, and Las Vegas was known for neither at the time. After all, who would try to compete with those ubiquitous inexpensive casino buffets?

One evening Don and I dined at a restaurant atop a spiral staircase in Caesar's Palace known as the Palm Restaurant. The food was mediocre, the service was condescending, and the bill was ridiculously inflated.

The next morning, after running for an hour on a treadmill in the spa, I found myself lying in the sun on the rooftop deck next to an older gentleman who appeared to have been around Las Vegas for a long time. He looked and sounded as if he might have been a New Jersey mobster.

Minding my manners, I asked, "Sir, you must know a good place to dine in Las Vegas? There's got to be someplace privately owned and operated outside the casinos."

His response sounded more like he was directing me to a hit job. "Go to Andre's French Restaurant on South Sixth."

Don and I made a reservation at Andre's for that night, but when we got into a taxi to go to the restaurant, the driver first acted like he had never heard of the place and then tried to talk us into going someplace else. But we persisted. Andre Rochat, the proprietor and head chef had refused, rightly enough, to pay taxi drivers an exorbitant fee for bringing patrons to his location. He had just opened his restaurant in mid-June 1980, having mustered out of the French navy and traveled to Las Vegas with only his knives wrapped in butcher paper. It was a fabulous restaurant with a warm, comfortable atmosphere, though in a challenging location, being near downtown on the edge of a residential neighborhood.

Andre and I hit it off from the very beginning and we remain close friends to this day. Andre loves to fish and has visited Shelli and me in Alaska a couple of times, fishing for pike and sheefish on the Yukon River, kings on the Kenai, and halibut and salmon on Kachemak Bay. If he's near water he's got a line in it. I refer to him as Andre Rochat, "Enemy of All Things Aquatic." In Las Vegas we would load his boat, the *French Tickler*, with gourmet food and fine wines and drive out to Lake Meade for an afternoon of water skiing, jet skiing, and bocce ball. Once, we even watched a Super Bowl game while anchored on the beach.

Andre became a culinary *tour de force* in Las Vegas and is the man who *single-handedly* proved that visitors to the city would pay up for fine dining. The mayor of the city instituted an Andre Rochat Day in recognition of his accomplishment. He opened Andre's French Restaurant in the Monte Carlo Hotel and Casino and a beautiful restaurant named Alizé on the top floor of the Palms Hotel and Casino. Most impressively Andre successfully competed with the best chefs in the world who were now flooding Las Vegas with high-end eateries.

Then came the global financial crisis of 2008, with Las Vegas, after a thirty-year boom period, being hit harder than practically anywhere in the country. Andre was not bragging or exaggerating when he once said to me, "I've worked harder than anyone." But he ultimately had to walk away from it all—just another of the millions of victims of unscrupulous Wall Street bankers, brokers and traders, and their government, political, insurance, and rating company counterparts.

Now in his mid-seventies, Andre still lives in Las Vegas but sells his expertise to others without the responsibilities of ownership. My own Chilkoot Charlie's did not escape the outfall of that debacle either, which practically destroyed the middle class in America. I now enjoy being retired, but it is not quite the retirement I had in mind.

Most recently, while I was still running the club, our bands came from the southern states of Texas, Mississippi, Alabama, Florida, Louisiana, and Georgia. Doran and I did a lot of driving around down there.

One time we were driving from Houston to New Orleans when we stopped at a mom-and-pop buffet-style restaurant along the way to partake of some southern food and loaded our plates with their small, soft, black crabs. When the nice elderly waitress stopped by our table to inquire about the food, Doran and I were crunching down on the crabs and he said the food was great, but that he especially liked the soft-shelled crabs, to which she replied, "Why, honey, them ain't soft shelled crabs." Could'a fooled us.

There were two large clubs smack on the beach in Panama City, Florida—Club La Vela and Spinnaker—that provided live entertainment and attracted big crowds of young partiers, so Doran and I travelled there multiple times to shop for bands. We were told the guy that owned Spinnaker was sent to federal prison a few years previous. He was apparently trying to sell the place and showed his two sets of books to what he thought was a potential buyer but turned out to be an agent for the Internal Revenue Service.

If we returned from one of these week-long trips with one new quality band ready to travel to Alaska, it was a successful trip. Returning with two or three new bands was a very successful trip, but of course things do not always work out the way they were supposed to. Sometimes the bands would break up or could not come as scheduled for various reasons, among them the possibility of a girlfriend or wife objecting to a member being gone for an extended period.

There was a band we saw named Hip Boot Joe. We originally saw them in Panama City, became pals with a couple members of the band, and scheduled them to come to Alaska. Then Katrina, the costliest hurricane in United States history, hit the Gulf Coast on August 29, 2005 and altered the lives of everyone in the band. We did manage to get the band up to Anchorage at a later date and, unfortunately, they did not draw very well.

Another large club down south that we haunted was The Swamp, in Fort Walton Beach, Florida, where we discovered Splendid Chaos, a band that was still playing the club regularly when I sold it to my employees in September, 2015. I learned early on that it is important to know your market and never to hire a band that you have not seen playing to a live audience in a club setting. It is imperative that you see a band playing to a live crowd and watch how they interact with the audience. I hired one band from a staged studio setting and I never did it again.

Anchorage's musical tastes have historically lagged a couple of years behind what is popular in the Lower 48. Doran and I saw a band called Mondo Bizarro playing ska music in Black Rock, Colorado. The club they were playing in was packed every night with young partiers. We were really excited at the prospect of bringing something different to town.

We signed a four-week contract with the band, brought them to Anchorage, but they were a total disaster. When they started playing the room emptied—every time. Anchorage was not ready for ska then, though it would be a few years later. We managed to get them work in a couple of smaller cities, including Valdez, in order to fill out their contract, but there was no way we could keep them on our stage. They would have put us out of business.

One group that Doran and I hired and used several times—sort of— was called Homicidal Supermodels. We had seen the lead singer, Randy, in Pittsburgh, Pennsylvania. But because of Randy's immature behavior on and off stage, he could not keep a band together. We finally ended up bringing just him to town and arranging for local players to back him up.

Though Randy was completely uninhibited and customers were entertained by his unusual movements and antics, we had to send him home in the middle of a contract because he was getting wasted on stage and creating potential liabilities for us, also throwing parties every night in the band house, and provoking fights between DJs and band members. Everybody loved the guy. He was fun and charming. But he just could not keep it together.

You get to know people when you travel with them on band trips. One time I took Rocky Fuller, my mentor Skip Fuller's nephew, who also was the lead bartender in the Show Bar for many years, on a band trip to Los Angeles. Rocky was a great guy, but he did not take very good care of himself and he is not around anymore because of it.

On that trip, I discovered Rocky was a walking garbage disposal. He would eat anything, anywhere, any time. I noticed one morning that he did not floss his teeth and gave him some dental floss, suggesting that he try it. When he started pulling it between his teeth his gums bled so profusely I thought I might have to spin off another long piece to use as a tourniquet around his neck.

On the Los Angeles trip, Rocky left to visit relatives and was not in the hotel room when I made arrangements to meet our agent at a particular restaurant at a designated time that night. So I wrote him a note in large letters on a standard sized piece of typing paper and left it on the floor where he could not possibly miss it, just inside the hotel room door. He walked right over it.

The next day, after Rocky had missed the appointment and the night out with us, he joked, "I thought you were getting messy, Gordon, leaving paper on the floor like that!"

But Rocky was the employee that perceptively announced one day, "Uh, oh, Shelli's got a desk!" With Shelli installed as the new Chilkoot Charlie's office manager, it was the beginning of the end of the freewheeling days of how personnel files, vacations, benefits, schedules, tenure, and the like had previously been handled.

Doran is a walking garbage disposal also. He cannot pass a 7-11 Store without stopping in, lives on junk food and has to be eating constantly. I do not know how he does it or why he doesn't weigh three hundred pounds. He is not overweight at all. And he constantly offers you some of his food. I called him a "food pusher."

When we traveled together, I would draw an imaginary line down the middle of the room. He kept his stuff on one side and I kept mine on the other. I also reminded him that I was not going to pick his underwear up off the bathroom floor for him. He would throw his clothes into a duffle bag before leaving town but still managed to look presentable by pulling a shirt out and ironing it before going out at night. My clothes were always neatly folded and could be found in the hotel dresser nearest my bed.

Doran and I have seen bands in places as diverse as Telluride, Colorado, and Key West, Florida. We found a reggae band named Satta in Aspen, Colorado, that ended up making four or five trips to Alaska. We brought another great band out of Vancouver called Faith and Desire and one from Montreal called Stand Clear, in which the very talented Colleen Codaic played. The band broke up and Colleen stayed in Anchorage enhancing the local music scene to this day.

If you are over twenty-five, you do not ever want to go to Panama City during spring break. We did it because it is a good time to see the best bands that play the area. Usually we would get a room in a motel off the beaten track, but once we ended up in a condo-hotel smack on the beach right next to the two big clubs there, Spinnaker and Club La Vela. The building was a half-circle with the open side facing the beach, and we were about halfway up its perhaps twenty stories.

College girls would be out on their lanais in bikinis and the guys all around and up and down the condo complex would be encouraging them to show their boobs. When they did, they got thunderous ovations and when they did not, they got booed. We were smack dab in the middle of a bacchanalian party.

The kids really trash that town. There are beer cans all over the streets and beaches and there has been local talk about not being the host anymore because it is damaging to property and property values.

We went to Austin once at the same time as the South by Southwest Music Festival, which is a very big deal for original music, but not such a great time to try to find cover bands. While there we saw and made the acquaintance of The Presidents of the United States of America, who later brought their popular song "Peaches" to the Chilkoot Charlie's stage. Austin has one of the liveliest original music scenes in the entire country and its downtown streets are packed with partiers that are much better behaved than our downtown crowd in Anchorage, but then our downtown is like an unsupervised street party and we don't have police patrolling on horseback.

In Las Vegas, where Don Fritz and I always stayed at Caesar's Palace, he was known as "Up 'til Dawn" by the bartenders at the circular bar downstairs. Fritz, who passed away from melanoma a number of years ago, was a very funny guy. He had previously played bass in Mr. Whitekeys' band. Whitekeys referred to him as "the mouth of the Yukon." Toward the end of an evening while shopping for bands in San Francisco, we found Robin Williams and the owner of a club on the Avenues out in front of the club discussing the format for Robin doing an impromptu show. Not long after we entered the club Robin got on stage and explaining that he wanted to hone his skills, invited members of the small late-night audience to make comments or ask him questions about prominent people and newsworthy events. Practically the entire hilarious dialogue was between Fritz and Robin Williams. Unfortunately, I can't remember any of it.

The Wave in Honolulu (where Shelli discovered the band Sonya) was a trendy club with an unusual mixed crowd of heterosexuals, gays, and military. One night while we were having a drink waiting for a band to begin a set, Fritz, an extrovert, made a comment to one of the military guys near him.

The guy said, "Get away from me, you faggot!" to which Fritz quickly replied, "I'm not gay, but (turning to point at me) my friend is!"

One of the more comical stories from any band trip, over all the years and different personalities involved, occurred on a trip when I had sworn off drinking for a period of about nine months. Going on a band trip is tough duty, but doing it completely sober is not as bad as you might think, especially when you bring along your own entertainment. I took Doran and Billy Yelvington, one of our long-time bartenders with a love of music, when we left for Chicago, St. Louis, and parts beyond. I didn't know where to stay in Chicago so I asked my friend, Walter John, who I knew had lived there before moving to Alaska. Walter said we *had* to stay at the Drake Hotel, so that's what we did.

The Drake is a beautiful, old-style, five-star hotel in the heart of Chicago though because of its age, the rooms are rather small. Doran and I were ensconced in the same room one door down from Billy's. The first night we went to dinner with our friends from *Playboy* magazine, and then they showed us around town. Chicago is a partying town. The bars have different kinds of licenses, some of which allow them to stay open all night. The popular clubs not only have a line to get in, but they have a VIP line as well. Our *Playboy* friends, with us in tow, went right to the front of the VIP lines, usually with a gift of an autographed photo of one or more of the doormen with a *Playboy* bunny taken on a previous occasion. The night is a bit of a blur, even though I wasn't drinking, but we ended it around 5:00 a.m. in a comedy club socializing with a female comedian friend who had played Koot's. The boys, Doran and Billy, were plastered.

During the evening our *Playboy* friends had suggested we leave the Drake to stay at the Omni, where they had an account, and we would not be paying nearly as much for a larger room. In the morning around 10:00 a.m. they called and told me they had made the arrangements, hence we had to check out of the Drake by noon.

Billy, I learned, had some strange habits. He could not go to sleep without a fan being on and he had to play video games while he worked up to bedtime. Both were professionally arranged for by the hotel staff. He also ordered some food from the hotel room service brought to his room. When he had played and eaten his fill, Billy, bare-assed naked, pushed the room service cart out into the hallway, holding the door to his room open with his raised foot. But the door slipped off his foot and closed—and locked—leaving him stranded in the hallway in his natural condition at around 7:00 a.m.

Doran was passed out, dead to the world. I was downstairs having breakfast. Billy pounded on the door and hollered to awaken Doran to no avail. Of course, he needed to pound and holler loud enough to awaken Doran, but he did not want to pound and holler so loud as to get the attention of other residents up and down the hallway. To Billy's immense relief, I returned from breakfast before his disturbance aroused any of the other guests, and I was able to get another key from room service. Doran slept through the whole thing.

Billy went directly to bed, but I had to awaken both him and Doran around 11:00 a.m. so we could check out of the Drake before noon. Both guys were in terrible condition. Doran was on his hands and knees, still drunk as he stuffed his clothes into his duffle bag and Billy was not much better. I feared one or both were going to throw up on the carpet as we struggled through the Drake's lobby. After checking into the Omni Hotel, Doran and Billy went straight to bed and neither of them got up until it was time to go out to the clubs again that night.

One of the trips Doran and I have taken in more recent years was to Miami's South Beach, which is very hip, but it was so hot we barely survived it. I used American Express in advance to make our reservation in what I thought was a nice hotel. When the lobby is very nice, but the inside of the elevator and the hallway you exit into are seedy, you know there is going to be a problem.

In this case our room, though expensive, was a dump. We had saggy beds, crummy furniture, a tiny bathroom and, worst of all, no air conditioning. We checked out immediately, determined to find a place on our own.

We ended up making do with a little hotel right on the strip that had an old-style water-based cooler that didn't work very well. But at least we were not paying a lot of money for a dump, and it was very close to our favorite place for breakfast in Miami, the News Café on Ocean Drive. Upon our return to Anchorage and hearing of the horrible, sensational murder of Gianni Versace by a craven serial killer, we learned that The News Café was also Versace's favorite. We may have been having breakfast at a table near him on the last morning of his life.

In later years I stopped going on band trips. At my age I was beginning to feel a little conspicuous in night clubs crowded with young people. It got to where I had to plan ahead even to stay out late at Chilkoot

Charlie's, especially since I had returned to doing the bartender banks, daily reports, and bank deposits in the mornings.

I did find it necessary to go on one last trip due to a band cancellation. We flew directly to Key West, Florida, had dinner and went out to see a band. The next morning we got up, flew to Tallahassee, had dinner and saw another band. The morning after we got up, flew to Reno, had dinner and saw another band, and the morning after that we got up, flew to Las Vegas, had dinner and saw yet another band. We were rewarded with not one band for our efforts. As they say, "It's a lousy job, but someone has to do it."

As for Shelli, she figured out how to deal with band trips: Either hole up in the Four Seasons Hotel, reading, watching movies and taking full advantage of room service while Mike and Doran drive around the countryside—or don't go at all.

There was a little shed/showroom/theatre beside Rusty Heurlein's log cabin in Ester, where he and Ruben had teamed up on that marvelous production called *The Great Land*. It was essentially a history of Alaska starting with the story of the Vitus Bering Alaska discovery years and proceeding, as I recall, through Baranof's Russian rule up to the pioneer gold rush years. The shed held a small seating area and an ingenious system of pulleys to showcase the large, original paintings by Rusty that depicted the various stages of Alaska's early history

As light flooded the paintings, Rusty, stationed off to the side, would pull the cords to move one painting out of the light and another into it, the movements synchronized to accompany a recording of historical narration by Ruben. It was a unique, quaint presentation by one of Alaska's best artists and one of its best writers. Rusty had me sign his guest book, already signed by such notables as author James A. Michener.

The duo produced another marvelous narrated exhibit called *The Big Stampede*, which at one time was presented in-the-round at Alaskaland in Fairbanks. Stephan Fine Arts later had the show on exhibit in Anchorage. I don't know what has happened to either of these exhibits, but they rightfully belong in a public museum. Hopefully some day they will be available to the general public.

Hogg Brothers Café

My friend David White was attending a community college in Hayward, California. He had just finished a cooking course, in the fall of 1976, when he decided to drive up the Alcan Highway to Anchorage. At the time he knew only one person in the entire state of Alaska—Michael Kerr, and although the state's economy was still booming, pipeline construction was nearly finished. The first oil would begin its journey to Valdez the next summer.

Upon arriving in Anchorage, David first acquired a job at La Mex, a very popular Mexican restaurant across the street from Chilkoot Charlie's on Spenard Road, and then worked as a manager for a while at Big Boy Burger, also on Spenard Road. One day he saw people loading food and supplies into a truck from a small restaurant wedged between two businesses: the Friendly Fireside Lounge and Spenard Bingo, both just to the north of Chilkoot Charlie's.

The former was the Swing Bar (today it is a pot shop) and the latter is now the main stage area of Chilkoot Charlie's. The movers said they were heading to Fairbanks and told David he could have the space if he wanted it—all he needed was money to replace the food and supplies they were removing.

Fifty feet away, on the other side of Spenard Bingo, I was operating Chilkoot Charlie's. At the time it was a bustling twenty-five-foot by one-hundred-foot raucous and rustic Alaskan saloon. My manager, Cliff Martin, aka Crazy Cliff, or just Craze, worked in a colorful Hollywood Indian outfit, including the big, black, high-topped hat sporting a big upright black feather.

I would show up at night wearing long-handled underwear, a fur-lined jock strap on the outside, bunny boots, an Australian Outback hat, and a kazoo in my mouth. Eventually, I found an authentic WW I infantry uniform, leggings and all, and a dark blue fabric flying helmet with goggles. Add a white scarf and presto—you had Rocky the Flying Mutherfucker—a XXX-rated Spenardian takeoff on the Rocky and Bullwinkle television cartoon series popular at the time.

If you remember Rocky paddling the canoe with Bullwinkle, Natasha, and Boris seated in it as the latter cried "Strook! Strook!" through a bullhorn in his Soviet spy accent, you are probably collecting Social Security checks each month.

When David and Michael approached me for a loan to start their restaurant, I happily staked them with $500 against future chili sales in the club. To promote business in their startup café, they both gamboled around the club in the inch or two of peanut shells on the floor serving hors d'oeuvres while wearing plastic porcine noses and oinking loudly. The practice might have been scoffed at by Madison Avenue types, but it worked, and another landmark operation had begun in the heart of Spenard.

David and his fun-loving roommates in the Bay Area had derived their gang's nickname from their refrigerator (filled mostly with beer) that had its brand name, Hogg Brothers Custom, emblazoned in metal letters on the front door. They were the Hogg Brothers and their name survived the lengthy drive up the Alcan Highway to become David's chosen name for the new Spenard eating institution.

David tells me the front window frame for the café came from an old mining shack in Hatcher Pass, adding an authentic Alaskan touch to the decor. The logo was three colorful oinkers, as I recall, and the place was decorated with porcine paraphernalia, large and small, lovingly donated by patrons. Shelli and I purchased and donated the stuffed head of a wild boar that we found at a garage sale, but the boys rejected it.

David said, "It looks like it died the death of psoriasis!"

Which reminds me.

Early-on in the history of Chilkoot Charlie's I came across one of the weirdest investments of a lifetime. A guy was selling his booth at the Alaska State Fair. It was a three-sided plywood structure with a curtain across the front; the whole thing was colorfully painted inside and out with depictions of a two-headed pig. Comments like AMAZING, ONE-OF-A-KIND, WEIRD and STRANGE in large black letters described what was on display inside. ONLY $1.00!!! A passerby would perhaps expect to see a real, live, two-headed pig in there.

There was, in fact, a two-headed pig inside the booth, but it was about a foot long and in a jar of formaldehyde. The pig and the booth were all mine for only $500. Though I never set up the booth at the club or the fair, I did put the pig in the jar on display behind the bar. I am told by a reliable source that it is still there.

The Hogg Brothers Café initially served sandwiches, burgers, and omelets all day long. They tried operating at night for a time, but it was too rowdy despite being, and remaining, sort of neutral ground where partiers could break bread in peace. Patrons who were 86ed from Chilkoot Charlie's had a habit of shifting their activities to the Friendly Fireside Lounge—watering hole of last resort—located on the other side of The Hogg Brothers Café.

My staff and I would sometimes sit cozily among these 86ed patrons in the café and although relations were naturally somewhat strained, as a credit to the establishment, I don't recall anyone ever breaking the peace.

The café eventually, and wisely, settled for the breakfast and lunch trade. It soon became everybody's favorite place to cure a hangover and goggle at a waitress named Angie, a pretty, vivacious young gal with a beautiful smile who was in the habit of wearing a see-through white blouse that profiled her full breasts. Not surprisingly, Angie's tip jar was the envy of all.

As if David's fun-loving, outgoing personality and Angie's smile and profile weren't enough to keep customers coming back, there was a permanent crew of characters installed at the Hogg Brothers, including Viene Yorke, Ready Freddie (Larry) Cole, and Garrett Hawkins. After about a year and a half, Mike left to take a job as a code violations inspector at the Municipality of Anchorage, a position that better suited his personality.

Underpinning everything was David's love of cooking and dedication to the quality of his ingredients. The place cranked out killer omelets and burgers. Portions were large and prices were reasonable. At any given time you'd find hung-over lawyers in suits sitting next to hung-over pipeline workers in Carhartt overalls listening to the blaring music of Led Zeppelin, their heads buried in their newspapers, glancing furtively at Angie's beguiling profile while pigging out on massive omelets accompanied by heaps of home-fried potatoes. My favorite omelet was the Tierra: cheese, avocado, tomato, Canadian bacon, and sour cream, $6.00. Add Tabasco. It was to die for.

There was nothing pretentious or fancy about the Hogg Brothers Café. It was a "greasy spoon," but it was everybody's favorite "greasy spoon." Not only were David and I such good friends that we made the yearly pilgrimage to the duck flats across Cook Inlet on opening day of duck-hunting season, but our employees were all friends with each other as well.

Chilkoot Charlie's had an annual holiday party that was held during those years at the Rabbit Creek Inn on the Old Seward Highway just beyond Rabbit Creek Road. Owners and staff of the Hogg Brothers Café, Arctic Music Co., K & L Distributors, plus our lawyer and accountant, were all invited. These were formal but raucous affairs with scripted agendas and some of the most fun I ever had.

We ridiculed one another, presented real and comical gifts, told off-color stories on employees that probably would end in a lawsuit today, and cured our hangovers in the morning over omelets at the Hogg Brothers Café. I am told that on one such morning we threw down shots of Jägermeister and danced around the kitchen. Just for the record, I can neither confirm nor deny that.

In 1985, with the original Hogg Brothers Café in Spenard doing well, David made a foray into the Kenai Peninsula by opening a location in Anchor Point. He operated there for about a year until he found a building on Pioneer Avenue in Homer. There, he had a restaurant/eating place license and by all accounts the place was successful. But he also had a sublease, and the guy with the lease jacked up the monthly payment on him. Unable to find another location, he just closed it up.

All good things do come to an end. The woman who owned the Friendly Fireside Lounge, who was David's landlord, sold out to me. A major Spenard character, Vern Rollins, threw in with David's ex-landlord and Viene Yorke, bought David's interest, and they moved the Hogg Brothers Café to Northern Lights Boulevard where the Spenard Roadhouse is now. It didn't last long. The atmosphere was gone. It felt like you were eating in a school cafeteria. Also gone were David's welcoming presence and his focus on quality, not to mention Angie's profile.

David left Alaska in 1988 and went to work as a neurology technician at Ohio County Hospital in Hartford, Kentucky, about an hour and a half west of Louisville. He is still chief technician and trainer there, but his love of cooking also landed him back in the restaurant business. For over a dozen years now he has owned and operated a Hartford restaurant named Capers. He has a full liquor license and serves dinners with nothing but five star reviews. Capers is open Thursday, Friday and Saturday for lunch and dinner and Sunday for breakfast.

A couple of years ago Shelli and I, after visiting with my daughter's family in New Mexico, flew to St. Louis to visit with Jack Kent and Jan, then went on to Tennessee to see one of Shelli's brothers. Since we were in the "neighborhood," we drove to Hartford, Kentucky to visit with David.

He hadn't changed a bit. He welcomed us with open arms and friends of his put us up in their comfortable home on pilings right next to the

Green River. We had the opportunity to dine at Capers several times, including breakfast the last day, but since I haven't eaten meat in over twenty years, I took a pass on the kindly proffered Tierra omelet.

"Cook's Tree"

This solitary birch

   stands in my mind as

   surrogate for history

   a hundred feet above

   the snow and surface

   time, a knowledgeable,

   highly-placed informant

   seeing at a glance the

   generations come and go,

   transforming their events

   to fit my fancy, never

   twice the same except for

   one invariable scene:

   Tanainas peering under

   painted brows beyond

   the misty inlet for

   marauding Aleuts and,

   to their wonder, seeing

   a great sailing ship

whose masts rise like

a forest from the fog

and Captain Cook,

on course toward tree

and watchers, sails

across the centuries

Collected Ruben Gaines II ©1988 Ruben Gaines

Bobbie McGee's

There are good, caring, generous people in the world like David White, and there are the others: the brutes, the knuckle-draggers, the ogres. Roy Mayer was one such. He was too simple-minded to have a sense of humor or to carry on an intelligent conversation, but he was big—very big—and built like a tank, weighing nearly 300 pounds. When he walked through the door, he blocked out the light. What he lacked in intelligence and sensitivity he more than compensated for with callous, reptilian aggressiveness. He was a bully—a thug.

I have harbored contempt for cowards and a hatred of bullies since conception and contend that the two are interchangeable and mutually reinforcing. Bullies do what they do because they are cowards, and at least some cowards do what they do because they are bullies. I quickly realized that Mayer, with only one thing on his mind—pounding on other people—was someone I didn't need or want around. No matter that we had mutual acquaintances and he hadn't posed a threat to me personally. Yet.

Mayer worked around Anchorage as a bouncer in the late '70s, which gave him ample opportunity to beat up ill-fated customers under the guise of "protecting" a licensed establishment. When he was not so employed he would roam around Spenard's nightspots, including Chilkoot Charlie's, pounding anyone who got in his way with his ham-sized fists.

One night he provoked a fight in Koot's when I happened to be only a few feet from the scene. After our doormen broke it up and hustled Mayer out the door of the club, I told them, "I don't want that stupid son-of-a-bitch in here anymore." I knew that was bound to present a problem for me when I encountered Roy elsewhere.

In January 1979, a new competitor arrived on Anchorage's nightclub scene, an upscale disco named Bobby McGee's, with a legal capacity of 500 customers. It was part of a chain operation headquartered in Phoenix, Arizona.

The flagship tenant of the financially-troubled International Marketplace on Tudor Road, a short drive from Koot's, Bobby McGee's was a popular destination but did not present a competitive problem for us at Chilkoot Charlie's. They closed their operation at 1 a.m., and the preponderance of our business was between then and the state's official 5 a.m. closing hour. In fact, many patrons and staff from Bobby McGee's arrived at Chilkoot Charlie's after McGee's closed for the night—a boon to our business.

It was a different story for Donovan's, near the corner of Benson Boulevard and C Street. Frank Reed, Jr. was the principal owner of that restaurant/bar, which was more of a direct competitor to Bobby McGee's and rapidly losing ground in the battle with the Outside operation, "Outside" being the definitive word.

I encountered Frank at the Bird House Bar on the Seward Highway one afternoon, and he complained to me about "these fucking Outside operations coming in here and robbing business away from us locals."

"I'm not going to take it sitting down," he said boisterously over one too many cocktails. And he sounded like he meant it.

I had been told that Mayer, now working as a bouncer at Bobby McGee's, had some sort of familial connection with the owners, and that they were in turn connected with another sort of family in Arizona. There was a fair amount of talk about "The Mob" in those days, and there were in fact attempts made by that element to infiltrate the local industry's topless dance clubs.

I was single at the time and dating a nice young lady by the name of Gaylene Brown, who I later discovered had been a school classmate and friend of my future wife, Shelli, at both Northern Lights Elementary and Romig Junior High School. One Sunday afternoon we were sipping on cocktails off to the left side of the main lounge area in Bobby McGee's when who should walk in the door of the nearly empty establishment but Roy Mayer.

I rarely describe myself as prescient, but as Mayer marked my presence, thudded directly through the middle of the club and right up to the bar, I sensed trouble in the offing. I could almost see those tiny wheels furiously laboring away in Mayer's melon-sized skull as he ordered and threw down a straight shot. He ordered another drink in a pint-sized glass while I watched him leering at us out of the corner of my eye, explaining to Gaylene that we were about to experience some real excitement of the dangerous, unpleasant, and thuggish kind.

Mayer left off his conversation with the bartender and strode over to the railing that bordered the lounge area, towering over Gaylene and me. After insulting my mother and my legitimacy, he asked, "Who the fuck do you think you are, 86ing me out of Koot's?" He made a less-than-polite comment to Gaylene and then doused us both with his drink. I immediately stood up, grabbed my drink in my right hand and looked up at the big galoot, who said, "You throw that drink on me and I'll fucking kill you!"

Splat! Without a moment's hesitation, I sloshed the contents of my drink directly into Mayer's face. Had it not been for the railing separating us he would have been instantly on me, but it took Roy some time to smash his way through seating and around the booth to get to me. By then I was in a position to defend myself, meaning simply trying to fend the guy off while rapidly back-pedaling and trying not to fall to the floor, which would have meant a trip to the hospital at best—to the morgue at worst.

On he came, closing in for the kill, until he finally had me against the west side of the building. Miraculously, I had backed into a fire exit door equipped with a panic bar. Accidentally impacting the panic bar hard with my rear end, I found myself standing alone in the parking lot, waiting for my tormentor to reappear at any moment. By then, however, the staff of Bobby McGee's had been able to restrain Mayer. I stood there, shaken but exhilarated, until the restaurant employees gave me the all-clear signal. I grabbed Gaylene and we got the hell out of there.

During his bar-hopping around town, Mayer made it known that he was not done with me. I made a point of avoiding places where I thought I might encounter him, partly because a couple of days after the incident at Bobby McGee's, Vern Rollins, an outlaw friend of mine and the person who later bought a stake in the Hogg Brothers Café, took me aside and, alluding to the alleged connection that Mayer had in Arizona, cautioned me against taking any action against him. He was obviously worried I might.

I said, "Listen Vern, I didn't start this problem and I don't intend to pursue it, but I'm not going to let Mayer push me around—or put me in the hospital—and I'll do what I have to do to protect myself."

That fall, when I opened the October 16, 1979 issue of the *Anchorage Daily News* over morning coffee and saw the front-page headline "Arsonist's Torch Destroys Bobby McGee's," I was as shocked as everyone else—though I had been more or less warned by my conversation with Frank Reed, Jr. at the Bird House Bar.

In the article, reporter George Bryson noted that the arson appeared to be a follow-up to a failed attempt made two weeks earlier.

Bryson went on to say that since the previous July, the developers of the center had been facing foreclosure proceedings by the Alaska National Bank of the North. The developers included Jack and Joyce Moore of Seattle, owners of Alaska's Qwik Shop stores; Terry Pfleiger (1943-2016), an Anchorage Realtor and friend of mine; and Robert Anderson, who had recently moved Outside.

The next day the paper announced that fire inspectors said there was going to be a "massive manhunt" for the arsonist. The *Daily News* reported that the damage to Bobby McGee's was estimated at $3.5 million, and there were three categories of high-probability suspects: disgruntled employees, similar businesses in Anchorage trying to eliminate competition, and owners of the building or the business trying to defraud their insurance company.

"'I can guarantee that some people are going to be upset with us before this thing is over,'" said John Fullenwider, chief inspector for the Anchorage Fire Department: "We're going to go after him…this was the largest incendiary fire we've ever had in the Municipality of Anchorage."

As it turns out it was not a disgruntled employee or a hard-pressed developer attempting to defraud his insurance company, but the owner of Donovan's, Anchorage scion Frank Reed, Jr., who was arrested along with his accomplices. Reed was charged with arson, conspiracy, a gun violation and using an explosive device. His trial became a lengthy series of plea bargains, convictions, appeals, overturns, exonerations, partial exonerations, and changes of venue.

Interestingly, the charges also involved an attempt to burn down Donovan's itself on December 31, 1979—more than two months after Bobby McGee's had been burned to the ground. The entire legal drama lasted five years, bringing shame and near financial ruin to one of Anchorage's most notable families.

Back when I attended Anchorage High School in the late '50s, there was no more prominent family in Anchorage than the Reeds. They were a wealthy, community-minded, pioneer banking family and the patriarch, Frank Reed, Sr., served as chairman of the Anchorage Charter Commission. At the time of his arrest Frank, Jr. was a prominent Anchorage stockbroker who the *Daily Sitka Sentinel* said, "was worth as much as $100,000 before Donovan's restaurant encountered financial problems." That's around $390,000.00 in today's dollars.

It took two trials, but Reed and another man, David L. Smith, were ultimately convicted on charges related to the burning of Bobby McGee's—however they were acquitted of attempting to burn Donovan's.

One night, years later, I encountered Frank Reed, Jr. in Chilkoot Charlie's. His arrogance was undiminished by his time in prison. After our short conversation, I reflected that bullies and arsonists (the deliberate sort—not the mentally disturbed arsonists who can't help themselves) represent different shades of cowardice. They first pick on people they perceive as unable to defend themselves and the latter resolve their problems illegally, at the expense of others because they cannot face up to their own failures.

When cowards run up against unexpected resistance they detour to the next victim, as Mayer did when I threw a drink in his face and Vern later reported to him that he was barking up the wrong tree. And a businessman who burns down his competition is, I suspect, capable of doing just about anything. Having once gotten away with arson, who knows what the next unacceptable inconvenience—or resolution for it—might be.

Another noted Alaskan artist, A. E. (Betty) Park (d. 1971), a friend and fan of Ruben's, did a masterful job of personifying Chilkoot Charlie and Six-Toed Mordecai and illustrating their titanic adventures in a couple of Ruben's publications of collected stories. She did the artwork for the cover of his two LP's recorded with Frank Brink (d. 2009), the "founding father" of Alaska theatre—*Vat I* and *Vat ll*. Betty also created a wonderful small, detailed clay model sculpture of Chilkoot Charlie at the behest of the Anchorage City Council. The statue was to be placed in front of City Hall on Fourth Ave.

She described the ordeal: "They told me his head was too knobby. Then they said, 'You've got to remove the liquor jug from his hand...'" In the end Betty, in need of money, sold it to Ruben's daughter Christine, who gave it to Ruben.

What the residents of Anchorage wound up with is a politically correct block of carved granite sporting a plaque commemorating William H. Seward that would offend no one other than those with artistic sensibilities.

Ruben gave Betty's model statue to Shelli and me during our last Christmas together. It will eventually belong to the Anchorage Museum, along with what the museum already has: the original mural behind the South Long Bar at Chilkoot Charlie's and the inserts representing different Chilkoot Charlie tales, such as *The Bear, The Mosquitos, The Tundra Boar, The Purple Goat* and *The Moose Mouse,* and a 4' x 8' painting each of Chilkoot and his nemesis, Six-Toed Mordecai. All were painted by Betty, at Ruben's insistence, for me to display in the club, and long ago were replaced with copies skillfully rendered by artist Michelle Wade.

Halibut Cove by Way of McCarthy

There are public museums that preserve and present art for the edification of the public. Then there are historic monuments that stand alone in their original setting—tangible reminders of bygone eras—like Kennecott Mine.

In June 1976, Lynn Cunningham and I were going to float the Gulkana River, which flows south from Paxson Lake to the Copper River just south of Gakona Junction. Lynn had floated the river before, but it was to be my first significant floating experience. The Gulkana is a clear water system offering excellent rainbow trout and Arctic Grayling fishing. We were excited to "get out of Dodge," and looking forward to the adventure. Problem was, when we got to Paxson Lake it was still frozen solid, so we could not launch our raft without the assistance of an ice breaker.

Lynn operated a successful upholstery shop on Merrill Field and was to be my first Chilkoot Charlie's independent franchisee. We were in the market. All we had to do was find him the right location.

Unable to float the Gulkana and since we were in the general vicinity, we decided to drive to Chitina, where we took in the sights such as they were, then decided to visit the historic little town of McCarthy and the adjacent, abandoned Kennecott Mine.

To get to McCarthy you drove northeast from Anchorage. Most of the 300-plus mile journey took place on paved highway, but the final 61 miles was over a rugged, unpaved four-wheel-drive road that required us to cross a river at a great height by driving over an old railroad trestle.

Then, just outside the town, we had to park the truck and cross another river in a seat fastened to a cable. We were then in the Wrangell Mountains which, being volcanic in origin, were notably different from the fault-block Chugach and Alaska Ranges I'd been raised near. The rugged heights of the Wrangells were a favorite subject of the master Alaskan painter, Eustice Ziegler, who created vivid, turn-of-the-century portrayals of miners leading mule-laden pack trains through misty valleys and across lively mountain streams.

On the road to McCarthy we stopped to sate our fishing desiderata at Silver Lake by catching some landlocked, stocked silver salmon.

Upon arrival, Lynn and I stayed at the historic McCarthy Inn where everything was an antique. We became friendly with the owner, Jerry Miller, and signed an earnest money agreement with him for the purchase of his business before leaving town. We had both fallen in love with the place and Lynn felt he had found his future Chilkoot Charlie's location. Remember, this was during pipeline construction. The future of Alaska looked very bright and prosperous.

For my part, I was so enchanted by the old Kennecott Mine, less than five miles away from McCarthy, I ended up purchasing the bunk house, the sauna house, the cafeteria, which still had table settings in place, and a house on "Silk Stocking Lane," where management had lived with their families when the mine was operational. My mortgage payment on the whole kit and caboodle was $500 a month.

The Kennecott Mine was named after the Kennicott Glacier inhabiting the valley below. The glacier was named after Robert Kennicott during the U.S. Army Abercrombie Survey of 1899. In a "clerical error," the "e" was substituted for an "i" in the incorporation papers. Either way you spelled it though, the mines—there were five of them—Bonanza, Jumbo, Mother Lode, Erie and Glacier, held the richest known concentration of copper in the entire world at the time.

With $30 million in financing from Daniel Guggenheim and J.P. Morgan & Co., the Alaska Syndicate was formed and the enormous, multi-faceted operation to deliver the ore to market was begun. It required the four-year construction of the 193.9 mile Copper River and Northwestern Railway from Cordova to the mines, as well as the formation of the Alaska Steamship Company. The first ore was shipped out by train in 1911. The peak year of production was 1916, during which copper ore valued at $32.4 million was shipped.

By the early 1930s, the highest grades of copper ore had been largely depleted and the mines started to close. The Glacier Mine was the first, in 1929. The Mother Lode closed in July of 1938, and Erie, Jumbo and Bonanza closed in September of that year.

The last train left Kennecott on November 10, 1938, and workers were told to be on it unless they wanted to walk out. That meant items in the cafeteria, bunkhouse, and other buildings I'd purchased, were left just as they had been, table settings and all. I figured the value of the antiques in the buildings I had purchased was more than what I had paid for the land and buildings, considering its remoteness and the lack of interest in the place at the time.

On the way back to Anchorage—the joke being, "Hey, mister, want to buy a town?"—we stopped to imbibe a few in Wasilla at the Lake Lucille Lodge, which we discovered was also for sale.

Well, that changed everything—with regard to the McCarthy Lodge anyway. Lake Lucille Lodge sat on property just outside the main part of Wasilla with significant frontage on Lake Lucille. We bought the place from Einar Hagberg, essentially as-is and on the spot. I wrote the earnest money agreement on a pad of yellow legal paper and we subsequently begged off on the purchase of the McCarthy Lodge, happily forfeiting our earnest money.

Before the deal on the Lake Lucille Lodge closed, two significant things happened: the residents of the State of Alaska voted to move the state capital to Willow and I ran away to Belize. That adventure is detailed in my memoir *Learning the Ropes.*

I had been making all the motions of a normal person, taking care of business and dealing with the recent death of my father. I was, however, disenchanted with both my partner in Chilkoot Charlie's, Bill Jacobs—for whom I could never provide enough money—and my second wife, Tiffany, the least empathetic person I have ever known.

When I snapped, I snapped like a broken forearm, driving down the Alcan Highway with one of our bartenders and all the money I could lay my hands on, intent upon becoming an expatriot dive shop operator on the world's second longest barrier reef.

Lynn expressed some interest in joining me but demurred in the end. Since it was my messed-up life that had created all the uncertainty over the deal in Wasilla, and since I did not want Lynn to have to deal with Tiffany, I took some Jack White limited partnerships from him in return for my half interest in the Lake Lucille Lodge. Then I left town in a cloud of dust and perturbation.

However, on my wending way to Belize I had to return to Anchorage twice for court cases. One case had to do with a personal injury claim at Chilkoot Charlie's and the other was to sue Einar Hagberg for specific performance, requiring him to live up to the terms of the contract I had written on that yellow legal pad.

When Alaskan voters chose to move the capitol of the state to Wasilla, it of course changed everyone's calculus of real estate values and business opportunities—especially those in Wasilla and Juneau. Most people thought the move would actually happen and Einar's brother, A.

E. "Bud" Hagberg (1929-1977), a successful business executive, told him not to sell.

I well remember their attorney dismissively brandishing our earnest money agreement in court, referring to it disparagingly as "this handwritten epistle." The court thought otherwise, however, and awarded the case in our favor. That meant Lynn had a bar of his own on Lake Lucille, though it was not destined to be a Chilkoot Charlie's because of an incident that temporarily tarnished the name. And I had a life of my own, tenuous though it was.

After six months of being on the lam I returned to Anchorage, filed for divorce from Tiffany, and started trying to rebuild my life and business. I decided it was best for me not to remarry anytime soon. I'd failed twice in marriage with seven years invested in each one.

Within a year or so, I did fall in love again with Shelli Shannon, my wife of thirty-seven years now. While we were living together, but before we married, I suggested driving to McCarthy and visiting the Kennecott Mine.

Although Lynn and I had begged off on the purchase of the McCarthy Lodge, I had still purchased the other buildings in Kennecott, and when I ran away to Belize I left them in the hands of Lynn's girlfriend, a real estate agent, in hopes she could sell them because I could no longer afford the monthly payments. She wasn't able to sell the properties, so they had been foreclosed upon—but I was still enamored with the area.

Shelli said, "Why don't we visit with Don and Vivian MacInnes, my best friend Debbie's parents in Halibut Cove instead?" Halibut Cove is a very small artsy fishing and retirement community across Kachemak Bay from Homer, aka "a quaint drinking village with a fishing problem." The Cove is accessible only by boat or plane.

We drove to Homer in September 1980, crossing Kachemak Bay in the ferry boat, *Danny J,* which is still running four decades later. We wore hiking gear and carried our belongings in backpacks as we walked a narrow trail that paralleled the beach, making our way to Don and Vivian's house. The locals referred to it as the Pizza Hut because it was in the shape of an octagon perched high on a knoll overlooking the bay. I made myself comfortable by immediately taking a nap on the living room couch.

When I awoke I asked Vivian, "Is there anything I can do to help out around here?"

She said in her Mississippi twang, "You bet! We need a new outhouse hole!"

I was immediately provided with a pickaxe and a shovel and set to work. To my dismay, the ground chosen near the house for the new outhouse, referred to as "Le Poopion," painted with colorful butterflies, was not dirt. It was rock and gravel—a major workout, but I was young and energetic.

The next day, after looking around a bit and discovering what a gem of a place the Cove was, I asked Don and Vivian if they knew of any property for sale in the vicinity. They did not, but they sent me and Shelli in their skiff, the *Kamikaze*—so named because it was very tipsy—around the island to the home of the Tillion family. Diana Tillion answered the door and in reply to my question, said, "We don't have any for sale, but Ray Miller, who lives on that little island there"—pointing to her right— does."

We were soon in Ray's skiff heading across the Narrows, the body of water between the mainland and Ismailof Island, to where he had four beautiful two to five acre parcels of "open-entry" waterfront land facing north. The parcels had sweeping views directly across the island isthmus, the bay beyond and the hills east of Homer.

Ray said, "I've got two boys and I can't get either one of them to make up their minds which parcel they want. So just pick the one you want and it's yours."

I chose the second one from the left, which had a prominence sticking out into the water. I also asked, "Is the one to the right of it available also?" It held a pretty little cove next to the prominence.

Ray replied, "How much land does one man need?"

Well, that was the end of that conversation. I did buy that other parcel years later, and I had to pay a lot more for it than I might have had I bought it from Ray.

I asked, "How am I going to get water?" The prospect of drilling for it did not look promising.

Ray said, "No problem. I'll provide that."

When we got back to the Millers' house, Ray covered the hundred-plus steps up from their dock with ease. Then he told me, "We've got one little problem. There's a couple that's supposed to be over here tomorrow to look at the properties."

I said, "Well, we're here right now and I'll pay you your asking price."

Ray said he hated lawyers, so I sat down at their manual typewriter and banged out an earnest money agreement, at which I was becoming quite proficient. I wrote a check to the Millers, and we opened beers to celebrate. The agreement included Ray's guarantee of water and also arranged for our money to be paid into an escrow at First National Bank of Anchorage until a cloud on the title could be removed. The Seldovia Native Association had sued the State of Alaska, claiming the state did not have proper title to the land at the time it had offered the "open entry" titles to residents who were only required to survey and stake it.

Ray turned to his wife, Judi, and said, "What are we going to do about that couple coming over tomorrow?"

She replied, "What do you mean 'we?'"

When it was time to return to the MacInnes' for the night, Ray said, "Watch out for that rock out there."

I said, "What rock?"

He said, "Oh, there's a rock out there in the middle of the channel."

I said, "Why don't you put a marker on it?"

Ray said, "What for? We know where it's at."

The next day Shelli and I visited the property again. It was a beautiful autumn day. The spruce bark beetles had not yet ravaged the Kenai Peninsula, and our property was covered with big, healthy, mature spruce trees with ground cover of moss, ferns and, of course, devil's club and alder.

Ray came panting up the trail to our knoll. He'd hooked up a ¾" PVC pipe to a larger pipe which ran down the middle of a stream that had been damned further up the hillside. He rolled the pipe onto our building site. The guarantee of a water source had been promptly completed.

That hill Ray struggled up was later dubbed Goat Hill. Just teasing, I said to Ray, "I'm surprised to see you huffing and puffing from surmounting that hill, since you live a hundred-plus feet above the water yourself."

"Every hill's different," he said.

I really liked the guy—what you saw was what you got. And Judi was a very nice lady, as well as a capable artist.

The following spring, some friends of mine came down for a weekend and helped build a crude platform on the prominence over the water amongst the aforementioned trees. We erected an eight foot by ten foot frame on spruce logs and placed a wall tent on it. Soon after, I built bunk beds, installed electrical extension cord "wiring," indoor/outdoor carpeting, a small refrigerator, a microwave and gravity-fed running water. Our hot water came from a banquet-sized coffee dispenser. We even had a small wine cellar.

After a few years we were able to install steel pilings, a three-piece floating dock and an aluminum ramp, with stairs running up to a stationary dock and on up to a deck, and yet more stairs to the porch in front of the tent. Locals nicknamed our spot "The Stairway to the Stars" because from a distance, all you could see was the dock and stairs leading up to the woods and the sky above.

In the mid-'80s, after Sheik Ahmed Zaki Yamani washed the Alaskan economy away in a tsunami of cheap oil, the stage was set for one of the most generous financial acts I have ever personally experienced. My business at Chilkoot Charlie's had seriously tanked. I worked out various arrangements on Deeds of Trust payments, bank loans, Alaska USA Federal Credit Union and Small Business Administration loans, and tapped every source of capital I could lay my hands on, as previously mentioned. Naturally, I made a phone call to Ray Miller, who told me he and Judi were going to be in Anchorage soon.

We met at our condo in Woodside East. I explained our dire circumstances and asked if there was not some way we could get a bit of relief from payments on the Halibut Cove property. Not only did Ray and Judy offer relief from payments, but since all the money we had paid over half a dozen years was sitting in escrow, they allowed us to remove all that money and start over on payments at the end of a year. It brings a tear to my eye when I think about it. Old Alaskans—real people. They were happy to extend a hand.

Shelli and I now enjoy living in Halibut Cove year-round, albeit in another location very near the old one. The *Kamikaze*, a gift from Don and Vivian, is now a flower bed full of beautiful purple poppies in our back yard, and I look out over the peaceful Narrows and the Isthmus as I type.

I will probably never float the Gulkana River, as Lynn Cunningham and I had planned. Sadly, Lynn died of a stroke years ago. Ray and Judi eventually moved to Oregon where Ray succumbed to cancer. I have never been back to McCarthy or Kennecott, and Shelli has no desire to

visit the place. But I still have a beautiful copper still that I brought out with me on my last visit—a vivid memory of that remarkable, historical vestige of a bygone era in Alaska—and we live happily in Halibut Cove.

"For the Late Alaskan Artist, Betty Park"

In this existence we who knew you knew a passing person only....

One who gave in fuller measure, surely who performed in better ways

And left behind more evidence of immortality than others not so blest....

Yet but a certain person in a certain life.

And so it ends; and those of us involved....

How deeply, we were not to know until the end occurred....

Face sorrow for ourselves

And deep regret that such a person occupying such a life

Should make such swift departure, leaving much undone.

You are recalled as standing on the constant verge of something new,

As though discovery were instinct for you,

Not reward for heavy labor.

But happily there's more; we'll learn

that nothing has been left undone,

That truths expressed in this, your closed-out life,

Are simple evidence of progress toward the ultimate,

Which is beyond this life's expression.

How, we wonder, putting sorrow out of mind

And leaving bleak regret behind,

Will then your work, released from this life's limitations,

Be, when next it's undertaken?

What strides, while in a resting place

Awaiting yet another signal to resume the journey toward the ultimate,

Will have been made?

Your concept, done with full commitment to the need

For other eyes to see and hearts to understand,

Of nature's beauties, her immensities, her greatness in the most minute,

How will they be put to canvas and engraved upon the spirit, then?

The things of nature were your greatest love in this existence:

No flight of bird was aimless, nor song without intent or meaning,

And these, instinctively perceived,

Were given us by you in clear translation.

A mountain's frame of mind:

Aspiring arrogance to humbleness

In countless downward variations and degrees,

Depending on the mood of yet the greater sky:

Of this we were apprized through eyes more keenly focused

On the ultimate, than ours.

And how will that be said by you in time, and time again to come?

We're well aware that nothing is unknown;

It's known in realms beyond, in this one only undiscovered

And so we have a comfort; there are those like you attuned

to sources of revealment and who, in moving on

And having learned profounder truths, will share the revelation.

And we wait on this.

Perhaps, since life is but an endless change of garment for man's soul,

You'll go unrecognized at first, when next we meet. But not for long.

The raiment will have changed but, lo, the soul will be the same,

And soon will be familiar. You, the passing person, will be found again.

And yet again give fuller meaning to another life

In this, the journey toward the ultimate, toward God.

Conversations Unlimited ©1972 Ruben Gaines

The Charleston Express

This tale is a perfect illustration of why the saying, "No good deed goes unpunished" is a truism.

The invitations issued by Alaska Pacific Mortgage Company announced that the "Charleston Express" was to depart from the Alaska Railroad Terminal in Anchorage at 6:30 p.m. on June 21, 1985. It would go all the way to Lake Lucille, then return at midnight.

The Anchorage economy was booming. It was the short period of time I refer to as the Glory Days when anything was possible and money was no object. Six months later Sheik Yamani was to open the oil spigots in Saudi Arabia sending the price of oil crashing and, as a result, the Alaskan economy. Few would be left standing.

The bank was hosting the event for the third year in a row as a way of thanking its customers: an assortment of real estate agents, mortgage brokers, appraisers, contractors and the like. Shelli was an associate broker for Fortune Properties. Her broker was Shari Boyd. Shelli directed her buyers to her friend, Terri Dubel (1951-1992), for financing. Terri was a mortgage broker who worked under Randy Boyd, Shari Boyd's husband. Randy Boyd was the President and CEO of Alaska Pacific Mortgage Company, which was a subsidiary of Key Bank.

Shelli's invitation to the event came from Terri Dubel. Terri was dating my lifelong friend, Norman Rokeberg, a leasing agent for Jack White Company—who accompanied her on the train—and of course Shelli brought me. Everybody who was anybody affiliated with real estate, as well as their spouses or special others, was on that train. We were all in high spirits and dressed to the nines in lavish costumes from the roaring twenties.

It was a lovely summer solstice evening and a hell of a shindig—the event of the year. I was wearing a striped, three-piece gray suit with black shirt, a white tie and a white fedora, and carrying a plastic Tommy gun. Shelli was wearing a beautiful knee-length red velvet dress with lace sleeves that I had purchased for her in Venice, Italy along with a string of red beads around her forehead, a la the fashion of the '20s.

Shelli had recently undergone a third surgery on her right ankle and had just been released from using crutches that day, so she sported a walking cast with a red sock over it. Shelli's friend, Terri, had recently had a mastectomy and was undergoing chemotherapy, so the girls were both in a rather fragile condition.

The train departed on time and the party was in full swing from the start. By then I had been the owner of Chilkoot Charlie's for fifteen and a half years and had been sued so many times that when people threatened me with another lawsuit, I'd tell them to "Get in line!" Ninety-nine percent of all lawsuits against my business were either for alleged over-serving by my staff or alleged heavy-handedness by my security—mostly the latter. Being the target of so many plaintiff attorneys, I could not help but notice that there was absolutely no control over the dispensation of drinks or the presence of even a modicum of security on the train.

There were perhaps ten or more railroad cars, and I would guess maybe four hundred partiers. Three of the cars were designated bar cars. The crowd was jovial, high-spirited, sophisticated, and taking full advantage of the free drinks. I remember seeing pre-mixed wine coolers being handed out singly and by the four-pack, and not by professional servers. The one-hour-plus ride to Wasilla is a bit of a blur. Suffice it to say it went by happily and rather quickly, and many aboard were bombed—or well on their way—upon arrival.

When the train stopped at Lake Lucille, everyone stepped off and walked the quarter-mile, or so, on the gravel road to Snyder Park, where the caterers had arranged a lavish spread of food and, of course, more drinks. Since Shelli and Terri were unable to keep up with the pace of the group, Norman and I went ahead to the park in order to acquire a table.

When the girls arrived we sat at a picnic table eating, drinking and socializing for a couple of hours. It was a perfect setting and the weather was pristine. Everyone was happy—talking, laughing and dancing without the slightest hint of impending trouble.

However, a couple of hours into the festivities, as recounted by Sharon Varner, a man named James Irvine approached her friend, Leslie Geleszinski, from behind and started playing with her hair. Leslie's husband was momentarily elsewhere when this happened. Sharon said Irvine then became very forward, asking Leslie personal questions as if they were friends.

The ladies said he was acting like a jerk, and Robin Varner supposedly told Irving he had better not play with *his* wife's hair. It was Robin Varner who then told James Geleszinski, Leslie's husband, about Irvine's behavior toward Leslie.

When it was time to reboard the train, everyone started slowly and leisurely strolling hand-in-hand back over the gravel road. In order to make it to the train on time, Shelli and I and Norman and Terri had started out early and were well ahead of the main body of the group. As we were nearing the train, we spotted a large man straddling—and pounding on—a small man lying in a ditch parallel to the road. It was not a fight. The big guy was just beating the hell out of the little guy, who was sprawled on his back against the other side of the drainage ditch running along the gravel road.

We hesitated, almost continuing on without interfering, but the scene was shocking. The little guy was screaming, begging, terrified and helpless. He was not putting up any kind of a fight, only trying to deflect blows to his head. Then the big guy forced his thumbs inside the little guy's mouth. So I did what I was used to doing in my nightclub operation—breaking up fights and preventing injury when possible.

I walked up behind the big guy, later identified as James Geleszinski, and slid my arms under his as he screamed in the face of the little guy, "I'm gonna rip your lips apart!" It looked like that was exactly what he was going to do. I pulled Geleszinski off of the little guy, later identified as James Irvine, and rolled over on my back, still holding onto Geleszinski to restrain him from doing further damage to Irvine. Geleszinski didn't fight me; he was passive. But it was obvious he was dangerous and I knew better than to let him go. He was playing possum.

Other partiers showed up on the scene, standing in the road watching Geleszinski and me on the ground, including Randy Boyd, president of Alaska Pacific Mortgage Company and organizer of the gala. James Irvine, got up and away from Geleszinski as fast as he could, and Randy Boyd, now standing above us on the roadbed, demanded that I release Geleszinski, later discovered to be a building contractor from the Valley.

At the same time, I was also violently confronted by Robin Varner, the friend of Geleszinski who had been the instigator of the attack on Irvine. He was screaming obscenities at me and demanding I release his friend. I told him to calm down, that I was not hurting his friend; I was just restraining him.

Randy Boyd now also insisted I let Geleszinski go. Well aware that it was Randy's party, I wanted to comply. I also wanted him to take control of the situation, so I said verbatim, "Fine. I'll let him go, but if I let him go and he hits me we're going to have a fucking problem."

On Randy's assurance that no harm would befall me, I let Geleszinski go. He got to his feet and Randy walked him up the road a little way, only ten or fifteen feet, where he reportedly told him he was not welcome on the train ride back to Anchorage. When I got up and was attempting to straighten out my clothing Varner got directly in my face, screaming and swearing at me again. When he took a swing at me, grazing my eyebrow, I parried with my left hand and punched him in the jaw with my right fist. His jaw broke, and so did my right hand. That was the end of Varner's active participation in the melee.

There was now a short peaceful interlude during which I furiously stomped around in the woods, swearing, grasping my broken hand, and again trying to regain my composure and straighten my disheveled appearance. Shelli made her way across the roadside ditch with some difficulty, thanks to her injured ankle, and tried to calm me down—no easy matter. But I soon walked with her back onto the roadbed where, surrounded by curious friends and fellow partiers, I attempted to answer their questions about what had happened.

Suddenly, out of nowhere, a left-handed, ham-sized fist burst through the crowd and smashed into my nose. Shelli said it sounded like an axe blow and that I went down like a felled tree. I did not slump to the ground; I was standing up straight and I fell backwards straight out. There was a smooth, rounded rock about a foot in diameter protruding slightly from the roadbed, and the back of my head landed right on it.

Shelli said later, "I thought you were going to get up and kill somebody."

I was out cold.

My face was pointed straight up at the sky, blood running from both nostrils, my unseeing eyes wide open, my pupils getting alternately larger and smaller, but not in coordination with one another. After a few seconds I regained consciousness, though I had no idea what had happened or even where I was.

Shelli, encumbered by her cast, helped me up and guided me across the nearby highway to a small mall. The mall was closed but she managed to get the attention of a young person working inside who allowed us the use of the men's room so I could be cleaned up. I was a bloody mess and my nose, which had been bent on one side of my face from my years of playing hockey, was now bent to the opposite side.

Although Shelli was overwrought by the condition of my face, all I could think about was how badly my hand hurt. When I saw myself in the mirror, however, I became for the first time fully aware of what had happened to me and I was furious. I wanted to know who had done this to me.

While Shelli and I were struggling through the effort of getting to the mall and getting me cleaned up, the melee on the gravel road grew exponentially. My friend, Norman Rokeberg got into Geleszinski's face, screaming, "Do you know who you just hit?"

Norman and Geleszinski exchanged blows that did harm to neither, but while attempting to hit Norman, Geleszinski hit Marilyn Warren in the back of the head, knocking her to the ground. Her husband, Charles, incensed and even bigger than Geleszinski, grabbed her attacker, threw him to the ground on the other side of the road and proceeded to pummel him.

Meanwhile, Randy Boyd was encouraging people to get back on the train. He managed to do that, sans Geleszinski and Varner, whom he had told to find other transportation home. Shelli and I were struggling to get back to the train before it left us in the middle of nowhere. The train was moving and slowly accelerating by the time we got to it, and we managed to get onto it only with the help of outstretched hands from Norman and others. Nursing my broken hand, we were certainly relieved to be settled on board among friends for the ride to Anchorage instead of being abandoned.

Randy Boyd, who had ordered the train to depart knowing that I, who had been seriously injured, and Shelli, who was wearing a leg cast, were on board, soon made his appearance and callously asked, without making even a cursory inquiry about my condition, "You're not going to sue us, are you?"

I stared at him; didn't say a word. But he had just made up my mind. You only get one chance to seriously mess with me.

Please do not get the impression that I am in total agreement with the extent of legal liability I incurred in my nightclub operation, or which the bank was incurring by throwing an event to thank their customers. That is better discussed at another time. But I believe in a level playing field. What's good for the goose is good for the gander. If public safety is what matters, why shouldn't a bank be held to the same standards as that of a nightclub?

You were required to be an adult to enter the doors of my establishment, but once you had, my business was responsible for everything and anything that happened to you or even that you did to yourself while on the premises or after you left because I had served you an adult beverage.

If you drank more than the legal limit for driving, then, even having been offered a free taxi, you drove anyway and caused injury to others or were yourself injured—I could be held liable.

Usually I ended up making "business" decisions to settle claims. Sometimes that was because the insurance company, which was charging me up the ying-yang, was afraid of going to court and sometimes it just made sense financially. Sometimes the cases were so fraudulent and bogus I demanded that the insurance company defend me, but I could not force them to do so.

Every time a fraudulent case was settled because it was considered a nuisance and a "business" decision to do so, my insurance rates would be jacked up and dishonest, gold-digging members of the public learned more about their "rights." If you thought you had a case against Chilkoot Charlie's any number of ambulance-chasing lawyers would line up to take it on a contingency. Why not sue? Just lie about your behavior and have your friends lie for you. If it came down to your word against that of the club's management, you won.

To combat such unconscionable transgressions we kept detailed logs of every evening. We had a security person carry a hand-held audio/video recorder so that evictions for over-imbibing and subsequent altercations were all on tape. The last thing a drunk wants to hear is that he has been cut off and has to go home. It was the spark that lit a lot of altercations. We instituted numerous operational procedures to prevent over-serving. We had an extensive security manual detailing their procedures and even had our security personnel trained by a nationally recognized nightclub security expert. We had cameras strategically placed around the premises, both inside and outside. Human nature being what it is, with abetment from the trial lawyer lobby, we still had incidents and we still got sued.

My insurance broker and I both got sued by my own insurance company one time over a highly publicized event involving a death. My broker had been merely photo-copying our renewal applications every year instead of going through them in detail with me, and there were some inaccuracies. In the normal course of events the inaccuracies would have been overlooked. The insurance company, Zurich, in a cynical effort to limit their liability, claimed that we had conspired to misrepresent liabilities. It was essentially a strategic move to compel us to have to participate financially in the settlement with the plaintiffs. It worked. I did kick in some money and I had to sue my broker, a friend, to recover my portion of the combined settlement. He understood. It wasn't my fault that the conditions had been created that allowed the insurance company to sue us.

Once, we received a demand letter from a lawyer representing a guy who claimed our doormen had "viciously, wantonly, with malice of fore-thought, etc., etc." beaten him up on the North Side dance floor "for no apparent reason." When we showed the lawyer our footage of the guy's friend picking him up, turning him over and dropping him on his head on the dance floor, we heard no more from him.

We had clearly posted rules, one of which was that you were required for your own safety to wear shoes inside the club. I ended up paying the emergency room bills of a woman who insisted on removing her shoes to dance barefoot on the South Side dance floor and cut her foot on broken glass.

There is a well-known case where two guys got into an altercation in the Taco Bell car service line. One was stabbed by the other and died. The one who did the stabbing had been to Chilkoot Charlie's earlier. Insurance company lawyers got the case dismissed on summary judgment in the lower court for what appeared to be an obvious overreach of liability. The Alaska State Supreme Court, in their wisdom, remanded the decision to the lower court, having divined some ill-defined shred of relationship between the guy having a couple of drinks at Koot's before going to Taco Bell for a late-night snack.

Taco Bell, on whose property the murder actually took place, was subsequently relieved of any responsibility. My insurance company forked over a settlement that neither side was happy about. The case reminds me of the cartoon I once saw of a farmer in overalls sitting in the witness chair in front of the judge and jury while the plaintiff's attorney shouts at him, "So you admit you planted the corn, that was turned into whiskey, that was sold by A to Z Wholesalers to Joe's Bar, that over-served my client, Mr. Smith!"

One night a big guy tried to do a pull-up on one of our fire sprinkler pipes. He jerked it out of the ceiling, broke a seam, and created a hell of a mess in the South Long Bar. He cut his head on the sprinkler head in the process, and that required stitches. You guessed it.

I am done with my rant. What I knew for certain in 1985 was had I been in charge of the "Charleston Express," there would have been no question in anyone's mind about who was responsible for what transpired. And I would have employed security personnel and professional servers, called the state Troopers at the appropriate time to intervene, done what I could to assist the injured. And I certainly would not have ordered the train to depart until everyone was on it.

Chilkoot Charlie's had lost a jury trial, one of the few cases we ever actually lost, a few years earlier. My doormen made up a story about how they thought the plaintiff was going for a gun when they hurt him, and the jury did not buy it. The plaintiff was represented by an attorney named Brian Shute, who I thought had been dogged in his efforts on behalf of his client. I called Brian, told him about my mishap on the train trip, and asked if he would like to represent me.

Brian said, "Sure! I'd rather represent you than sue you any day."

Brian retained Michael Buckland, a private detective, who during the month of July interviewed numerous participants in the evening's events and concluded his report thusly:

"It is my opinion that we have a rather solid foundation at this point. We have acquired a considerable amount of information and evidence concerning Mr. Gordon's damages and the various joint tortfeasors responsible. Having established the relationships between the parties, the applicable standard of care can be determined through legal research."

On August 5, 1985 I filed my lawsuit against Alaska Pacific Bancorporation and Alaska Pacific Mortgage Company, its subsidiary and James Geleszinski.

"WHEREFORE, Plaintiff prays for judgment against Defendants for the following relief:

1. For general and special damages as proved at trial;

2. For punitive damages as proven at trial.

3. For pre-judgment and post-judgment interest at the maximum legal rate;

4. For costs and attorney's fees; and

5. For such other and further relief which the court deems just and equitable."

Geleszinski retained the law offices of Kay, Christie, Saville & Coffey and counterclaimed that I "started an altercation with Mr. Geleszinski by initiating contact with him, by harmfully and offensively touching him inter alia by grabbing him and throwing him to the ground and holding him there." They claimed that my actions, "constituted an assault and battery upon Defendant (Geleszinski) for which Defendant is entitled to recovery in an amount to be proven with particularity at the time of trial."

They went on to claim:

"4. After throwing and holding Defendant Geleszinski to the ground, Plaintiff [me] then attacked one Rob Varner who was being held with both arms behind his back. Michael Gordon at that time and place began to beat Rob Varner about the head and face while Mr. Varner was defenseless.

5. Defendant Geleszinski made an effort to defend Rob Varner, and to prevent serious physical injury to him from occurring.

6. As a direct and proximate result of his efforts to defend Mr. Varner, Mr. Geleszinski suffered physical injury to his person which required medical treatment and resulted in lost wages, the costs of which were in excess of $10,000, the amount to be proven with particularity at the time of trial."

7. Defendant Geleszinski is entitled to special and general damages against the Plaintiff in a sum in excess of $25,000 to be proved in particularity at the time of trial.

SECOND COUNTERCLAIM

8. Defendant Geleszinski adopts and incorporates all preceding paragraphs of his first counterclaim and further alleges as follows:

9. Plaintiff Gordon's actions as above described were wanton, willful and reckless, and warrant the imposition of punitive damages in favor of Geleszinski against Plaintiff in a sum to be proven at trial."

A third counterclaim was that my conduct was negligent, and Defendant Geleszinski's damages were the direct and proximate result of my negligence.

This was a totally fabricated representation of what transpired on the way to the train from Snyder Park the evening of June 21, 1985.

A year later, on July 9, 1986, David J. Schmid of Kay, Saville, Coffey, Hopwood & Schmid, wrote to Brian Shute:

"I have been given the authority to offer $3,000.00 to dismiss my client from the litigation. While this sum may not be substantial from the view of Mr. Gordon, it is quite substantial from the Geleszinski's point of view. Similarly, if the offer were accepted, I would be willing to provide you with some information which could be helpful in your action against the bank that is otherwise privileged and non-discoverable. While I can't reveal the nature of this information, I can say that it would bolster the allegations of your Complaint against the bank which in my view are now unsupported by any evidence obtained through formal discovery.

The advantages to settling with Mr. Geleszinski are several. It would reduce Mr. Gordon's costs of proceeding with its litigation against the bank, it would eliminate the necessity of defending against Mr. Geleszinski's Counterclaim, it would insure at least some recovery against Mr. Geleszinski, it could bolster the remainder of your client's claim, and leave the deep pocket for further recovery."

And my parents wanted me to be a lawyer?

Randy Boyd's deposition was taken on March 24, 1986. Two days later Brian Shute sent me a letter describing the deposition, which follows in part. I spotted three lies from Randy in the very first paragraph.

"1. Mr. Boyd said that (Lie #1) he, Mike Burns, and yourself all arrived at where Mr. Geleszinski was sitting on top of Mr. Irvine. Mr. Boyd said that Mr. Geleszinski appeared to be striking or ready to strike a blow with his fist to Mr. Irvine. Mr. Boyd recalls that (Lie #2) the three of you pulled Mr. Geleszinski off of Mr. Irvine, and that thereafter Mr. Boyd took custody of Mr. Geleszinski and walked him ten or fifteen feet away to calm him down. Mr. Boyd has (Lie #3) no recollection of you saying anything with respect to apprehension about Mr. Geleszinski hitting you.

2. Mr. Boyd says that he then (Lie #4) saw you with a full nelson hold on Mr. Varner at the same place where Mr. Geleszinski and Mr. Irvine had been. Mr. Boyd said that he then had (Lie #5) you release Mr. Varner to him whereupon he again walked Mr. Varner away to calm him down.

3. Mr. Boyd's next recollection is that of Mr. Warren fighting with Mr. Geleszinski. Mr. Boyd has no recollection of you being hit, nor does he have any recollection of you hitting Mr. Varner. Mr. Geleszinski testified in his deposition that Mr. Boyd was holding Mr. Varner while you hit Mr. Varner. Mr. Boyd specifically refuted this and said that it did not happen.

4. Mr. Boyd indicated that the only person he saw in an intoxicated state was an employee of the bank who had to be carried onto the train. (I guess you only see what you want to see.) He indicated that he was the person responsible for the organizational decisions, and that contracts for catering were made by Susan Tebo in the marketing department.

5. *Mr. Boyd indicated that there was no consideration given by him to providing security for crowd control, first aid, etc., other than that provided in the contracts for the catering and railroad service. He said the reason for this was that he did not see a necessity for it given the professional status of the guest list. He admitted the alcohol was served free, and that there was no attempt to check the tickets, and that anyone could have gotten on board the train. He indicated that he further didn't see any reason for security because there had been no incidents in the two prior years the event had been held. Finally, he indicated that the bank was not planning on holding the event in the future for three reasons: 1) the litigation you have brought against them, 2) the expense, and 3) the bank can't invite all of its customers and they had bad feelings generated in those who didn't receive an invitation.*

I believe Mr. Boyd's deposition went favorably for our case. At the conclusion of the deposition, Mr. Geleszinski's attorney approached me in private and wanted to know whether we would be willing to settle the matter on a reasonable basis. I told him that I knew you had somewhere around $9,000 in hospital bills, and that a minor portion of those were attributable to your hand. Mr. Geleszinski's attorney indicated he felt his client's case was weak, but that his client had limited funds available for settlement."

In their Motion for Summary Judgment, dated August 6, 1986, Richmond & Quinn, attorneys for Alaska Pacific Bancorporation and Alaska Pacific Mortgage Company, citing various legal precedents, asserted that Alaska Pacific Mortgage Company was not negligent, nor was it vicariously liable to the plaintiff (me) for the acts of Geleszinski. They concluded by saying:

"Alaska Pacific Mortgage Company acted reasonably under the circumstances (and) under the circumstances could not have foreseen this bizarre set of facts. It took no acts which proximately led to the injury. It is also not vicariously liable for the acts of Geleszinski as a matter of law. For these reasons, the Alaska Pacific Mortgage Company and Alaska Pacific Bancorporation should be granted summary judgment."

On September 19, 1986, with the Superior Court decision approaching, Brian Shute received an Offer of Judgment from the bank through their attorneys, Richmond & Quinn, for $6,000, plus all allowable costs and attorney's fees. I rejected the offer as too little, too late.

In October 1986, the honorable Superior Court Judge, Joan M. Katz, in her wisdom, ruled in favor of the bank, its subsidiary and James Geleszinski, approving their Motion for Summary Judgment. Judge Katz ruled that there was no material issue of fact regarding whether the bank was negligent in not providing adequate security and that there was no material issue of fact regarding whether the bank was vicariously liable under the theory of respondeat superior.

On October 20, 1986, Brian Shute made on my behalf an Offer of Judgment to Robert Richmond of Richmond & Quinn for $14,000. In a cover letter Brian explained:

"As you can see from the enclosed memorandum, Mr. Gordon and myself believe that the Trial Court erred in the grant of summary judgment. Mr. Gordon will, if the Motion to Reconsider isn't granted, or if this offer isn't accepted within 10 days of your receipt of this letter, appeal the decision of the Trial Court.

I believe that, given the authority cited in our memorandum opposing the Bank's motion for summary judgment and supporting our Motion for Reconsideration, there is a substantial likelihood of reversal.

However, even if the Motion to Reconsider is granted, the Plaintiff has lost the momentum of its trial preparations, and even though he is not happy with the amount of the settlement, he would accept it as offered herein. On the other hand, if he either prevails upon his Motion to Reconsider or is forced to go to the expense of preparing an appeal, he would no longer consider the enclosed offer." Our offer was rejected.

Before Judge Katz's decision in favor of the bank I settled my suit against Geleszinski for $10,000. I received from Brian Shute's trust account the $6,000 balance after a contingency fee of 33 1/3 % and other expenses.

In October 1986, Brian Shute filed on my behalf a Motion to Reconsider the Granting of Summary Judgment in Favor of the Bank. It was rejected by Judge Katz, so I was now in the position of not only owing my own attorney expenses, but those of the bank, as well as the expenses involved in appealing my case to the Alaska Supreme Court if I was finally going to prevail. It was never about money with me, other than my expenses; it was about principle. I had been seriously injured. I felt it was the bank's responsibility, and I was incensed by the bank's callous attitude toward me. Also, as I have said previously, had the roles been reversed there would have been no question of responsibility.

Adding insult to injury, after the granting of Summary Judgment to the bank by Judge Katz, Randy Boyd showed up at Chilkoot Charlie's to celebrate the bank's victory by dancing on the North Side dance floor and laughing in my face.

It was time for a new legal team. My choice was Paul Davis of Boyko, Davis, Dennis, PC and C.R. Baldwin, PC. I had had previous dealings with Paul and had a lot of faith in his legal capabilities. In a letter dated November 20, 1986, to Robert L. Richmond of Richmond & Quinn, representing Alaska Pacific Bancorporation, et al, Paul informed him that his law firm had entered its appearance on my behalf, that he was sure that Judge Katz's decision was as much of a surprise to Richmond as it was to Shute, that there was a better than average chance that Katz's decision would be reversed upon appeal and that the amount needed from the bank to settle matters was now $25,000.

Paul submitted our Opening Brief to the Alaska State Supreme Court on March 12, 1987. In the brief, without citing all the case law, Paul argued:

"THE SUPREME COURT MUST REVERSE A SUPERIOR COURT DECISION IN GRANTING THE MOTION FOR SUMMARY JUDGMENT IF THERE IS A GENUINE ISSUE OF MATERIAL FACT OR IF THE MOVING PARTY IS NOT ENTITLED TO JUDGMENT AS A MATTER OF LAW.

THE HONORABLE JOAN M. KATZ ERRED IN HER FINDING THAT THERE WERE NO MATERIAL ISSUE OF FACTS REGARDING WHETHER THE APPELLEES WERE NEGLIGENT IN PROVIDING ADEQUATE SECURITY TO THE APPELLANT.

THE HONORABLE JOAN M. KATZ ERRED IN FINDING THAT THERE IS NO MATERIAL ISSUE OF FACT REGARDING WHETHER THE APPELLEE WAS VICARIOUSLY LIABLE UNDER THE THEORY OF RESPONDEAT SUPERIOR."

On April 6, 1988, the Alaska State Supreme Court, comprised of Chief Justice Warren Matthews, Justice Rabinowitz, Justice Burke, Justice Compton and Justice Moore, rendered its decision.

In doing so it found:

"Alaska Pacific does not argue that it was not a possessor of Snyder Park when it hosted the party there. In our view a jury question is presented as to whether Alaska Pacific should have reasonably anticipated altercations among its guests. If the answer to that question is in the affirmative, the jury could find that Alaska Pacific failed to take reasonable precautions which would have prevented harm to Gordon.

The jury could find a duty to anticipate outbreaks of violence on the following facts. There was a large crowd of people to whom large quantities of free liquor were given. No effort was made to limit dispensation of alcohol to those apparently sober. One of the activities was a dance, where jealousies, proposals for sexual transactions, and social slights might play a motivational role.

We conclude that the rule of exemption has no application to this case. Gordon's claim is not that Alaska Pacific is liable because it served people who were intoxicated. His claim is that Alaska Pacific had a duty to provide protection, knowing, among other things, that intoxicated people would be on the premises. The source of the intoxicants is not critical to this theory.

Gordon also argues that Boyd had a duty of reasonable care because Boyd undertook to protect him from Geleszinski. If Boyd breached this duty, Alaska Pacific is liable for Gordon's injuries under the doctrine of respondeat superior. Alaska Pacific contends that Boyd did not undertake to protect Gordon. The trial court apparently ruled that Boyd did undertake to break up the fight, but concluded that he exercised reasonable care as a matter of law.

Even though one person is otherwise under no duty to another, if he voluntarily undertakes to protect the other he may be liable for his negligence in doing so.

Gordon testified that, after he pulled Geleszinski off Irvine, he would not let Geleszinski go until someone came along, because Geleszinski was "mean." When Boyd arrived and asked Gordon to release Geleszinski, Gordon replied, 'fine, but if I let him go and he hits me, we're going to have a …problem.' Gordon wanted to make sure that Geleszinski would not turn on him when Gordon let go. Gordon assumed that Boyd or other people 'got hold of' Geleszinski and led him away.

Boyd agreed that he 'took charge' of Geleszinski after Gordon let go of him; he walked him ten to fifteen feet up the road, because Boyd did not want the altercation to start all over again.

Reading this testimony in the light most favorable to Gordon, we conclude that a jury might find Boyd undertook to prevent Geleszinski from fighting. This undertaking could be found to give rise to the correlative duty to protect those with whom he would foreseeably fight. Gordon was one such person.

Gordon argues that Boyd breached his duty because Boyd simply released Geleszinski fifteen feet up the road. Alaska Pacific contends that Boyd exercised due care because Geleszinski appeared calm when Boyd released him. The trial court ruled that Boyd exercised due care as a matter of law because it was undisputed that Geleszinski appeared calm when Boyd released him.

Although Geleszinski was calm when Boyd released him, this occurred within ten to fifteen feet of the site of the first fight. In contrast, after Geleszinski struck Gordon, Boyd walked him through the woods, across an open field, across the railroad tracks and across the highway to a mini-mall, where Boyd informed Geleszinski and his wife that they were not getting back on the train to Anchorage. Moreover, Geleszinski did not struggle against Gordon's restraint, yet Gordon did not release him until someone appeared to take charge of the situation, because Gordon suspected that Geleszinski was 'just playing along.'

Whether particular conduct is negligent or reasonable is a question of fact for the jury, if reasonable minds could draw different inferences from the evidence presented. We believe that reasonable minds could differ on the question whether Boyd exercised reasonable care in releasing Geleszinski so soon, and so near the scene of the struggle, despite his calm demeanor. We therefore conclude that the trial court erred in concluding that Boyd exercised due care as a matter of law.

Alaska Pacific argues that neither lack of security guards nor Boyd's release of Geleszinski was a proximate cause of Gordon's injuries as a matter of law. Further, it argues that Gordon's and Geleszinski's acts are, as a matter of law, superseding causes. We conclude that there are genuine issues of material fact, and conflicting inferences which can be drawn therefrom, which precluded summary judgment on proximate cause. Further, we conclude that Gordon's and Geleszinski's acts are not superseding causes.

If there had been security guards one could have escorted Geleszinski safely away from the area of confrontation while another could have quelled the Gordon-Varner altercation. This would have prevented some of the injuries Gordon suffered. Similarly, the presence of security personnel might reasonably have obviated Gordon's intervention in the Geleszinski-Irvine altercation. Moreover, Boyd's release of Geleszinski did have as its result the attack by Geleszinski on Gordon. A jury could readily find a proximate cause relationship between these acts.

The prevention of fights, whether in self-defense or not, is one reason why security guards may be required under section 344 of the Restatement (Second) of Torts. The fact that they occur cannot therefore be regarded as a superseding cause, for they are within the scope of the foreseeable risk.

As to the theory that Boyd was negligent in releasing Geleszinski, the risk was that he would continue to fight. Gordon, as the person who had restrained Geleszinski, and who because of this was then involved in a fray with Geleszinski's friend Varner, was a foreseeable target. Thus on the theory as well, Alaska Pacific's superseding cause theory fails.

REVERSED AND REMANDED."

On April 12, 1988, Brian Shute wrote Paul Davis:

"Dear Paul:

Congratulations on your reversal of Judge Katz's absurd decision in Mike's case. I note that your office jousted with Richmond's office on the Bank's motion for attorney fees, and substituted as counsel for me.

Hopefully the Bank will now get realistic about this case and settle it like they should have done a long time ago. Please let me know.

In reviewing my file, I see that I have my trial note book with outlines of witness testimony, pleadings digests, etc. prepared. It would save some trial preparation time, if the bank insists upon going forward with the matter. Again congratulations. Mike deserves his justice.

Very truly yours,

Brian R. Shute"

In addition to my broken hand, I suffered from a brain concussion that required medication and psychiatric counseling. I had screaming nightmares that woke me and Shelli up for weeks on end. My nose was so severely broken that it had to heal completely in its broken state in order to be re-broken and repaired in a surgical procedure.

Key Bank did make restitution.

In the pre-trial interview of Jim Irvine conducted by Michael Buckland on July 10, 1985, Irvine sums the whole story up perfectly, "I know that—I think when they were—whoever it was that was trying to help me was doing it in a mild way. It wasn't like jumping on him or anything like that. And for what he did for me and for what happened to Mike and I thought Randy—man alive, there was just no call for it, absolutely no call for it."

Ruben, I am certain, in spite of all his other talents, wanted to be remembered for his poetry. I recited this one to express my feelings at Ruben's memorial.

"Comfort"

When I am young

and suffering my first

unthinkable reverse and,

wounded to the core, go

crawling to another who

will listen to it all,

I hope I find no

counselor, who robs

me of my grief and tells

me disappointment is a

simple seasoning and

failure an adjustment

and the grinding misery

is just the firm caress

of God, but one who will

agree that it's the end

of everything and wisely

wails with me and follows

in my stumbling, broken

path awhile

Collected Ruben Gaines II ©1988 Ruben Gaines

Betrayal

Having experienced betrayal in romantic relationships, I knew how it felt. I also knew that in spite of the pain, there is a sweetness to it—something deriving from the complex stew of love gone wrong. It hurts plenty, but not so much as the cold evisceration by a trusted, lifelong friend that leaves you dumbfounded and senseless. Love is the foundation of one; friendship itself the other. A friendship should outlast a love. Most of us understand that for a marriage to last a lifetime, our spouses should also be our friends.

Imagine being best friends with someone from junior high school until your mid-sixties. I'm talking about someone with whom there were no secrets, someone who visited you while you were living in the dorm in college and brought a case of beer. Imagine someone with whom you ran a dozen marathons and with whom you trained almost daily for the majority of them, sharing and competing over the endless hours of running the local trails. Imagine someone with whom you joked about things you could never joke about with any other person on earth, even—or perhaps especially—your spouse; a person you were in fact closer to than your spouse in significant ways.

Imagine someone with whom you had business relationships involving large amounts of money and serious responsibilities spanning decades, where there was never the slightest concern about trustworthiness by either party. There was total trust, because you *knew* this person and he *knew* you. This was a person upon whose shoulder you cried when experiencing excruciating personal difficulties. Certainly, I stood by him during difficult times as well, but did he ever cry on my shoulder? He may have, but I actually do not recall that he ever did. Perhaps it had been more of a one-sided relationship than I realized.

One night, while drinking in the Swing Bar at Chilkoot Charlie's, this person confessed to me that for an entire year he had found excuses for not doing things with me, or agreed to do something and then canceled at the very last minute, or had simply stood me up. The confession was unprompted and apparently made because he felt guilty about it. I asked him why he had done it and he said, "Because I'm an asshole."

I went home and said sadly to Shelli, "I wish he had never told me."

I had noticed the pattern, but I naively never considered that it was intentional and calculated. That had never even entered my mind. One possible explanation was my friend's new wife. She had worked with Shelli at the FDIC after the bank they both worked at was taken over by the Federal Deposit Insurance Corporation. Shelli introduced her to him. Lo and behold, they got married. I was his best man. He had been my best may when I married Shelli. But from the day of the marriage things between the four of us began to change. Though we were outwardly friendly she became standoffish. His relationship with us became more distant, which was not to be unexpected, but there was more going on than that. Perhaps his new wife had put him up to it or had at least created the atmosphere from which his new routine evolved. No matter. We had been lifelong friends. He had known her for a few years. And he had made a choice.

When he tried to make up I reminded him that he had made a choice and that my friendship was not something he could turn off and on like a faucet.

"C'mon Mike. Let's hug and make up. You've been my best friend forever," he said.

Nope. Not anymore. I simply could not make myself overlook a year-long binge of him intentionally injuring me, week after week. The more I thought about it the more it annoyed me. I missed the relationship, but there was no way I could bring myself to forgive him.

What made him do it? Perhaps I took the relationship for granted? Did I see myself as the main character and he in the supporting role? Could he have been that manipulated by his new wife? Actually, that's not hard to imagine. I asked him if there was anything I had done that had precipitated his behavior and he said there had not been. Was my wounded pride all that stood between me and a relationship that lasted for fifty years?

My lifelong friend had cut a hole in me that could not be filled simply by forgiving him and stitching him back into the fabric of myself. At least not in the short term. I began to think about reaching out to him, but pride is a powerful force. It creates its own complex defenses and the internal struggle lives in me to this day. So many years have now passed since he died that any further contemplation is academic, but it is there still.

I did try to call him once, but his phone number had been changed. Perhaps he had already passed away. I was unaware of his death until long after it happened. As far as I know there was no memorial, and I never saw anything in the newspaper. I learned about it in a phone conversation with Dan Sullivan, the ex-mayor of Anchorage, who knew we had been lifelong friends and thought I might have some details.

I have discussed my feelings with Shelli and a number of close friends. The nearest I have gotten to a solid answer to my quandary was from Charlie McAlpine, who replied, "Mike, some acts are unforgivable."

Perhaps. Maybe that's why it has taken me so long.

But I forgive you, Glenn. Rest in peace.

"Let's Relive it again...."

Precious few are left who remember the great Fishwheel Gold Rush of 1949, a Fairbanks phenomenon. Fishwheel was the ad-lib name of the locality where some grains of gold were supposed to have been found, and the rumor started a fake stampede. The find was alleged to have taken place in the country around Ft. Yukon where that river breaks up into a thousand separate sloughs and backwaters, near a fishwheel operated by a local native.

There were still numbers of old Dawson and Nome stampeders around, all of them yearning for a rerun of the thunderous old days, when men were men and Nellie the Pig was not necessarily so ugly if the lighting was right; and a nifty little fever grew in the space of a few days. The Affair Fishwheel was on a minute scale compared to Dawson but one got a fleeting glance at how fire gets lit under the imagination and melts the thought process. There were loud afternoons at the Wagon Wheel and other Fairbanks bars, and much questioning of oldtimers who were now automatic authorities. They hadn't had it so good for half a century.

Oh, there were cynics who said that local bush pilots were responsible for spreading the rumor, and were charging big fees for hauling greenhorns up to Ft. Yukon. But oldtimers were wallowing in renaissance, their fans were bent on reliving history and nobody was interested in debunkery. People were bound to get to Fishwheel and there was no other way to go, than to fly.

The fever was on and, as a radio reporter, I went to the diggings to cover the story for the local radio station, maybe even network coverage, equipped with a tape machine and generator to motivate it, microphone and heavy clothes. The bush pilot hauled me and the gear to Fishwheel, the literal end of the earth, now snowbound and swallowed up in a galaxy of look-alike sloughs of the Yukon.

There was the native's fishwheel, all right, frozen in the ice, and a few pitched tents, the vanguard of the stampede. A couple of them were already occupied by prospectors who had flown north to stake claims, usually in behalf of ones who stayed at home in the Wagon Wheel and other warm saloons. It was almighty cold in the main tent where my equipment sat, and the adjoining one was stocked with racks of men's clothing, the first merchandising intended for Fishwheel.

I beheld the little plastic vial that contained the few flecks of gold, the original discovery. On the program hastily set up I questioned old-timers, natives and newcomers about the ultimate prospects, and comparisons with the stampedes of the past.

And somewhere in the proceedings the ethereality of the whole event emerged. Once hinted at, the phoniness quickly grew as crystal clear as the glint of the sun on the snow outside the tent. The evasiveness in the eyes of those doing the talking was evident, and I saw the interest of the Dawson oldtimers subside and noted the reticence of the natives, especially the one who ran the fishwheel. The program itself was growing phony because the generator that ran the tape machine froze; when played back the voices of the interviewees slowed in an audio sump or rose to a staccato babble like Donald Duck.

I wish the Fishwheel Gold Rush had lasted longer; everyone in Fairbanks did. History never even had time to *begin* repeating.

Collected Ruben Gaines ©1987 Ruben Gaines

The Rokebergs: Norman, Mel, Ruby & Tang, early '60s.

Mike in his ROTC uniform, UAF, 1961

Mike demonstrates the difference in size between a king and a sockeye salmon, Kvijack River, 1961.

I

Augustus Chidley

Tommy Rocker and Mike, company party, December 2004

Hogg Brothers Cafe poster

The Kamikaze as flower bed, 2020

Shelli and Mike dressed for Charleston Express, August 1985

Mike finishes the Honolulu Marathon, December 1, 1979.

Mike, Grete Waite, and two members of the Anchorage Running Club, Marathon, Greece, 1983

Mike recuperates from finger degloving injury, October 2010

Henry and Nalani Kreutz, Halibut Cove, June 1, 2002

Back row: Kevin Kuster, Mike Gordon, George Georgiou, Tom McCulloch.
Front row: Frank Gurtler, Doran Powell

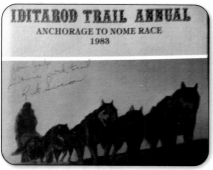

1983 Iditarod Trail Annual signed by Rick Swenson

Vivian MacInnes and Uncle Larry, June 1986

Dick Lowell, Mike, Dan Lowell and Doran Powell, Uruguay, May 1995

David Mayberry, "Doctor Bob" Warren, Halibut Cove BBQ, September 2011

Charlie and Cullen McAlpine

Polka Dan "honks kordeen" at Mike's book signing at Writer's Block Bookstore and Cafe, 2019.

Wanda Prince, "Mayor of Spenard," in the Bird House Bar inside Chilkoot Charlie's, circa 2015

Sherri Jaussaud, (1960-1983)

Phesdo House

Phesdo House and grounds

Callaloo Resort postcards

Mike with barracuda, Los Roques,
Venezuela, 2002

Arsentiev Sergei, Todd Burleson and Mike,
summit Mt. Elbrus, August 19, 1991.

Tibetan pilgrims to Lhasa,
Chinese artist, purchased in
Bejing, China, October 2010

Mike and Leonard Hyde at the
Taj Mahal, April 2012

Mike & Walter John, Mike's Rotary sponsor.

Dick Grace and Mike at a Pillars of America event, Egan Convention Center

Mike's son, Michael, shows off newly acquired food supply, 2020.

Ruben's shower cartoon from original Halibut Cove residence, September 1992

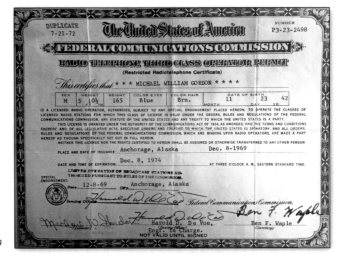

Mike's FCC Radio Telephone Third Class Operator Permit, issued December 8, 1969

USS Funston

Cabaret, Hotel & Restaurant Board (CHAR), back row Frank Lanson, Skip Fuller, Jack Griffin, front row Mary Powell, Mike O'Neil, Mike Gordon, Unknown circa 1970

1983 photo of Chilkoot Charlie's, Spenard Bingo Hall to the left

Mountain Mike's Retirement Party Announcement, September 2015

Koot's with double rainbow, October 2, 2017

Shelli, Tiny Tim and Mike

Uncle Larry Lawrence and Shelli, March 1991

Peter Ettinger performing at Chilkoot Charlie's

Arsentiev Sergei with our BBQ
lamb near Elbrus village

Leonard Hyde with snake, New Delhi, India

Mike shows off the Soviet Walk, Chilkoot Charlie's.

Mike & Shelli with Mike's memoir,
Learning the Ropes

*Ruben Gaines attends Chilkoot Charlie's
company party, December 9, 1991.*

Mike & Nick Fuller

Ruben Gaines with Chilkoot Charlie
ring, Halibut Cove, September 1992

Oleg & Mike enjoying "tea",
cruiser Aurora, Leningrad

Oleg, Lenin and Chilkoot
Charlie's slogan

Mike & Ruben, late 80s

1982, Ruben's 70th birthday gala, Mike's sister, Pat, Ruben, Mike & Shelli

Diana Tillion, Mike, Shelli & Clem Tilllion, October, 10, 2008, Halibut Cove

Halibut Cove Gothic, October 1, 2011

Attempted Robbery

The '70s and '80s were pretty crazy in Anchorage. Some of it spilled over into the '90s.

Jon A. Woodard was fascinated by Steven Segal—the 6' 4", pony-tail-sporting actor, martial artist and stuntman. Jon mimicked Steven's appearance, including the trademark black clothes and ponytail. Woodard wanted to establish a reputation for himself as a tough guy—as an outlaw. Eminently successful, he wound up convicted of robbery and second-degree murder and was sentenced to 66 years in prison.

The sorry tale of this callow, delusional twenty-seven-year-old's crime was well-covered in the local press: He murdered a hapless Loomis guard while attempting to rob the Carr's Aurora Village grocery store located in Spenard between Northern Lights and Benson Boulevards. What was not covered was that before Woodard's fateful grocery store misadventure he had tried to rob Chilkoot Charlie's.

In the aftermath of the attempt at Koot's, I learned that Woodard and accomplices had visited the bar on several occasions during the day shift to case the place. He had casually asked a lot of questions of the bar staff. He knew that the person who counted the bartender banks was named Olga (Cwikla). He knew that she performed her duties in an office across the hall from a set of bathrooms toward the rear of the club, and just inside the back door where the janitorial crew exited in the mornings to take out the trash. He knew that Beth Berke sometimes helped Olga with counting down the banks and filling out the daily reports. He knew there would be a lot of cash in the safe from the Friday, Saturday, and Sunday nights of the upcoming three-day Memorial Day weekend. He knew Olga's approximate arrival and departure times.

Woodard chose the morning of Monday, May 25, 1992 to strike. He waited in the alley for the clean-up crew to open the rear door to dump the trash, then forced them back into the club at gunpoint and into the lady's room across the hall from the office. He then kicked in both office doors—inner and outer. In the outer office he found two locked and secured safes, one for dropping night bartender sales, the other a gun safe compartmentalized to accommodate a dozen bartenders' banks. In the inner office he found two desks, the master safe locked like the others, and some security equipment—but no Olga.

"Where's Olga?" Woodard demanded of the terrified clean-up crew who were being held at gunpoint by an accomplice.

"She's off today," they replied in unison.

"Where's Beth Berke?" he barked.

"She's not here either," they said.

It was a holiday Monday. The banks were closed. Olga and Beth had taken the day off. Our general manager, Doran Powell, had done the Sunday night banks after closing early Monday morning, then gone home to bed. None of our management was present. The only people on the premises were cleaning up from the night before and of course none of them had combinations to the safes, all of which were secured in their respective locations. Woodard had miscalculated. Unmentioned in the press because no money had been taken and no one had been shot, and undeterred by his lack of success at Koot's, Woodard chose his next target.

Two weeks later, on the morning of Monday, June 8, 1992, Woodard, wearing a mask, strode into Carr's Aurora Village. Again, he had help. Twenty-six-year-old Sean Pierce, a convicted forger, was the lookout. Twenty-five-year-old David Van Housen, a Carr's employee who stocked produce on the midnight to eight a.m. shift had familiarized Woodard with the store layout and told him when the guard would be making his cash pickup. Twenty-three-year-old Karl Bohlin allegedly helped hide some of the cash after the robbery.

At the time there was an open-air box-shaped cubicle that acted as an office in the middle of the front area of the store. It had shoulder-height Plexiglas windows on all four sides and was only about five feet tall. Terrence Becker, the Loomis guard that fateful day, was inside collecting cash for transport to the bank. At his height Woodard could easily reach over the top of the cubicle to point his gun at Becker. When he did, and demanded cash, Becker started to reach for his own gun.

Woodard warned, "Don't do that."

Becker, for some sibylline reason, did it anyway. Woodard shot him in the side of the head and escaped with about $50,000 in cash.

When Doran Powell learned later in the day of the May 25th attempted robbery of Koot's he was afraid whoever had tried to rob us might come back before we could make our deposits at the bank on Tuesday morning, so he took evasive action. Imagine Shelli's surprise that Monday evening when after returning from a trip to Canada to visit her great-aunt Ferne, she opened the dryer in our condo to find bank bags bulging with nearly $100,000 in cash. It was a clever place for Doran to hide the money. The condo was secured with an alarm system, Shelli was in Canada, and I was not yet home from my second attempt at summiting Mt. Everest.

Returning from Nepal the following week, I immediately went about tightening security procedures. We installed solid oak doors in metal frames in both the inner and outer offices. Both doors were equipped with security bars and the intercom system was upgraded. Whoever was working in the inner office was never to let anyone into that office until they had first been let into the outer office and reinstalled the bar on the outer office door. If a person was leaving the office instructions were to close and lock the inner office door behind them before removing the bar and opening the outer door. Any person left in the inner office was to put the bar back up before the outer office bar was removed. There was never to be clear–and-open access to the inner office. Though I warned Olga—and others—many times, human nature being what it is, I was generally the only one who always followed the procedures.

Woodard was to learn the problem with accomplices: they talk. None of them had anticipated 48-year-old Terrence Becker being shot in the head. The *Daily Sitka Sentinel* reported on September 4, 1992:

"A convicted forger who admitted serving as lookout during a June supermarket heist that left an armored truck guard dead has pleaded no contest to armed robbery.

Sean Thomas Pierce, 26, entered the plea in Anchorage Superior Court on Thursday.

In return, Pierce will be given immunity from prosecution for murder, and he will receive no more than four years in prison if he testifies against his friends, who allegedly carried out the deadly robbery."

The same paper reported on August 12, 1993:

"A man who helped his friend with a 1992 supermarket robbery that turned fatal has been given two and a half years in prison.

David Van Housen, 26, an employee of the Carrs supermarket, gave inside information to Jon Woodard, who robbed the store of about $50,000 and killed an armored-car guard.

Judge Karen Hunt sentenced Van Housen to the short term, saying he was genuinely sorry for his act and had excellent prospects for rehabilitation."

On September 27, 1993 the *Sitka Sentinel* wrote:

"A man convicted of killing an armored car guard during a super-market robbery has been sentenced to 66 years in prison.

Jon Woodard, 28, was sentenced Friday for second-degree murder. He was convicted earlier this year in the June, 1992 shooting death of Terry Becker.

Judge Karen Hunt rejected the prosecution's request that Woodard be given the maximum 99 years, saying, "While he is dangerous, he doesn't qualify as a worst offender."

"Woodard is to stand trial later this year on two other robbery charges, and he is accused of federal weapons violations.

The 66-year sentence means Woodard can apply for parole in 22 years."

Woodard, in fact, the last time I checked was residing in a federal halfway house in Anchorage. Terrence Becker, born on May 19, 1944 in San Mateo, California, left behind a widow, Gail Ito; a son T.J.; a mother, Mary Becker; two brothers, John and Stephen; and sisters Mary Ellen Becker and Margaret O'Brien, none of whom will ever see him again. Terrence had worked for Alaska Mountaineering and Hiking for 15 years. Three years before his death he took a job with Alaska Security, which became Loomis. His hobbies included hiking, ocean kayaking, downhill skiing and practical shooting, none of which he will ever do again.

Though I am not one to question the wisdom of Judge Hunt's sentencing decision, I do wonder what Woodard would have had to do to qualify as a "worst offender." Since he was convicted of second degree murder I surmise he would have had to commit first degree—premeditated—murder, though the line between the two is sometimes fuzzy.

I have often pondered what the outcome would have been had Woodard not miscalculated in his attempted robbery of Chilkoot Charlie's. What if the nexus of potential lethality had occurred there instead of a few blocks away?

When Ruben died, I did not want to be comforted by how he did not suffer greatly in the end or how lucky I had been to have such a steadfast, gifted friend as he. I know at times he simply tolerated me; I could be arrogant and bull-headed, but I have a good heart and I usually try to do the right thing. Ruben knew that. He stood by me during some difficult times, like when Chilkoot Charlie's was the focus of bad publicity. He never chastised me, criticized me, or questioned my integrity. And he didn't allow himself to be used by the press for that purpose, which they tried to do at least once that I know of.

So I know how Ruben felt when he penned the above lines in "Comfort." I wanted to wail out loud about the loss of my dearest friend, a mentor, a man who treated me like a son, whom I shall miss every day of the rest of my life.

I did not want to hear about what a long, productive life he had lived, and I spoke emotionally about it during his memorial at the Senior Center that Ruben referred to affectionately as "Gaffersville" on April 7, 1994.

After Ruben's son, Phil, announced that, "Alaska has lost Ruben Gaines," and given a proper panegyric, like an eldest son would do, the room was somber but emotionally under control. By the time I had finished talking next there wasn't a dry eye in the room.

I felt—and feel—unworthy and unequal to the task of remembering a man who stood head and shoulders above most of the men I have ever known. Ruben was pure of heart and soul. There was not an ounce of malice, greed, meanness or arrogance in him. He loved and respected all things. Politically, I would argue in vain about some position steadfastly presented by he, who cared only for the welfare of his fellow man. The devil with practicality. He would respond with, "That's just an excuse, man!"

Marathons

I have done some dumb things in my life—but I have also done some smart ones. The dumbest thing I ever did was start smoking. The smartest thing I ever did was quit. Of course I must have quit a thousand times over the fifteen years I smoked, only to find myself smoking the broken and twisted cigarettes I'd gently teased out of the crumpled pack I'd retrieved from the garbage can where I had tossed them just an hour before. Sometimes I would throw a pack out the window of my car and then stop at a store to buy more on my way home. But when I watched my dad die from esophageal cancer in 1977, something inside me changed. Dad never smoked cigarettes. He derisively called them "pimp sticks," but he smoked and chewed cigars.

It was a certainty that I was either going to quit smoking or die prematurely. I hated knowing that I was addicted, and I had begun to experience the effects upon my stamina while skiing. Reality really hit hard when I was scuba diving with a dive buddy—which I did a lot of during the seventies—and had to return to the surface sooner than my buddy was ready because I was nearly out of oxygen.

The time was right when I spotted a new product on the market that made a lot of sense to me. It was called "One Step at a Time" and it was manufactured by Waterpik. The product consisted of four filters; the first removed twenty-five percent of tar and nicotine from the cigarettes you smoked; the second removed fifty percent; the third removed seventy-five percent; and the last one removed ninety percent. The instructions were simple: smoke as much as you want, but do not smoke without using a filter. Use each filter for two weeks, and do not accelerate or decelerate the process. For the last two weeks you were getting only ten percent of the tar and nicotine into your system, so a person had to find it easier to put them down at that point. I thought to myself that if I couldn't quit with such a sensible program, I was surely doomed.

At the time, I was working the floor at Chilkoot Charlie's five nights a week with my security staff. The place was jammed with smokers and people razzed me about the "sissy" filters I was using. I learned early to have spare filter sets handy—one at home, one in the office, and one in the car because they were easily misplaced and, following the rules, if you did not have one you could not smoke. I was religiously faithful to the program and by God, it worked.

As fate would have it though, the very last night of the eighth week while working in the club I misplaced my filter halfway through the shift. I am not sure why, but I did not have a handy replacement, so in desperation I stuck a swizzle stick in my mouth and chewed on it. I made it through the night without a cigarette, and I have never smoked one since. I chewed swizzle sticks for weeks, but I was done with cigarettes. My bar manager had bet me that I couldn't quit, and I still have my winnings—a one hundred dollar bill—framed and hanging on my office wall. I will not try to mislead you, though. Quitting smoking was the hardest thing I ever did.

It wasn't until the last day of 1978 that I met Shelli. In 1977, I had a girlfriend in the aftermath of quitting smoking who liked to jog a bit and she convinced me to accompany her. Amazingly, I began to enjoy those outings. While smoking I couldn't have run around the block, but I found myself running farther and farther distances until one day I ran ten miles without stopping. I was elated.

During the '70s and '80s I spent a lot of time in Hawaii. At one time I had two condos there—one on the top floor of the Royal Kahana on Maui and one overlooking Waikiki Beach in the Ilikai Hotel in Honolulu. My favorite hangout in Honolulu was the Chart House restaurant and bar, right next to the Ilikai, overlooking the small boat harbor. I knew the whole crew there.

I was in Honolulu in December of 1979, soon after I had completed that first ten-mile run, and it happened to be a few days before the running of the Honolulu Marathon. I knew nothing about training for a marathon, much less signing up for one, but I found out where the headquarters was located and tried to enter. They laughed at me. It was too late.

That evening at the Chart House I mentioned the experience to my friends and, lo and behold, one of the bartenders—an Okinawan named Guy Maynard—had signed up to run the marathon, but had decided not to. Guy kindly offered me his race bib so I ran my first marathon under an assumed name. Race officials will ban you from the race for life for doing what I did, but I didn't care because I didn't know at the time that I was destined to run the race twice more.

You can imagine how well I did in that first race, so it's just as well I wasn't running as Mike Gordon. It took me four hours and fifty-seven minutes to complete the course. I did fine until I "hit the wall" at twenty miles; the next six-point-two miles were absolute misery in the heat and humidity, as the elderly and the obese whizzed past me in bright flashes of flopping flesh and cellulite. But I did finish and even mustered enough energy to look good for the photograph crossing the finish line. The best thing about a lousy time in your first marathon is that there is lots of room for improvement.

So began my years of marathoning. Shelli and I would plan our vacations around them. We even incorporated a marathon into our honeymoon. I sponsored—and joined—a small group of runners from the Anchorage Running Club to run the original marathon route from Marathon to Athens. All marathons since the original are in commemoration of that run by Athenian-born Pheidippides (530 BC- 490 BC), who ran 26.2 miles to inform the archons in Athens that the Athenians had defeated the Persians on the battlefield at Marathon.

Pheidippides had already run to Sparta the day before to ask for their assistance fighting the Persians—a request they declined—so he had run a total of one hundred fifty miles in two days. After delivering his message of the victory at Marathon to the people of Athens, he promptly fell over dead.

I always do better physically and emotionally when I have some sort of long-range goal out in front of me, and since training for a marathon takes at least six weeks on top of a pretty good running base, the whole program was a good fit for me. All told I ran fifteen marathons over a period of about fifteen years, the last few extending into my five-year attempt to climb the highest mountain on each of the seven continents. I ran the Honolulu Marathon three times, the Mayor's Midnight Sun Marathon in Anchorage three times, the Glacier Marathon (starting from the turnoff to the Alyeska Resort in Girdwood) twice, the Seattle Marathon twice, the Pittsburgh Marathon twice, the Long Beach Marathon, the New York City Marathon, and the Original Marathon.

When I started running, Bill Rogers was winning the Boston Marathon regularly. I was a big fan of Bill, and went to hear him speak in the old Central Junior High gymnasium when he visited Anchorage. My goal was to achieve a finish fast enough to qualify for the Boston Marathon, but I never succeeded. The race I chose twice as my qualifying race, the Glacier Marathon, turned out to be a mistake.

It was an out-and-back course that started from the turnoff to Alyeska Resort and proceeded south through Portage almost reaching the point where the highway starts to ascend into the mountains before you turned back toward the starting point. I'd chosen the course because it was absolutely flat—but there was also a crown in the roadbed. You would run out on the left hand side of the road and back on the left hand side as well—the angle of the pavement downward to the left the whole way.

On my first attempt I was well on my way to a Boston Marathon qualification, but by the time I reached Portage on the return I had developed a large blood blister on the ball of my left foot. I sat down on the side of the road and cried.

On my second attempt I developed an acute pain in my left hip, had to slow way down around the twenty-mile station, and ended up hobbling across the finish line. Even so, I turned in my best-ever time. Before the award ceremonies were over at the Indian House, an ambulance had to be called to take me back to Anchorage. The Seward Highway was under major construction and the temporary roadbed was the railroad tracks. You can imagine my discomfort as I bounced most of the way back to Anchorage with what turned out to be a stress-fracture in my left femur at the point where it bends to enter the hip socket.

The upside of these two painful experiences is that I learned from a "jock doctor" that my left leg was two-thirds of an inch shorter than my right leg, which had exaggerated the stress on that leg from running on the angled road surface. I had suffered regularly from various structural ailments once I started running long distances, but after my diagnosis I ran with a lift in my left heel and never had another problem. It is funny how you get so used to some things that you never even notice them. Once I knew my left leg was shorter than my right, I realized how I tended to pivot around the shorter leg while standing.

When our running club group of five showed up at the starting point of the Original Marathon, we discovered to our dismay that the local Marxist/Leninist Party, which had already desecrated practically every paintable surface in the country with their red hammer and sickle, had decided to pull an inconsiderate bone-headed publicity stunt. They scheduled their own marathon over the same course starting at the same time as the Original Marathon that had drawn thousands of people from all over the world. To avoid an international incident, the managers of the Original Marathon postponed the start of our race until the course was free again.

As with many difficult circumstances, there was a silver lining. During the hours-long wait we got to meet and have our photos taken with Grete Waitz (1953-2011), who was also running the race. Grete was the Norwegian schoolteacher who won nine New York City Marathons, more than anyone else. She set a world record for women in the 1978 New York City marathon, finishing in 2 hours, 32 minutes and 30 seconds, subsequently lowering it three more times. Waitz was the dominant female distance runner of her age.

While we waited, we hid from the blistering sun behind stone walls, drinking Heineken beers. We didn't get to start our race until midday. Though it was a much hotter race than I had anticipated because of the late start, I did well and once we neared Athens there were nice crowds along the route, waving olive branches to welcome us. The race ended dramatically with a lap around the inside of the Colosseum.

Running and training to run marathons produced many other interesting moments for me. The second time I ran the Pittsburgh Marathon, while crossing the finish line, the announcer said, "And here comes Mike Gordon from Anchorage, (long pause) Arkansas!"

I have a lot of relatives in Pennsylvania. Ancestors of both my father and mother immigrated through Baltimore and settled in Western Pennsylvania. People I met in Pennsylvania are some of the nicest but most parochial people in America. On this same trip, Shelli and I were having dinner with a group of my cousins and I mentioned we were going to New York City next.

One cousin, older than I, said, "I've never been there."

The look on my face must have effectively expressed my reaction.

He then said, "Why would I want to go there?"

New York City is less than a six-hour drive from Pittsburgh, or an hour-and-a-half flight. I had no response.

We have visited relatives in Pennsylvania twice, but there has never been a reciprocal visit. You might as well suggest they take a spaceship to Mars as suggest they visit Alaska.

Once I got into climbing I used to think about running a marathon after returning from a big mountain like Everest. I would go to Nepal weighing one hundred eighty-five pounds and return weighing one hundred and fifty pounds, looking more like Bill Rogers than Mike Gordon, and in incredible cardiovascular condition. It seemed to me I should have been able to run a record marathon by doing so, but the timing of the return, my work schedule, and an available race date just never conveniently lined up for me.

I have always been competitive but I am by no means a gifted athlete; consequently I have preferred competing against myself. Hockey is the only team sport, other than little league baseball, that I ever participated in enthusiastically because I was too small as a kid for basketball or football. I found my good skating skills to be a great leveler of the playing field. Mostly I have enjoyed individual sports such as skiing, scuba diving, mountain climbing and distance running. I was not particularly good at distance running but I am capable of long-range commitments, and I can take a lot of punishment.

At age fifty, after my third attempt on Mt. Everest in the spring of 1993, I started running again. It didn't go well. I experienced painful shin splints, and though I tried to run through them day after day as I had been able to do in the past, I simply could not overcome them. After a frustrating extended period of painful attempts, sometimes with long stretches of walk-and-run intervals, I simply gave up on it. My subconscious has never given up though, since I still have frequent dreams in which I run long distances. Sometimes my legs move and I wake up with cramps in my calves from the effort.

Maybe I should just acknowledge my subconscious, purchase a new pair of running shoes, and give it another try. Nah. With a rolling lawn that takes hours to mow and one hundred and five steps from the water to our home—after the ramp—I get plenty of cardiovascular exercise.

Mike Dunham wrote a wonderful article about Ruben, titled "Conversations Emeritus," which was published in the Lifestyles section of the February 27, 1994 *Anchorage Daily News*. The occasion was that Ruben had announced his intention to become a "snow goose."

"'A lot of recent stuff has come from staring out this window,' the 81-year-old broadcast legend said. But I think I'm through with winter up here. The protracted length of cold weather really gets to my emphysema and creaky joints.

His mobility severely limited by an old hip injury, his children and grandchildren ('They're all gifted') living out of state and imploring him to join them, it's easy to understand why Gaines might decide to spend winter in California and return to Alaska in the summer. 'I've known any number of gaffers who do it that way,' he said.

An accidental fall 10 days ago put urgency into his deliberations. He slipped, twisting his knee, and couldn't get up. He stayed on the floor for a day and a half before help arrived. From his hospital bed, sounding hoarse but alert, he said, 'I kept thinking about glasses of water.'"

Evil Presence

As mentioned, some of my running experiences were unpleasant. Some were downright scary.

On September 7, 1994 the *Anchorage Daily News* broke the story of the brutal murder of Alexi O. Kaptanian, a 22-year-old UAA student who had only arrived in the state the previous month. He was killed by a paroled ex-con named Ray E. Rice who had been recently released after serving seven years for stabbing a complete stranger. Kaptanian met Rice at the Java Joint, a popular coffee house in Spenard at the time. The student had left his mountain bike chained at the Crazy Horse, a strip club just below Fifteenth Avenue between Gambell and Ingra Streets, and as they left the coffeehouse Rice offered to show him a shortcut through the woods.

Anchorage Police Sergeant Mike Grimes said the two men walked into the woods just west of where Gambell Street crosses Chester Creek when the ex-con attacked the student "to get his cash and an expensive leather jacket he was wearing." Rice stabbed Kaptanian in the eye with a Leatherman, robbed him, and rolled him into the creek where he then stood on the young man until he was sure he was dead. The subsequent autopsy verified that Kaptanian had, in fact, died from drowning.

Rice made an extensive admission of the crime saying that he had "an irresistible impulse" to kill. Police reported Rice was a follower of the occult and was wearing a T-shirt that had *End of God,* the title of an album by the satanic metal band, Decide, emblazoned on it.

Kaptanian's father, Pierre, of Aurora, Colorado, was naturally aggrieved over his youngest son's death. He was reported as saying that Alexi had come to Alaska because he liked the outdoors and because his older brother lived in Alaska, although in Petersburg, an island community in Southeast Alaska. Except for attending a small college only a few hundred miles from their residence, Alexi had never been away from home before. He was shy, trusting, and withdrawn—conditions resulting from a rare malady that had left him bald at the age of five.

For over twenty years I had resided in Woodside East, a high-end planned unit development about a mile west of where Kaptanian was murdered. I lived there for roughly another ten years after the incident. My home overlooked and had easy access to the Chester Creek bike trail, and when I started running marathons in 1979 I spent many a joyful and/or toilsome hour running long distances—up to twenty miles—both east and west of my location. If I ran east I was only a short distance from the Lake Otis Drive underpass and the Goose Lake overpass, and if I ran west I was less than a mile from the Seward Highway underpass.

Over my more than fifteen years of running in various states, numerous countries, and on different routes in Anchorage, Girdwood, and Homer I have absolutely no recollection of any seriously frightening or disturbing incidents except those I encountered on the Chester Creek bike trail between the Goose Lake overpass and the C Street underpass, but of them there were plenty.

One sunny afternoon I was running west toward the Seward Highway underpass alongside the softball park and could not help but notice two young boys and a girl playing very near the entrance to the underpass as I approached. The kids were pre-teen and would not normally have presented a threat, but there was something unusual and disturbing about their behavior and the furtive way they looked at me.

I had to run between them to get to the underpass, and as I drew closer I heard one of the boys say to the others, "Let's beat him up and take his stuff." I seriously doubt that those three kids could have made good on their threat, but the threat was real nonetheless, and as I whisked past them I simply stated, "I don't have any stuff."

When I came back through the underpass from the other direction on my way home the kids were gone. As the elderly (to them) object of such cruel contemplation expressed out loud by three feral pre-teen children—one a girl, I couldn't help but wonder what the world was coming to.

During an early evening run in the fall one year, I was returning from a long run on the Tony Knowles Trail. Immediately after crossing the bridge over Chester Creek I passed two teenage boys and a teenage girl who appeared to be heading to a concert at the Sullivan Arena just to the north of our location. They were milling around suspiciously. After passing the teens I could hear unmistakable footfalls behind me.

Not wanting to be attacked from behind I stopped abruptly and spun around, fists out, ready for a fight. Looking the teen who had been stalking me right in the eye I asked, "What the fuck do you want?"

He stopped, shrugged his shoulders and turned back to his two friends who had been watching. I continued on my way home. Had I not turned around and faced him, would he have pushed me or hit me in the back of the head? I believe it is highly likely he would have.

Another evening I was again returning from the Tony Knowles Trail, had crossed under the Seward Highway and was just entering the woods at the east end of the softball field on the south side of Chester Creek. Two pre-teen girls were walking westward on the trail toward me, one of them swinging a four-foot alder bough. Again there was something disquieting about the scene and when I got just in front of the girls, about to pass them on the right, the girl with the bough swung it very hard, right at my head. I was ready for it. I caught the bough in my left hand, yanking it out of hers, and chased her to the ground on the other side of the trail.

Both girls were screaming as I stood menacingly over the one who had attacked me, holding the weapon high as if to strike. I would never have hit her, but she didn't know that. I growled at her, "I should whip the daylights out of you. If you ever do such a thing again I really hope it happens to you." I tossed the branch into the woods and continued on my way home, dumbstruck and furious.

The next incident is quite different, but lends further credence to my assertion of an evil presence in the area.

I have been in Alaska for nearly seventy years and have been attacked by a moose only once. It happened at the Seward Highway Chester Creek underpass along the Chester Creek trail. Once again, I was returning from a long run on the Tony Knowles Trail, only this time it was in February during the festive carnival of Fur Rendezvous. It was dark but the overhead trail lights were on, casting weird shadows on the snow.

There had been a lot of recent snowfall and though the trails had been groomed, there was deep snow just off the trail. There was also a four-foot high temporary wood-and-wire picket fence rolled out on either side of the trail meant to act as a funnel into the culvert for the dog teams that used that part of the trail for the Fur Rendezvous dog team races.

I crested the hill and was fifteen or twenty feet into the chute created by that picket fencing when I fortunately happened to look up and into the dimly-lit underpass I was approaching. There, right in the middle of the underpass, was a bull moose with a small velvet rack. We spotted each other at the same time and I could see his head lower as his hair stood up along his neck.

I did not actually see his charge because I was already moving as fast as my legs and hands could carry me back up the slope, around the outside edge of the fencing chute, and out into the deep snow on all fours—but I know there was a charge.

When I recovered my composure and realized I wasn't going to be trampled and gored to death, I looked around and saw the moose standing in the middle of the trail. It was about twenty-five yards away, at the top of the small rise over which I had just recently passed on my way to the underpass. He had not covered that distance that quickly in a casual saunter and he was then just looking around while I sat there in the deep snow, waiting for him to wander off across the creek and up the other side. There was absolutely no question about whose trail it was.

More recently, on March 29, 2015, just past noon, a woman was knocked unconscious and stabbed on the same trail near Goose Lake. Having just crossed the pedestrian bridge over Northern Lights Boulevard, she was walking and texting on her phone when she was attacked from behind and knocked unconscious. Regaining consciousness, she realized she had been stabbed in the lower back and that someone was rifling her pocket. According to *Alaska Dispatch News*, police said her attacker then fled on foot, taking nothing.

Even more recently, one morning in May 2015, a 43-year-old cyclist had just crossed the Goose Lake overpass on his way to work when he was attacked by one of three teenagers loitering by the trail. The teen had a five-foot long two-inch-diameter branch he was using as a walking stick. As the cyclist passed the teenager swung the stick, hitting his victim square in the face. The hapless cyclist suffered a broken nose, fractured right orbital bone and a fractured skull. He was lucky to have survived the assault.

The *Alaska Dispatch News* identified the cyclist as Tim Kirk. Julie Saddoris, Kirk's girlfriend, said that the teenagers had not appeared menacing to Kirk, and that he had not anticipated any trouble:

"'…it happened all of a sudden, just kind of random,' Saddoris said.

Kirk continued to ride away, then eventually lost control and went into a ditch, Saddoris said, where he got out his phone and called 911.

Passersby stopped to help him, and Kirk was then picked up by an ambulance, Saddoris said."

Kirk received twenty-three stitches just to the bridge of his nose and more under his injured eye. He said the teenagers walked off toward East High School, but Kirk was able to provide descriptions to the police.

Fortunately, as with the attack by Ray Rice upon Alexi Kaptanian, the ogre was identified and arrested. According to the *Alaska Dispatch News*, Anita Shell, a spokesperson for APD, said the police coordinated investigative efforts with East High School resource officers, found video footage of the teens skipping school that day, matched their clothing and descriptions, and noted their inconsistent stories. The fifteen-year-old assailant was lodged in McLaughlin Youth Center.

Surely, I cannot be the only one who thinks it is more than coincidental that all these incidents occurred in a single stretch of trail not much more than a mile long. I do not believe I have overstated my case. There is the nearby Sullivan Arena that attracts large crowds—some on foot. There are a couple of housing developments nearby too, and East High School a short distance to the east of the area that might be considered a source of trouble. But there are also nice subdivisions in the vicinity, ball parks, and a portion of the wooded area of the University of Alaska Anchorage campus, as well as Goose Lake.

I am absolutely convinced there is some sort of evil presence in the area. Whether you agree with me or not, be vigilant if you ever find yourself alone on that stretch of trail. Better yet, take my advice and just avoid it altogether.

Of course these incidents beg the questions, "What is going on in our community?"

"What is it that would cause preteen children to wantonly, physically attack strangers, so avidly?"

One sunny summer day a few years ago I left my home in Spenard and as I crossed the street to the parking lot where I park my truck, a pint-sized thug no more than four feet tall or ten years old walked up to me and said, "Go home old man."

"Mrs. Maloney and the Diptera"

This story begins...say it detonates, rather...

When Mrs. Maloney, awash in a lather

From reading exciting reports of the north,

Packed shotglass, chemise and spittoon and set forth

To distant Alaska. The articles stated:

For him who took off at a pace double-gaited,

Gold nuggets the size of a railway caboose

Abounded, plus farmland the color of snoose.

The Kenai Peninsula...that's where she squatted...

Is lovely in May. One can even get potted

Inhaling the air, which is flavored like brandy.

Mrs. M. set to work feeling perfectly dandy,

Though fierce are the hazards of homesteading there;

There isn't much future inside of a bear,

Of which in the Kenai are several brands,

Majority standing some thirty-odd hands.

But her? When a bruin approached through the hops

Anticipatorily licking his chops

She grabbed him barehanded and fetched him a clout

And while he was stunned, turned the beast inside out.

Horticulturally, Mrs. M. was proceeding

To raise enough produce to handle the feeding

Of all of Alaska, and even to sate

The hunger of most of the South 48.

But not being made of philanthropist stuff,

She ate what she raised; it was barely enough.

She hoed with one hand, and the other probed soil

In various spots with a ramrod, for oil.

Betimes in bare feet she was scratching the ground

To see if perchance there were nuggets around.

The noises and earthquakes and winds, as she dug,

Dispossessed all the animals but one small bug;

This insect belongs to the *Diptera* group,

According to science. An ignorant stoop,

However, will know that it flies by magneto

And carries a spear and its name is mosquito.

The first one of summer, aware of its mission,

Zoomed in. Mrs. M., in bent-over position

And blissfully ignorant, hacked at a weed.

The visitor hovered, and then took a bead.

The beasts lifted ears to such sounds as, bedad,

Meant only one thing: Mrs. M had been had.

The insect, they all realized with a grin,

Would soon be inviting its relatives in.

Awaiting a sight that was sure to transpire,

They didn't wait long; like a wheatfield on fire,

Mrs. M. thundered past, being busily skewered

By every mosquito from Portage to Seward.

Perhaps she is still being chased, but who cares?

The thing that annoys both the people and bears

Is the fact that when Mrs. M. left on the run

She took along every mosquito but one,

And that's all it takes to repropagate same!

They're as thick once again as they were when she came.

Collected Ruben Gaines ©1987 Ruben Gaines

Glory Days

Construction and planning of the Alyeska Pipeline took place from 1969 to 1977 and employed roughly 70,000 people. The actual pipeline construction started on March 27, 1975 and was completed on May 31, 1977. The first oil flowed down the pipe on June 20, 1977, traversing 800 miles from Prudhoe Bay on the north coast of Alaska to the port town of Valdez on the southern coast. And on the evening of August 1, 1977, the SS *Arco Juneau* sailed for the Atlantic Richfield refinery in Cherry Point, Washington with the first tanker full of black gold.

Once pipeline construction was complete, most of the workers from that boom time returned to the Lower 48, and it took a while for Alaska's economy to recover. But in the early '80s the state entered the period I refer to as the Glory Days

The pipeline craziness was over and the speculative craziness ramped up. Alaska was on a roll. Anything was possible and money was no object. Banks were lending money by the truckload and real estate developers with limitless credit were building shaky empires on Anchorage's unstable, earthquake-prone soil. There was only so much property to be had in the Anchorage bowl, and conventional wisdom held it would never be worth less. No one had ever lost money investing in Anchorage real estate—and never would.

Awash in petro-dollars, the State of Alaska eliminated the personal income tax and instituted the Permanent Fund Dividend. Legislators representing localities far and wide carved out big bucks from the state budget for an array of capital projects. Anchorage's Project '80s massively increased the city's infrastructure and quality of life by funding the expanding Coastal Trail, the Alaska Center for the Performing Arts, the Sullivan Arena, the Egan Convention Center, the Loussac Library, and more.

There was a cheering squad for any big project, no matter how grandiose—like moving the capital to Willow, building a domed city in Denali Park, and turning the 874-foot-high Bodenburg Butte into an international destination with a tram hauling tourists to a fancy restaurant on the summit.

One real estate speculator, Pete Zamarello, told me (in such a way that I felt he was talking about me personally) that because of increasing property taxes, the average Anchorage business person soon would no longer be able to afford to own the property upon which his or her business was located. About that time his ubiquitous, unimaginative strip malls sprang up like invasive weeds. They did not sport Pete's name on them, but everyone knew who was building them. They were—and still are—an eye-sore and blight on the community, though admittedly housing some fine local small business operations.

Pete lived in a purple-colored mansion out near Turnagain-by-the-Sea subdivision. Like Pete, the house was loud, garish and didn't fit comfortably into its surroundings. Pete hated bankers. He bought a block-size tract of land across the street from National Bank of Alaska to the south—where GCI, Arby's, and the Matanuska Brewing Company are now—and bragged to me that he was going to erect a building higher than National Bank of Alaska so he could "piss down on Elmer." Elmer Rasmuson, (1909-2000), the president and chairman of that bank, was a former mayor of Anchorage and an unparalleled Alaskan philanthropist.

My nightclub, Chilkoot Charlie's, was booming. I was building a big new condo in Woodside East overlooking the greenbelt, and I was adding property and seating capacity to the club operation. I owned and stayed frequently in my two condos in Hawaii. Western Airlines had hooked a whole bunch of us Alaskans on Hawaii with their "triangle fare." If you were flying to Los Angeles you could stop over in Hawaii for nothing. Zero. Nada. I used to visit the islands whenever my tan would start to fade, for which I now pay the price of regular visits to my dermatologist.

I became close friends with a musical duo named Cecilio and Kapono, popularly known as C & K, who were all the rage in Hawaii during the '70s and '80s. They both looked Hawaiian, though Cecilio was Mexican as his name suggests. Henry Kapono is the only one-hundred-percent Hawaiian I ever met. He is also a world-class musician. The gods must have introduced C and K. I always compared their style of music to Seals and Croft. How they could harmonize! They successfully brought traditional Hawaiian music into the world of pop music but sadly were never able to make the leap to the mainland and national recognition.

One day out of the blue I received a phone call from Henry Kreutz, C & K's manager, asking if they might play a gig at Chilkoot Charlie's. I didn't have a suitable stage at the time. I hadn't yet added the Spenard Bingo Hall to the north, nor had I incorporated what used to be a fenced-in yard at the far southwest corner of the building, which is now the area occupied by the Ice Bar on the ground floor and the Russian Room upstairs.

I told Henry if he came to Anchorage he could stay at my home, and I'd see if I could get the boys a gig at Alyeska Resort in Girdwood. He and a friend named Mel Mossman did come to Anchorage, stayed with me, and I managed to get the duo a gig at the ski resort. Years later C & K played Koot's on several occasions. My niece, Teri, was fortunate enough to have the boys sing at her wedding reception at my Woodside East townhouse.

They once visited our little cabin in the woods on a wild adventure to Halibut Cove and many years later, in the role of "Pastor Mike," I performed the wedding ceremony for Henry Kreutz and his bride, Nalani, at our present home in the Cove. More recently, Henry's son Olin became a celebrity in Hawaii by playing center for the Chicago Bears. Henry went from being famous in his own right to being referred to as Olin's father. And proud father he was.

A lot of my friends were in the real estate business—several at Jack White Company—the top real estate brokerage firm in town and were amassing multi-million dollar portfolios. My wife, Shelli, and I earned real estate licenses ourselves. I hung my license at Jack White Company—an attempt at business diversification and to distance myself from the liquor industry. I naively thought I could hand off the operation of my nightclub to my management but I found that, as the saying goes, "When the cat's away the mice will play."

Around this time, but when I no longer had my license hanging on their wall, I was invited to an afternoon holiday party at Jack White Company along with a lot of other investors, contractors, bankers, brokers, and the like. It was a nice affair with no shortage of beer and wine, so by the time I and a handful of my friends departed for the Chef's Inn we were pretty lit up.

The Chef's Inn, owned by Dale Mormon, was a hot spot at the northwest corner of Arctic Boulevard and Northern Lights Boulevard. It later became Blues Central and is now the Anchorage Billiard Palace, owned by my Irish whiskey drinking pal, Paul Schuldt. Dale always had amazingly good bartenders, any one of whom could individually serve the entire club when it was packed with people drinking heavily. The house specialty was roast beef French dip sandwiches that you prepared yourself. Another draw was the elevated dance floor. During the day patrons sat around it to eat lunch and dinner, and after dinner it was great fun for those who wanted to kick up their heels—that is until Dale's insurance company put the kibosh on it.

Ever notice that insurance companies are no fun? They also put the kibosh on the once-flourishing hot-air balloon industry that festooned the sky above Anchorage with colorfully decorated orbs, the magnificent Chugach Range framing the background. As far as I know there had not been a single covered loss. Maybe I am delusional, but doesn't that look like a business opportunity for insurance companies? Anyway, balloonists couldn't afford the premiums, which let the air out of the fledgling industry.

Dale was an excellent bar operator and was married to a beautiful woman, but he had a monumental drinking problem, like a lot of operators of the era. He would regularly go to sleep with his head on the bar during business hours and had the uncanny ability to somehow or other remain aware of what was going on around him, lifting his head to rejoin a conversation or to give an order to an employee out of the middle of what appeared to be a coma. One afternoon a woman, upset about something or other, stepped over Dale—who was sprawled out on the floor in the middle of the aisle in front of the bar—and demanded to talk to the owner. The bartender said, "You just stepped over him, lady."

Our group that afternoon at the Chef's Inn was Terry Pfleiger (1943-2016), an agent at Jack White Company; Kris Gratrix (ca. 1945-2012), a commercial building contractor; Norman Rokeberg, then a leasing agent at Jack White Company; probably Buster Newton, a real estate developer; and yours truly. There might have been one or two others I can't remember. I've already admitted we'd been drinking.

Kris Gratrix was a successful contractor, and beneath his gruff exterior pumped a kindly heart. But in junior high and high school he had been what might be called a "problem child." My dad grew up on the rough streets of Pittsburgh, and as a coach at Central Junior High always gravitated toward kids like Kris, and they toward him. Kris remained friends with my dad until my dad's death and would visit us every so often to pay his respects.

Kris was boisterous and tended to brag about his accomplishments. He had been gasconading for a good while at the Chef's Inn that day and receiving a fair amount of ridicule because of it when Terry Pfleiger finally said, "Kris, I've figured out how to make a fortune." Kris, in his cups and unsuspecting, took the bait.

"Yeah? How's that?"

"I'm going to buy you for what you're worth and sell you for what you think you're worth."

Well, that brought a lot of laughs from people around the table, but Kris was not one of the sources of laughter. He was a big, tough guy. And he was very pissed off. He stood up, grabbed the table around which we all sat and dumped it on end—all our drinks and glasses crashed to the floor. Then he headed straight for Terry, chairs and stools flying in every direction.

I leapt to my feet, getting myself between the David-and-Goliath mismatch that would have occurred if Kris made it to Terry. Kris was coming on like a bull with a full head of steam when we collided and both lost our balance, falling into the wall with the full impact of both of us on my right shoulder. That incident was roughly forty years ago and I still can rarely go to sleep on my right side. I also suffer from restricted movement, chronic pain, and visible atrophy. As with the Charleston Express incident: no good deed goes unpunished, right?

Kris departed the havoc he'd created spewing a stream of curses and threats and piled into his brand new orange Corvette. We all watched as he threw it into reverse, stomped on the gas pedal, and roared backward smacking into a big unforgiving metal light pole in the club's front parking lot. Then he swung the mangled car around and roared off down Northern Lights Boulevard, leaving steaming black tire marks and thick smoke in his wake.

The drinking probably resumed once the mess had been cleaned up, as did the rampant real estate speculation—until the mid-1980s oil glut and subsequent economic crash.

In an effort to chasten wayward members of the OPEC cartel, or as some might assert, to crater the Soviet economy, Saudi Arabia's oil minister opened the spigots in the desert kingdom and flooded the world market with black goo. Few were left standing in the aftermath of the financial tsunami that hit oil patches everywhere, including Alaska with it's almost totally oil-dependent economy.

Alaskans in search of work began leaving the state in droves. They'd just drop their house keys off at Alaska Housing Finance Corporation on their way south and haul what, after a garage sale, remained of their personal belongings down the Alcan Highway.

People have said to me, "Well, people still drink. It mustn't have been a problem for Chilkoot Charlie's."

Wrong. Just for the record, the bar business depends on expendable income. People still drink when the economy sours, but they find less expensive ways to do it—like going out once a week instead of two or three times, drinking a six-pack in their car in the parking lot before entering the bar, hiding a pint bottle in their coat, or going to a house party instead.

From Yamani's figurative opening of the Saudi oil spigot in the fall of 1985 to Joseph Hazelwood's literal ramming of the *Exxon Valdez* into Bligh Reef in March 1989, I suspect one of the only people turning a profit in Alaska was the one who owned the U-Haul franchise. Ironically, Hazelwood's colossal ineptitude created such a mess that Exxon's efforts to clean it up rejuvenated the Alaskan economy.

By the time the economy did come around again, I was on my third banker. I had done a work-out with the Small Business Administration and Alaska USA Federal Credit Union, I had borrowed all my life insurance cash values, emptied my IRA account, taken a second mortgage on my home, and sold those two lovely condos in Hawaii. I sold one to a Japanese buyer for cash, deposited the money in my business checking account, and watched it disappear like a diamond ring down the bathroom sink.

As Cecilio might have said in his native tongue, "Adios."

"Chilkoot Charlie and the Bear"

This tale is roughly titled, "Chilkoot Charlie and the Bear."

How innocent that title sounds, while sitting smugly there.

Before we're half way finished with our hero and his battles

We'll wail in anguish, one and all, like brats who've lost their rattles.

The thing commences in a most deceptive gentle vein:

Old Chilkoot found a grizzly cub who shivered in the rain,

And took him to the cabin, where he fed him muskeg soup

And bundled him in blankets, so he wouldn't catch the croup.

He fixed a bed of sacks and ancient curtains made of chintz;

He dealt with him as kind as Doctor Dafoe with the Quintz.

The mother bear had doubtless passed away among the sticks,

Assisted by some lout who shot a thirty-point-ought-six.

So Chilkoot nursed the waif with all the means he had at hand;

There never was a more repulsive mother in the land.

The spring and summer passed away, and autumn came in focus.

The cub had grown to urchin size, and certain hocus pocus

Would greet old Chilkoot when he ambled in from all the traps:

At times he thought he'd like to make a pair of grizzly chaps.

The waif would knock the cans from all the cupboards, and cavort

In other ways of mischief, doing things he hadn't ort.

But urchins will be cubs, and Chilkoot Charlie didn't moan

As long as grizzly junior left his liquor stock alone.

If Junior had as much as pulled a cork from off a jug

Old Chilkoot would have had, that very day, a brand new rug.

One day our hero went abroad to gaze upon his traps

And gather in the mink which make them thousand dollar wraps.

Before he left, he'd fixed a bed for Junior in the kitchen;

He'd looked a little beat; for hibernation he was itchin'.

So then, when Chilkoot snowshoed back, a week from when he'd started,

And looked inside, there came a roar from where his beard was parted.

Young Junior's place beside the kitchen stove was bare. Instead,

He hibernated happily in Chilkoot Charlie's bed!

That there was quite enough. Old Chilkoot kicked him in the nether

But Junior didn't move. He only snored hell bent for leather.

By now his grizzly pal weighed, oh, nine hundred pounds, I'd wager,

And lay there smugly like a colonel. Well, at least a major.

To say that Chilkoot's rage was great would only be a trifle;

He cussed a mighty oath, and then he lifted up his rifle.

Then Junior opened up one eye, and calmly as you'd cough

Reached out and grabbed old Charlie's gun, and broke the barrel off.

While Chilkoot looked in horror at the stock within his hand,

Young Junior, with a grizzly smile, returned to slumberland.

What Chilkoot must have thought while stewing in his rocking chair

And gazing at the bed, which now contained that thieving bear,

Had better not be stated unabridged, I rather think.

The censor folks would pull the plug and send us down the drink.

There's one thing for sure—while Junior slept and Charlie meditated,

The air around him grew so thick it felt like marinated.

At last old Chilkoot's hand stole out and grabbed a two-blade axe.

He rose and slithered like a snake across the floorboard cracks,

But when he raised the axe to start the stroke that meant the end,

Young Junior opened up an eye, which plainly said, 'Why, Friend!'

And that's the way it went, so help me, right on through the season,

Till Chilkoot lost the bolts that held the hinges of his reason.

Each solitary time that Chilkoot had 'er figgered out

The bear would open up that eye, and put the plan to rout.

So Chilkoot Charlie gave it up; he settled in his chair

And drank a jug of booze a day, and gazed at that there bear.

The Spring rolled 'round. One day our hero wakened from a doze,

And looking at the bed, he saw that Junior had arose.

He had shambled to the kitchen, and was busy at the moment

Fomenting all the trouble it was possible to foment.

Not only had he ate the grub while Chilkoot was in snooze;

He'd pulled a couple corks, and sat there soused on Chilkoot's booze!

The pain of that discovery unmanned our ancient buddy;

Had Chilkoot weaker been, he would have wept the Chugach muddy.

He only sighed a gutsy sigh, whose tone was resignation,

And then he mixed some hotcakes, to forget the situation.

No sooner was he seated at the steaming hotcake stack

When Chilkoot felt a nudging in the lumbar of his back.

And there stood Junior, frowning. His expression said, 'Say, Rover,

You got no decent sense of hospitality? Move over!'

He guzzled Chilkoot's hotcakes, while his host sat there bereft.

From hence, this happened every meal. He ate what Junior left.

Old Chilkoot suffered through the spring, attending on young Junior,

The situation grimly growing loonier and loonier:

Although it's not a common trait for normal grizzly bars,

This guest grew fond of Chilkoot's hoarded stock of fine cigars.

When Charlie finished feeding him, young Junior settled back

And gestured with his paw, and took his snort of White and Black,

And then his host produced a light. This smug and shaggy Jonah

Would arrogantly fill the air with buck-apiece Corona!

This problem was a sticker, any imbecile would own:

Old Charlie had no weapon, and that Junior was full grown.

He never let the trapper get beyond suspicious sight;

He followed on the trapline, and he watched him through the night.

Young Junior knew a good thing when he saw it, that's fer shore;

No other bear had ever had it quite so good before.

He grew quite independent, too. This mattress-haired buffoon

Had learned to light his own cigars, just like a fat tycoon.

So now we have made contact with the climax of the play:

We lift the loving curtain on a certain night in May.

The customary scene prevailed, with Junior fatly lounging,

And poor bedraggled Chilkoot in the kitchen, sadly scrounging

Among the pots and pans, and getting noticeably thinner

While cooking like a slave to get this lazy slug his dinner.

He fried the customary sourdough hotcakes on the griddle,

While Junior drooled and rubbed his big fat paws upon his middle.

Without a decent grunt of thanks, when Chilkoot set the table,

He licked the platter cleaner than a Derby Winner's stable.

While Chilkoot served him faithfully, the way the poet says,

Young Junior should have heard the click of empty cartridges.

They clanked in Chilkoot's pocket, as he shambled through the room,

And played a rattling prelude to the grizzly villain's doom.

When Junior wrecked the rifle, he should never have forgot

The bullets still were...hold it; we'll decapitate the plot.

The meal was done. The bear was full of hotcakes, had his booze,

And now the fat cigar, before his nightly one-eyed snooze.

The bear bethought it strange; when Chilkoot offered him the stogie

He quickly turned and ran, just like a shark pursues a pogie.

He scuttled through the door and barely paused to lift the latch.

Young Junior shrugged in wonder, then he reached to get a match.

When Chilkoot got say thirty yards beyond the cabin's rear

There came a great explosion, and it knocked him on his ear.

He looked to see the joint go up in shambles through the air,

Then down again with nothing left but sundry bits of bear.

Then Chilkoot started in to laugh; he chortled and he cackled;

He giggled and he chuckled as the ruins burned and crackled.

And though the rain began to fall, and things were rather drizzly,

He made a fricasee, right there, of late, exploded grizzly.

He wiped his chin, then took those empty bullets from his pocket

And kissed each one. It looked as though his mind had sprung its sprocket.

Without the powder in it, what's the value of a cartridge?

It wouldn't shoot the feathers off a wooden-legged partridge.

The powder's work was done. Old Chilkoot's laugh resounded far.

Young Junior never should have lit that buck-apiece cigar.

Chilkoot Charlie ©1951 Ruben Gaines

The Class Ring

In the fall of 2010, I returned to the University of San Francisco to finish off the seventeen credits I needed to complete a bachelor of arts in political science with a minor in philosophy. After five jobs, eight businesses, three marriages, two children, seven grandchildren, three dogs and four cats, I found myself back in college, graduating in the spring of 2011—48 years late. The first-ever directed studies graduate from USF, I walked at the head of the class, followed by a roomful of young adults, as we crossed the stage of the magnificent St. Ignatius Church on the USF campus. Watching from the crowd were my wife, Shelli; my daughter, Michele; my son-in-law, Jerry; two of my college roommates, Jim McCartin and Rick Fischer; and Rosie, the widow of the third roommate, Gerry Lombardi (1942 - 2005).

To say that I was proud would be the understatement of my entire life so, of course, I had to have a class ring. On the ring I had imprinted political science on one side and philosophy on the other, with a chunk of topaz, my birthstone, set in the middle. For the year of graduation I had 2011 stamped on one side instead of the year I should have graduated—1964. It was a beautiful ring and I wore it all the time in place of the Chilkoot Charlie's gold nugget ring I had been accustomed to wearing for many years.

Near the end of September, 2015, I was wearing that class ring on my right ring finger and my wedding ring on my left ring finger as I pulled my 25-foot Bayweld, the *Ruth Isabel*, up to our floating dock in Halibut Cove—something I've done by myself too many times to count. It was near the end of the season. I was thinking about all the procedures that went into closing down for the winter, like shrinking the perimeter of our compound and draining water systems. It was a nice afternoon. There was no weather with which to contend. The tide wasn't roaring in or out. I wasn't in a hurry, and I was as sober as a judge.

As usual, I approached the floating dock at an angle with the port side of the boat's bow, turning the steering wheel sharply to the left, then reversing and goosing the engines to swing the stern in and align the boat with the dock. I put the engines in neutral, rushed to the stern and grabbed the port stern line with my left hand while with my right I grabbed the waist-high railing on the port side of the cabin to steady myself. Then I stood up on the port gunnel as the boat eased slowly sideways, awaiting the right moment to leap over about a foot and a half of water onto the floating dock.

There was a 4' by 8' piece of 1/2" treated plywood on the boat, leaning upright on its long side between the port transom railing and the cabin. I was bringing it over to replace one of two pieces of plywood that covered our hot tub in winter because it had been used as building material. But the presence of that sheet of plywood meant I had to reach around and behind it to grab the railing. That slightly awkward circumstance manifested profound and immediate consequences.

The Tonight Show host and comedian, Jimmy Fallon, was forced to cancel his June 26, 2015 program taping because of a ring avulsion injury. He tripped over a braided rug that he said, "my wife loves and I can't wait to burn." After catching his wedding ring on a counter as he tried to stop his fall, the late-night host wound up in New York's Bellevue Hospital, where he underwent six hours of surgery and ten days in the ICU. He was able to regain feeling and movement in his finger only because a micro-surgeon implanted a vein from his foot into his hand. Fallon warned his television audience *not* to Google "ring avulsion" and I can attest to the wisdom of that advice. They are not pretty pictures. The less precise, but more descriptive, name of the injury is degloving.

Back in Halibut Cove, I leaped from the gunnel to the floating dock with first my left foot, followed immediately by my right. That's when I discovered my school ring had become stuck to the inside of the waist-high railing. I was jerked back forcefully onto the port gunnel, breaking ribs eight, nine and ten. My right leg was now dangling in the ice-cold water of Kachemak Bay, the *Ruth Isabel* slowly drifting seaward as I writhed on the gunnel, reaching out frantically with my left foot to hook the tie-off railing that ran along the edge of the floating dock. I'd prefer not to consider the consequences had I not been able to do so. It was my first lucky break of the day.

Having pulled myself and the *Ruth Isabel* back to the dock with my left foot, I extracted my hand from the cabin railing and got off the boat, suddenly realizing the extent of my finger injury. I had what can best be described as a "Terminator finger." All of the skin had been peeled off to the tip of the finger and I could clearly see the inner workings.

But unlike Terminators, which have no feelings or emotions, I went immediately into shock. Though I was reeling and staggering, holding onto my injured hand and unable to fasten the boat to the dock, I did have the amazing wherewithal to slip the ring from the degloved portion of my ring finger back over what little flesh remained at its base. I really don't know why I did it, other than the ring looked unseemly rolling around the bare bone and sinew—but that action probably prevented more bleeding, which was minimal.

There was no one around, so I looked up toward our home, a hundred-and-five steps above the boathouse. I was still weaving about, moaning audibly, holding both the stern line and my right hand to my chest. In my second lucky break of the day, Shelli, who was in her night robe on her way to the shower, heard my moaning and appeared above, looking down on me from the porch.

I said quietly, "Honey, I'm really hurt." Since it was calm and I was on the water, she heard me plainly and hollered for me to sit down because the way I was weaving around she was afraid I was going to fall. I felt better standing up, which I was still doing when she got to the dock with towels and two bags of frozen corn to put on the wound. I'm not sure what I'd have done had she already gotten in the shower and not heard me.

Shelli immediately tied the bow of the boat to the floating dock. But after seeing my injury she went into shock herself and couldn't manage tying off the stern line, so the *Ruth Isabel* now drifted toward a perpendicular angle to the dock. She could barely punch in the numbers on her iPhone to call our neighbors, the Thurstons, who lived only minutes away with a large, fast catamaran named *The Far Side* tied to their dock. Jim and their son JT were over in nothing flat. They secured our boat, hustled me into their boat, had me lie down—which I was able to do only briefly because of the pain of the three broken ribs—and, abandoning the "No Wake" rules inside the Halibut Cove Narrows, roared out of the channel heading for Homer.

No sooner had we left the Narrows when I had to call a halt. The waves in the bay weren't very large, but at high speed *The Far Side* was banging jarringly hard upon them and the pain in my right side was excruciating. Slowing down would have taken us too long to cross, so we turned around and headed for the isthmus of Ismailof Island, tethered the boat and walked up onto the gravel. Shelli got another Halibut Cove neighbor, Dr. Martha Cotten at South Peninsula Hospital in Homer, on her mobile phone while JT managed to get a helicopter on its way from Homer. Jim's wife Jan sped over in her skiff to learn why we had returned. She then decided to accompany us to the hospital to support Shelli while Shelli supported me.

Meanwhile I was being driven insane by no-see-ums crawling all over my face and around the brim of my baseball cap, about which I could do nothing—one hand injured and the other holding a bag of frozen corn. That summer was, incidentally, the worst season for bugs that I can recall in Halibut Cove, having been preceded by a very mild winter. In desperation, I finally sprinted for the cover of the boat to wait for the helicopter.

The pilot landed Shelli, Jan, and me in the painted white circle on the roof of the hospital. We exited the helicopter and rushed down to the emergency room, where there must have been a total of eight physicians and assistants waiting for me. Dr. Cotten had called in an orthopedic surgeon and had a ring saw on site.

It seemed to take forever, and in fact did take perhaps half an hour for them to remove my class ring. One doctor sawed through the bottom of the ring with my palm up, bone and sinew clearly visible, then Dr. Cotten stuffed a length of dental floss through one side as Dr. Brent Adcox, the orthopedic surgeon, stuffed another length through the other side. Then they began pulling in opposite directions.

It was a big, tough ring, and it did not cooperate readily, but after a number of tries they finally managed to pry it apart far enough to pull it over the diminished circumference of my finger. Meanwhile, I had been injected with some sort of anodyne, could feel no pain, and according to Shelli, was keeping everyone in stitches with my comments on the procedure.

Later, on a trip Outside, Shelli and I gave the ring to her best friend, Deborah Spencer, a goldsmith with a high-end jewelry store in Lake Oswego, Oregon, to have it repaired. Not that I'll ever be able to wear it again because my finger is now too large and misshapen to accommodate it. Deborah suggested it would have been much easier to remove (and to repair) the ring had the doctors cut it on either side and just taken it apart. Her assessment seemed so logical and obvious, but it never occurred to me, Shelli or any of the doctors. I am looking forward to passing her comments on to Dr. Cotten when I see her, so the next person visiting ER in Homer with a ring avulsion might have an easier time of it.

After a little over an hour in surgery, I awoke in my hospital bed with Shelli by my side. Dr. Adcox kept me in the hospital for three nights, worried about a possible onset of pneumonia because my broken ribs had bruised my lungs and my kidneys, the latter not functioning one hundred percent.

I was unhappy about the extra nights because of the cost, and because I felt fine except for my broken ribs, which required me to sleep on my back, take pain pills regularly and avoid coughing or laughing at all costs. But no doubt, it was the right decision. I was still taking half doses of pain medication and a full dose before bed ten days later when we visited the doctor in his clinic just below the hospital in Homer. I was goofy all the time and couldn't finish a sentence half the time, but I was in excellent spirits.

A nurse ushered Shelli and me into Dr. Adcox's office, where he had us both sit down before preparing us for the worst.

He said, "It's going to be ugly. The skin will be black around the edges of the wound."

Then he began to unwrap the bandages. When the finger was uncovered he was visibly shocked and said emphatically, "You're a good healer! Most deglovings require *amputation*, even after surgery."

Now let me tell you—that was the first time Shelli or I had heard that word used in reference to my injury, though it was obviously something that had been discussed behind my back.

Fortunately, I had closed down our guest cottage before the accident, which requires crawling around in the dirt under the building. But both Shelli and I were worried I would be unable to complete the rest of the closing without major assistance. Still, I managed to do it all—including draining and winterizing the hot tub—with a plastic bag covering my hand, held in place by a big rubber band. Again, my ribs were more of a problem than my finger.

In retrospect I am grateful, in spite of my severe injury, that I was able to hook my dock with my left foot; that my boat didn't drift away from the dock, as I would almost certainly have fallen in the water minus a finger and possibly my life; that Shelli hadn't entered the shower; that Jim, Jan and JT Thurston were home; that the ring removed the flesh of my finger all the way out to the tip, but did not take veins or tendons with it; that Dr. Cotten had the ER staff and equipment ready and waiting for me when I arrived; that the finger could be reconstructed, albeit misshapen and stiff, numb and too big in the middle, tingly on the end; and—most importantly—that as Dr. Adcox exclaimed, I'm a "good healer."

As Mike Dunham went on to say in his article on Ruben Gaines:

"Weeknights at 6 (the time shifted as Gaines moved from station to station) the town paused and leaned close to its glowing radio dials for *Conversation Unlimited*. Ken Flynn, Gaines' supervisor at KHAR from 1966 to 1983, described it as five to 15 minutes of pure poetry, absolutely free-form, whatever he wanted to do.

There were no bounds to the subject matter. It was commentary, reminiscences, silly and serious poems. Dry reference books became fodder for whole series of programs. The man would read from geography texts, record books, the dictionary, pulling out items which caught his eye and launching into long-form wordplay which kept the listener swallowing clear pictures, digesting and smiling.

Reading old scripts of these shows provides only a dim shadow of what the program was actually like to hear. There was a pacing, inflection, enunciation, the thousand unquantifiable elements that go into creating a satisfactory performance. Broadcasters and listeners always refer to Gaines as a complete professional, one of the few top-notch announcers to work the market. But that doesn't explain why people who left the state 25 years ago still chuckle as they recall verbatim a piece of their favorite *Conversation Unlimited*."

Dick Lobdell, currently (in February, 1994) the morning host on KENI, remembered, 'He and Ed Stevens were doing all these goofy things. They'd read the football picks right off the gambling card. They did 'The Cow Hour' with awful country music and corny lines like, 'At the sound of the tone the time will be three-quarters to the bottom of the jug.' They did 'The Spenard Sim-Phony with more bad music. Then Gaines would come on'—Lobdell's voice takes on a tone of high sophistication with Conversation Unlimited. No one else even attempted to duplicate it.

The day Gaines flies south, Alaska will lose a piece of its cultural history. To many Alaskans whose memories encompass the decade prior to and following statehood, the man is a living treasure.

As uttered by Gaines, a single word could release oceans of meaning. Often, after expounding on peculiar Alaska place names or a list of historical oddities, he would conclude the program with the phrase, 'Students. Er, students?' leaving a razor sharp image of the rambling professor who has just looked up from his tomes to find the classroom has either departed or fallen asleep on him.

A hell of a lot of enthusiasm went into writing those 15 minutes,' Gaines said."

Coleman's Big Fishing Adventure

When Coleman McDonnough (1938-2019), the son of one of my father's older sisters, showed up at our office door, I was in my mid-sixties. I had never met Coleman, or even seen a photo of him, and I suddenly felt like I was looking in the mirror. That's a strange experience, especially that late in life. One evening after we'd eaten sushi with Coleman at our favorite sushi bar, Shelli pointed out that Coleman not only looked like me but wore the same style of clothing and had the same mannerisms.

He cracked us up when he related the story of how he had walked into Chilkoot Charlie's one night without me. He swore he'd never do that again because customers and even some employees thought he was me. I could just imagine him trying to explain to a persistent customer who'd been imbibing for a while, "I'm not Mike Gordon. I just look like him. I'm his first cousin." Right.

Until Coleman died recently he and I referred to one another as "your double." Talk about validation.

One August, Coleman came to visit us for a week so we could spend some quality time together and, after having dinner in Anchorage with some good friends, we spent the rest of our time together in Halibut Cove.

There is a silver salmon personal use set-net fishery in Kachemak Bay in August each year in which Shelli and I successfully participated for a number of years. The fishery is for residents only, so Coleman couldn't assist in the actual fishing or receive any of the catch, but we thought it would be interesting for him to observe and participate to the extent he could by law.

When Shelli and I first became involved in the fishery, almost ten years earlier, we had no idea what we were doing and experimented with a number of locations. We fished out in front of Halibut Cove, along Glacier Spit, up the bay beyond Glacier Spit, and even on the north side of the bay. The most popular locations are right off the end of the Homer Spit, but the competition for those beaches is fierce and you have to contend with others running right over your nets in their speeding boats as they travel to and from the halibut fishing grounds.

Our results were mediocre, catching mostly pink salmon or nothing, until we decided to try Eagle Beach, just west of Peterson Cove, across the bay and southeast from Homer. We hit a bonanza and for several years we were alone in that location; no one competed with us for the beach. The rule was that the fishery opened at 6:00 am, and the first person with their gear in the water after the opening had the right to the location until the end of that opening.

We were allowed up to thirty-five big, beautiful silver salmon during each twenty-four hour period. They were fresh from the ocean and as large as small or medium sized king salmon—gorgeous glittering tor-pedoes. I learned to fillet salmon with the speed and skill of the best of them, and Shelli and I had an abundance of fillets, canned smoked salm-on, and pickled salmon for the rest of the year, and more.

One year our closest neighbor in Halibut Cove, a commercial fish-erman born and raised in the community, unexpectedly beat us to our favorite site on Eagle Beach. From that year on, it was a race to see who could get to the prime spot first. Our neighbor had the fastest small boat suitable for set net fishing, and when he saw us leaving he would whiz past us to secure the spot.

Some years weren't particularly good fishing at the secondary loca-tion we had to settle for, or at the primary location, once our neighbor had caught his fill and pulled up his nets. So one year I slipped out of the Cove and slept in a tent overnight on the beach with a friend and his kids, ready for the 6:00 a.m. opening. I was sporting a big, wide grin when our neighbor exited Halibut Cove and, seeing me on the beach, immediately spun around and headed home.

The fishery is at a time of year when there are generally very high tides that pull debris from the beaches and very low tides that suck a lot of seaweed and kelp from the bottom. Much of this junk gets caught in your fishing nets, making life miserable. It's one thing to deal with the debris if you're catching a lot of fish, but it's quite another if you're not. Before taking Coleman out to see how the fishery worked, we had experienced seasons of debris sans fish and chosen not to participate for a couple years.

With Coleman on hand and not wanting to waste my time, I needed the prime location for the first opening. Since I didn't know whether the neighbor was going to participate, I opted for the overnight camping routine again. Coleman and I motored to the beach in Shelli's aluminum riverboat. It is very heavy and slow, but its bow is perfect for pulling the net over while picking fish. We set up the tent, and I had all the gear ready to be first in the water at 6:00 am, but what I had not considered was that the tide, near high when we arrived, would be going out all night while we intended to sleep.

As the tide began to recede, the heavy boat was repeatedly at risk of being left high-and-dry on the beach. If it had gotten even halfway dry, Coleman and I together would not have been able to get it back into the water and would have had to wait until the next high tide to float it. The last thing in the world I wanted was to miss the fishing period, stuck on the beach while someone—especially my neighbor—launched his net in the prime spot.

Coleman helped me manhandle the boat back into the water a couple of times, and then I just stayed awake and did it myself the rest of the night, walking down the steep gravel beach and back in my hip boots and underwear. Then around 4:00 a.m. Coleman volunteered to sit in a folding chair and tend the boat, now quite a distance below us, for a couple of hours so I could get some sleep. Though I did not realize it at the time it was a brave gesture for him, fearful of being attacked by a bear.

Finally, 6:00 a.m. arrived. I pulled the one hundred and fifty feet of net out into the bay, dropped the anchor and returned to camp without a hitch. No one else had even shown up to lay claim to the location. We crawled back into our tent to get some badly needed sleep.

At noon, Shelli began to worry about us. We'd been in such a hurry to depart that we had not taken our cell phones with us, so she couldn't call and was afraid something had gone wrong. After a few hours of rest we closed down our camp and I checked the net. It was empty. Coleman and I left the net in place and motored back to Halibut Cove, arriving just as Shelli was contemplating calling 911.

Since Coleman could not lawfully help with tending the net, Shelli and I went over to check it that evening by ourselves. It had a lot of crap in it: branches, twigs and seaweed, but no fish, so we spent an arduous couple of hours cleaning it up. The next day we went over to check the net again. It was high tide and full of crap again, only far worse, and still no fish—so we decided to just haul it in and call it quits.

Since there was no way we could remove all the limbs, stumps, seaweed, and a log nearly as long as the skiff as we pulled in the net, I untied the beach end and put it in the boat. Then we started hauling the boat along the net line in the direction of the net buoy and anchor, pulling the net in as we went. About halfway through this arduous process of piling a net full of wet, heavy debris into the bow of the boat the weather changed—quickly and dramatically—for the worse.

We were now frantically pulling the net into the boat. When we finally got the net and anchor on board, a herculean job under the circumstances, we were seriously overloaded and in dangerously rough water.

Shelli was steering the boat back toward Halibut Cove and I was on the starboard side of her trying to organize our load when, as we were cresting the top of a large wave, the boat started to slide backwards into a deep, dark low point between waves that would surely have swamped us. Shelli didn't have the motor on full throttle, and there wasn't time to communicate. I just reached over with my left hand and shoved the throttle forward as hard and fast as I could, moving the boat forward to keep the stern in front of the following wave. It was a very close call. Had that following wave caught up with us, it would certainly have filled the stern of the boat with water and swamped us.

As we rounded Peterson Point and approached the entrance to Halibut Cove we saw our neighbor, Marion Beck—owner of The Saltry Restaurant—in her big aluminum skiff departing the Narrows for Homer. That is, until she saw the condition of the water and turned immediately around. She looked at us like we were crazy and shouted over, "What the hell were you guys doing out there?"

We hollered back, "It wasn't like this when we went out to our nets. We got caught by surprise!"

The next day Coleman helped with picking through the nets, but it took weeks to completely clean them. Coleman was long gone by the time Shelli and I got to the bottom of the pile, which had become a rotting, stinking mess. There had been one fish in it, an unlucky silver salmon that had been caught near the shore: because of the wave movement of the net against the beach, it was practically fleshless.

There were several potential disasters in trying to save the net that day, not to mention the near swamping of the boat on the way home. You don't actually pull the net to the boat, you pull the boat to the net, and we wouldn't have been the first to capsize while being whipped up and down on the waves, like a carpet being shaken by an energetic housekeeper, trying to save a net. Under such circumstances it's also not hard to get buttons on your clothes or snaps on your hip boots ensnared in the netting and end up pulled overboard as a result.

While Coleman was still alive he and I would tease each other about going set-net fishing again. I don't recall that he stopped eating fish, but he'd seen all he needed to of the other end of the process.

Shelli said to me after the incident, "I think we're getting a little old for this."

I replied, "Maybe we should burn those nets so we're never even tempted to use them again."

We never burned them, but we haven't ever used them again either, with or without Coleman.

All the gear's for sale if you're interested: nets, ropes, buoys, and anchors—cheap.

"Clarence"

To watch a seagull in flight is pure edification. It sits practically with knees crossed on the bosom of a gust and wafts well above the smog level, its mind seemingly on higher things. Without gulls, poets would lose 50 percent of their inspiration. Man, watching the bird fly, has enfranchised it with beauty, virtue and grace beyond most others in the natural kingdom.

In character they're something else. Being chary about their propaganda and aware of their gluttony, my eardrums sandpapered by their eternal screeching, I had never cottoned to gulls. As a onetime Ketchikan, Alaska, resident, I knew them well. Certain hyper individuals stood out from the crowd, though all shared a common greed. Any flotsam, just so it looks edible and floats, automatically belongs to ol' No. 1, and mayhem is the preferred way to get it. In Thomas Basin, that city's harbor, I watched one divebomb a fishing schooner. The object of its attention was a half barrel of bait herring...the skipper told me the details later...and the barrel had a lid with a hole in the cover no bigger than the gull's head; but the bird saw the herring through the hole, and assaulted the barrel several times at Kamikaze speed, stunning itself each time. I was told the gull, on one last bombing run, finally grabbed a herring, but stayed stuck with its head in the hole, like a sinner in the stocks.

Awed by such greedy zeal, I described the act on the radio, and soon got many stories back from listeners. It seemed this dive bomber was not out of the ordinary. I told the stories and got more. Some classics emerged, like the one about the gull who, plummeting toward the water after a piece of flotsam, spied a bigger piece at the last moment, changed direction with a misguided wingover, and wrung its own neck. A man wrote a profane report, not usable on the radio, about his trout-fishing trip: he had turned his back to clean a knife when the gull, descending fast out of nowhere, seized the record-sized rainbow he'd caught, and to which the fly and line were still attached, and soared aloft. The last the man saw of his prize catch, line, expensive bamboo rod and triumphant frame of mind, they were crossing the Tongass Narrows toward the Pacific.

From the wealth of letters a pattern emerged: an individual gull weaving in and out of most of the accounts, issuing from the composite like the drawings of a described felon for the police records. I named this celebrity Clarence. Two characteristics remained constant in the stories: Clarence's greed, and deep distaste for human beings.

Time passes, and so did Clarence and Ketchikan. That is, I *thought* he had passed. Decades later I ran across this press wire item: *Picture this: a golfer is approaching the fourth tee on an Australian golf course more than three miles from the sea, when he is suddenly hit in the head with a fish. Fellow golfers say they saw an eagle circling above, and they believe the fish slipped from the bird's claws.*

What eagle? That bird...neither eagle nor albatross or other flier of the southern hemispheres, but 8000 miles removed from Thomas Basin, Ketchikan...is Clarence. That, in every characteristic, frame of mind and detail, is him. Or *he*.

Collected Ruben Gaines I ©1988 Ruben Gaines

Playboy Magazine

The cover of the May 2000 issue of *Playboy* magazine sported a photo and the headline "Hef's Twins, Naked as Jaybirds." The cover also touted an interview with Pete Rose, an article on "The Modern Mafia," and one on "Tantric Sex Made Simple: She'll be Screaming." Not mentioned on the cover was an article titled "Critic's Choice, The Best Bars in America, which culminated in a list of the 23 best bars in America according to *Playboy's* blue-ribbon panel of publishers, editors, writers, critics, chefs, restaurateurs and raconteurs.

The very first bar on the list is Chilkoot Charlie's of Anchorage, followed by J-Bar, Hotel Jerome, Aspen; Mumbo Jumbo, Atlanta; Continental Club, Austin; Casablanca, Boston; Gibsons, Chicago; Samba Room, Dallas; Lili's 21, Detroit; Mercury Room, Key West; Red Square, Las Vegas; China Grill, Miami Beach; Napoleon House, New Orleans; Campbell Apartment, New York City; Greatest Bar on Earth, New York City; Continental, Philadelphia; Froggy's, Pittsburgh; Bix, San Francisco; Coyote Café, Santa Fe; F.X. McRory's, Seattle; Timber Wolf, Tempe; Madam's Organ Restaurant and Bar, Washington, D.C. and Skybar, West Hollywood. Now, you gotta admit, that's a helluva list to head up.

The magazine next, in alphabetical order according to bar name, writes a few descriptive sentences about each bar.

> **Chilkoot Charlie's,** 2435 Spenard Road, Anchorage (907-271-1010). The nights get long in Alaska, but Chilkoot Charlie's, in Anchorage's historic Spenard District, makes them seem a lot shorter. In fact, by the time you get to all three stages, three dance floors and eight bars in this 30-year-old establishment, the night may not be long enough. (Chilkoot Charlie is a fictional Alaskan character made famous by Ruben Gaines, a writer and radio personality.) At Chilkoot's, you can rock to the music of the Beach Boys, the Doobie Brothers, Megadeth and Van Halen, or retreat to the Forties Swing Bar and dance to big band music or sip a martini and watch a black-and-white movie. Just be careful not to sip too many. You might get the women and the grizzly bears mixed up when it comes to wrasslin' time.

Finally, the magazine printed a whole page listing its "Choice Critics," that helped them identify the top hangouts—seventy-one critics to be exact. I won't bore you with the whole list, but here are a few examples:

Eric Azimov, restaurant critic and food writer, *The New York Times;* Anthony Dias Blue, wine and spirits editor, *Bon Appétit,* Los Angeles; Dale Curry, food editor, *The Times-Picayune,* New Orleans; Ray Foley, publisher, *Bartender,* Liberty Corner, NJ; Richard Carleton Hacker, smoke and spirits editor, *Robb Report,* Beverly Hills; Michael Jackson, beer and spirits writer, London; John Mariani, restaurant critic, *Esquire* and *Virtual Gourmet,* New York City; Ron Marr, editor and publisher *The Trout Wrapper,* Ennis, Montana; Mike Mills, barbecue champion, owner 17th Street Bar and Grill, Murphysboro, IL; Michael Schachner, senior editor, *The Wine Enthusiast,* New York City; Jasper White, chef and owner Jasper's Roadhouse, Cambridge, MA.

The *Anchorage Daily News'* gossip column, the Alaska Ear, heralded our inclusion in the list with a single line: "Way to go Big Mike!"

During the summer of 1999, a small group of *Playboy* employees visited the state of Alaska, as they did every other state in the union, to photograph local female talent for their millennial issue. They had reserved rooms and planned to do their photo shoots at Anchorage's Sheraton Hotel on East Sixth Avenue. Much to their chagrin, they discovered the Sheraton's management was unhappy with being selected as the site of their activities and, further, quite uncooperative.

Local publicity for the millennial photography was being handled by radio station KHAR, with whom Chilkoot Charlie's staff had a good working relationship. When the *Playboy* folks complained to their KHAR counterparts about the lack of cooperation from the Sheraton management, they were told that the photography could just as well be arranged at the club. When we got the call I was thrilled.

Over the course of a week or so, all the girls who wanted to represent Alaska in the millennial edition of the magazine had their photos taken at Chilkoot Charlie's. As if it wasn't enough to have pretty young women walking in and out of the club all week, we got all the good publicity from the event that the Sheraton had not wanted. The Sheraton actually got some bad publicity because they were perceived as being too uppity to host the activity. My crew and I also became good friends with the two main *Playboy* staffers in town from Chicago: an editor, Kevin Kuster, and photographer, George Georgiou, both of whom absolutely fell in love with Chilkoot Charlie's and expressed a desire to return to Alaska for a fishing trip. We told them, "You'll catch fish so big you'll shit!" (Unless your name is Coleman!)

Lo and behold, the next summer Kevin and George did return for some of those big fish, bringing with them Hefner-style *Playboy*-branded silk pajamas for me and my upper management. They also had the inside story of how they had made sure that Chilkoot Charlie's was included in the above list of famous American bars. It seems there had been another well-known bar in Anchorage—the other must-visit one—that was being considered. Our friends, having actually visited both, had forcefully responded, "No way!"

I thought it was appropriate for me to send a "Thank You" note to Hugh Hefner and some sort of gift, but what sort of gift do you give to the world's most iconic playboy who has got absolutely everything—right down to a photo of his twin blonde girlfriends plastered on the front of his world famous magazine? I sent him the only thing I figured he didn't have—an oosik—accompanied by a couple of CDs of my short stories and "Ode to an Oosik," author unknown, which reads as follows:

Strange things have been done in the Midnight Sun,

    And the story books are full—

But the strangest tale concerns the male,

    Magnificent walrus bull!

I know it's rude, quite common and crude,

    Perhaps it is grossly unkind;

But with first glance at least, this bewhiskered beast,

    Is as ugly in front as behind.

Look once again, take a second look—then

    You'll see he's not ugly or vile—

There's a hint of a grin, in that blubbery chin—

    And the eyes have a shy secret smile.

How can this be, this clandestine glee

That exudes from the walrus like music

He knows, there inside, beneath blubber and hide

Lies a splendid contrivance—the Oosik!

"Oosik" you say—and quite well you may,

I'll explain if you keep it between us;

In the simplest truth, though rather uncouth

"Oosik" is, in fact, his penis!

Now the size alone of this walrus bone,

Would indeed arouse envious thinking—

It is also a fact, documented and backed,

There is never a softening or shrinking!

This, then, is why the smile is so sly,

The walrus is rightfully proud.

Though the climate is frigid, the walrus is rigid,

Pray, why, is not man so endowed?

Added to this, is a smile you might miss—

Though the bull is entitled to bow—

The one to out-smile our bull by a mile

Is the satisfied walrus cow!

I knew exactly where to take the boys fishing for the promised "fish so big they'd shit"—the Tanana and Yukon Rivers out of Manley Hot Springs.

My friend Frank Gurtler took us on an overnight river boat trip down the Tanana Slough to the Tanana River, into the Yukon River, and 125 miles or so down the Yukon to the village of Ruby. We caught huge pike along the way, mostly at confluences where smaller rivers like the Zitziana joined the Tanana or Yukon, their tea-colored waters mixing with the larger streams' silty glacial-fed water like oolong tea poured into milk. At Ruby we caught our fill of sheefish using the old standard Dardevle lure.

Sheefish are beautiful. They look like freshwater tarpon—scales and all—though they don't grow to the size of tarpon. I baked one for dinner one time and found it to be inedible. It looked wonderful lying on the platter surrounded by sautéed vegetables, but we just could not eat it because it was too damn fishy. I unceremoniously dumped it in the garbage. Later, I discovered that interior locals, like Frank and his wife, Diane, cut their sheefish up into bite-size chunks and deep fry them. Frank deep fried some for us on our return trip to Manley Hot Springs. They are actually pretty tasty prepared that way.

Interestingly, sheefish inhabit the same waters as those huge pike that are like alligators without legs, but sheefish have no teeth in their mouths. Maybe they're the only other fish the pike refuse to eat, since they've never had them deep fried. You can literally stick your fist in the mouth of a sheefish and move it around without getting a scratch.

Don't try that with a pike. You need a good pair of pliers just to unhook the pike from your lure. Pike will hit any kind of lure—anything that moves, for that matter. There are bodies of water in Interior Alaska where nothing else is alive. Nothing else moves above or below the surface, and if it does, it's dinner. A duck landing on the surface is a meal in nothing flat. Whoosh!

Northern pike occur naturally in most of Alaska, but they are not indigenous to South Central Alaska, where they are considered an invasive fish. They are territorial, aggressive and will decimate the population of other fish, like trout.

Some of the pike we caught were so big you could drape them over both arms held out in front of you and they would hang halfway down to your knees, weighing upwards of 50 pounds. And unlike their pretty, toothless neighbors, pike are packed with succulent, tasty white meat. If you're ever fortunate enough to eat pike prepared on the banks of the Tanana Slough by Las Vegas Chef Andre Rochat with a French white wine sauce and capers, accompanied by a glass of Sancerre, you'll know what I'm talking about.

Suffice it to say, our pals from Chicago had the time of their lives up north. Frank, a handsome part Alaska Native man with a large scar around one eye that tempts you to ask, "How big was that bear?" good-naturedly put up with all our shenanigans, including throwing away the cap on a liter bottle of vodka and requiring him to stop along the shore of the Yukon so we could catch a bee—don't ask me why; you had to have been there—to put in the bottle before emptying its contents.

Not long after the boys had returned to Chicago, I received a letter from *Playboy* magazine. It was hand-typed and signed by Hugh Hefner himself.

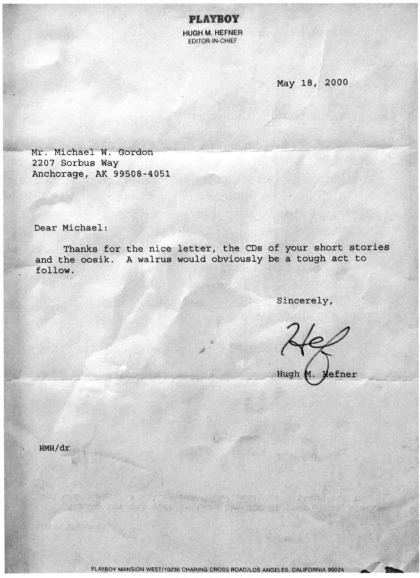

Hugh Hefner's letter to Mike

More from Mike Dunham on Ruben:

For most of his radio life Gaines ran morning shifts crowded with news, temperature, interviews and characters of his own creation. Music was secondary. Ken Flynn remembered that at KHAR, 'Ruben was unpredictable and unmechanical. I'd show him how to handle the records carefully and he'd nod. I'd go back to my office and hear a noise on the air, then Gaines saying, 'Hang on, ladies and gentlemen, let me get my record off the floor.' He'd cue records on the air. He'd make up sponsors. I was a 24-year-old fledgling program director, wanting to have everything roped in, trying to be mature and he kept calling me 'kid' all the time.

Gaines called everyone 'kid.' His boss, Patty Harpel, recalled that when he told her he was retiring in 1987, he said, 'I have to, kid. I'm starting to sound like Pop!'

Just for the record, Ruben called me "kid" once in a while also, though he expressed it in such a way that it felt endearing.

Charley Horses

The phrase "charley horse," describes an involuntary muscle cramp—usually in an athlete—and is actually a piece of baseball jargon. Some say it had to do with a lame horse that pulled the lawn roller at the White Sox stadium. Others insist that it came about when the Providence Gray's pitching Hall-of-Famer Charley Radbourn, whose nickname was Old Hoss, suffered the condition during a game.

Now it was my turn at bat, so to speak.

"Ahh! Ahh! Ahhhhh!" I screamed at the top of my lungs.

"I've got a charley horse in my right leg!" If I bent it at the knee it cramped and I *had* to straighten it.

It was November of 2003 and we were on our way home to Anchorage in our big, fully-loaded Ford 250 with a cab over the full-size bed. The charley horse struck as we were approaching Tern Lake, a favored layover for stately white swans as they migrate through in spring and fall. Due to my pain, I was using my left leg for both gas and brake pedal, holding my right leg out as straight as possible.

Shelli and I had just finished a brutal eighteen-hour day closing down our Halibut Cove summer home—later in the season than normal, so it had been freezing cold with snow on the ground. And it was practically dark when we motored away from our dock for one of those far-less-than-placid crossings of Kachemak Bay on the way to Homer.

Shelli has always claimed there are one hundred and five steps up to our home, after you've climbed the aluminum ramp from the floating dock to the boat house level. The ramp itself, depending on the tides, can vary from horizontal at the highest tides to practically vertical at the lowest. It alone measures about thirty steps. Someone said recently that there are actually one hundred and ten steps. I count only in segments: eleven steps, then thirteen, thirteen again, then eight, seven, six, and so on. I am not enough of a masochist to total them. Who cares if it's one hundred and five or one hundred and ten? It is helpful, though, to know how many are in the different segments when carrying heavy loads and when footing, visibility and/or both are challenging.

"Ahhhh! I can't drive," I screamed again as I pulled awkwardly into the Tern Lake parking lot.

I managed to struggle out of the truck, swallowed water from a plastic jug, and paced wildly around in circles in an effort to subdue the spasms in my leg. After ten minutes or so of limbering up, I tried to climb back into the truck.

"Ahhhhhhh!" "Ahhhhhh!"

I had bent my right arm as I reached up for the handhold above the open door and had bent my left leg as I placed it on the running board. Now I had a charley horse in both my right and left legs, *and* my right arm.

"Ahhhhh!"

At this point I was frantically stomping straight-legged around the gravel parking area while flailing my cramped arm, holding it straight out from my body. I no doubt looked and sounded like a shell-shocked madman or a zombie in the throes of a maniacal tantrum. I can't positively recall the reaction of the swans to my dance performance.

Shelli said, "You're going to have to let me drive."

That was becoming apparent even to the madman. The problem was how to get myself back into the truck. Shelli has a reconstructed ankle from a high school auto accident and having had to resort to this method more than once during her rehabilitation, suggested I keep my legs straight as I backed myself, butt first, into the passenger seat, simultaneously pulling myself in with my arms.

I managed that with considerable difficulty and a few more agonized outbursts, ending up seated with both legs and both arms straight out in front of me like a fearful car crash dummy anticipating a head-on impact with a brick wall. Tears streaming down her face, stifling laughter, Shelli drove off into the night, turning the truck north on the Seward Highway toward Anchorage.

The proximate cause of all this drama was piled into the back of the truck under the canopy. In addition to our load of personal effects there were at least sixty cases of jams and jellies in four, six, and twelve ounce jars: "Shelli Jelly."

We have what is best described as a compound in Halibut Cove. It is two acres, mostly landscaped. And to describe Shelli as a gardener would be an understatement. She is a farmer.

It all starts with the four compost piles, scientifically managed with tender loving care—turning in the proper amounts of carbon, nitrogen, oxygen and water. Nothing goes to waste on our property, not even brush we've cleared. Most of our neighbors burn brush on an open area of their property or on their beach when it's raining but we have a chipper/shredder for that and the resulting material makes for great layers in the compost piles. If we have too much material we use it to fill in sunken areas of the lawn or to expand the domesticated perimeters of the property.

As an aside, I follow a pescatarian diet, eating seafood, eggs, cheese, vegetables, and fruits, but no meat or fowl. Composting wasn't the cause of my dietary choice, but it was the confirmation of it being the right choice—that and the fate of a college roommate's wife. When you put any kind of seafood in a compost pile, it heats the pile up and burns like an oven inside. When you put meat or fowl in a compost pile, it putrefies. Think about it.

My college roommate and his wife were in England on an extended road trip. They stopped at a bed and breakfast, and in the morning they were offered an English breakfast of eggs with blood sausage. Rick declined, but his wife accepted the offer.

She died a horrible, untimely death from mad cow disease.

I'll never have to worry about that.

Back to the Halibut Cove compound, where we had—and still have—rolling lawns, a lot of beautiful deciduous trees, a couple of ponds, rock gardens, shade gardens, a vegetable garden and an herb garden, as well as a lot of decorative annuals around the main house and guest cottage. We also have a windmill—not quite as large as the one in Spenard. It came with the property.

We have apple trees and Evans cherry trees and rhododendrons, but mostly we have berries. We've got the world's most prolific red currant bushes. We also have white currants, Swedish black currants, and indigenous black currants. We have blueberries, low-bush cranberries and high-bush cranberries, four varieties of gooseberries, lingonberries, Josta berries, Gogi berries and salmon berries galore.

There are mountain ash trees (a member of the apple family bearing pommes, not berries), elderberries, choke cherries on the Mayday trees, Saskatoons and honey berries. And finally, there are scads of red and golden raspberries.

Importantly, we have enough varieties that Shelli can make up a twelve-jar gift pack with cherries or a different berry variety in each jar, all grown on our property, and bestowed with names like Blu-Saska-Rhu, Toasted Gold, Razapeno, Christmas Consort, Ginger-Rhu, and Polka Dot Jelly, though in recent years we have concentrated more on making juices and liqueurs.

Fall season is when we tend to visit more with Halibut Cove neighbors. Most of the tourists and guests are gone. Early mornings in October are spent writing, then shrinking the perimeter—closing down the guest house and hot tub, bringing in hoses and yard decorations, raking leaves, composting annuals, cutting back perennials and covering their beds with the raked leaves and cut stalks. Geese trim up their flying wedges in preparation for their long journey south, as noisy flocks of crows descend upon the mountain ash trees and elderberry bushes in front of the house.

The elderberries have fermented by now, so the birds get sloshed and hang upside down, clowning around clumsily as they squawk loud, bawdy barroom crow songs. Seals and sea otters, in anticipation of winter, start taking over the floating docks. They're not potty-trained and—especially the seals—have perpetual diarrhea, so you have to start being careful where you step down there. Jacques, our standard poodle, has taken it upon himself to run off the sea otters, but they still manage to slip onto the floats at night and leave their mess behind them.

Jacques has not yet figured out the difference between sea otters and river otters, to his detriment. Recently two adult river otters—large members of the weasel family—got him by the tail and tried to drag him into a pond and drown him behind our guest cottage. They were protecting their young.

A few days later the same river otters were hanging out in salt water under our floating dock. As Jacques searched for them, they grabbed him by the nose and pulled him into the salt water. They were working him over and would have killed him had not the same two neighboring teenagers who saved him the first time been on the scene to grab him by the collar and haul him, soaked, bleeding and battered, out of the frigid water. One of the otters actually climbed up out of the water and onto the dock after him. That saltwater assault required a trip to the veterinarian in Homer where he was given antibiotics for his twenty-plus puncture wounds.

Fall afternoons and evenings, with the absence of guests, are spent talking, reading, listening to music, and stirring jams and jellies on the stove while the soapstone fireplace crackles away keeping the place toasty warm. Also, since we moved full-time to the Cove a few years ago we've installed a television and have been known to binge on a Netflix or Amazon series.

But preliminary to all this, the cases of empty jam and jelly jars have to be purchased and hauled to Halibut Cove—from the store into the truck, from the truck down the ramp and onto the boat, from the boat up the ramp to the tram—which did not exist at the time of this story. Then, from the tram it's up another long flight of stairs to the house. Once stacked, the cases fill a space large enough for an overstuffed living room sofa. And let's not forget the seemingly endless twenty-five-pound bags of C & H Sugar: ditto the journey from the store into the truck, ramp, boat, ramp, tram, stairs and house.

In any photo of hunters and gatherers I am with the hunters—every time. I love hunting and fishing. But when it comes to picking berries I'll be honest. I would rather watch televised golf, paint drying, or listen to pampered college students at Yale screaming obscenities while whining about their latest perceived injustice.

Shelli, though, never tires of asking me—with an irrepressible grin on her face—if I'd like to pick berries with her. Sometimes I actually agree to do it, but I'm thrilled when my daughter, Michele, or a female friend arrives and is excited to venture into the bushes with her.

One fall season I drove to Soldotna with Shelli, attended a Daughters of the America Revolution luncheon—at which I was, not surprisingly, the only guy present—then got up the next morning, drove to the Johnson Campground area and picked high-bush and low-bush cranberries all afternoon. Now that's true love. It's not that we actually needed the berries. We already had two freezers chock-full of berries in Homer and two more in Halibut Cove.

The 2003 season produced a bumper crop of berries. We stayed late and made lots of jams and jellies, as mentioned earlier—sixty to seventy cases. We invented several great new recipes that year. But then I had to carry all those cases, not to mention the loads of leftover food, orchids, clothing and gear down to the boat over the slippery snow-covered lawn and the stairs that only reached halfway to the house at the time. A single case of a dozen twelve-ounce jars of jam or jelly is heavy, and there was no one to help me.

I tried to make light of my misery by making up berry jokes. While picking up the next load I'd report to Shelli, "I'm berry nearly done!"

"Do you know the way to (San Jose) Saskatoon? Bumpatabump-bumpbumppadadabump! I've been away so long!"

Our 25-foot Bay Weld is generally a stable boat, but once fully loaded it was top-heavy and listing drunkenly from side to side.

I wondered aloud, "Whatever happened to Mike and Shelli?"

Answering myself, "Oh, they overloaded their boat with jams, ran into a Swedish black currant, and jelly-rolled 'er!"

What else could I do?

Thanks to my herd of charley horses, Shelli wound up driving all the way to Anchorage. After using the facilities at the gas station at the intersection outside Girdwood and thinking I was back to normal, I volunteered to drive the rest of the way home. But it was not to be. As soon as I bent an arm or a leg I was instantly and painfully cramped.

With less than two months before Christmas, we spent many evening hours wrapping case after case of jam and jelly, mailing them to friends and relatives all across America and labeling many more for the dozens of employees of Chilkoot Charlie's. People loved the gifts. Some recipients wrote extensive e-mails and dutifully cleaned and returned the empty jars, hoping for future deliveries.

We don't go through quite the same routine every year anymore because we live in the Cove year-round and we don't have all those employees. Thank God, because I'm not getting any younger. The stairs go all the way to the house now and we have a boom as well as a tram. We make more juice and liqueurs, which we consume ourselves, than jams and jellies. We still deal with the routine of stairs, ramp, boat, ramp, truck, house for anything we transport, and we've planted even more cherry trees and berry bushes, yearly harvesting more than we can use.

No matter because, you see, there's a double standard for berries and cherries around here. When you've caught too many fish for smoking and filleting you stop fishing, but when you've picked too many berries and cherries you just buy another freezer.

Ruben loved my wife Shelli. I used to joke with her, not without a certain uneasiness, that if Ruben had been thirty years younger he and I might have had a real problem. When I would pick him up to go out to dinner and Shelli was not in the car with me, the first thing out of his mouth would not be, "How's it going?", but "Where is she?" Early on I gave up trying to confide in Ruben any sort of grievance with Shelli because he would invariably announce, "I'm on her side, man." And he was right to be.

Speaking of going to dinner with Ruben—most people don't realize that Ruben might have been part Japanese. He claimed to be Volga German—and actually was—Hagelganz being his real family name. I used to call him Hasselblad to get his goat. But I wouldn't be surprised if there was Japanese heritage in there somewhere. We used to take him to different kinds of ethnic restaurants for the sake of variety until one night, about ten years into the program, we thought "Why not?" and took him to a sushi bar. Eureka! Ruben was never exactly a virtuoso with chop sticks, but he took to sushi and sake like a fish to water.

For a guy who never forgot any other thing he learned in his life, he could not for the life of him remember what to call any of that stuff. All he knew was that he loved it and for ten years, roughly once a month, we'd eat at a sushi bar. Just so you know, that's about 120 orders of maguro sashimi, 240 hotategai, maybe 50 orders of amaebi, 100 orders of suzuki usuzukuri, 240 orders of tobiko with uzura no tamago, and 2,000 servings of sake, not to mention the plum wine and green tea ice cream for dessert. Ruben is not only missed by family, friends and avid followers, but by the Sushi Bar Association of Alaska.

One night after a feast of sushi, Ruben said, "It's a wonder a guy doesn't grow gills, dagnabit!"

The Windmill

After the early 1980s, when for a few years Alaska's economy knew no bounds, I was made an offer I couldn't refuse by none other than Mafia Mike. That's how I became the custodian of an important local historical icon. Had I known at the time what a maintenance nightmare it would present I'm not sure I would have accepted the responsibility, regardless of the obvious promotional potential.

In April 1941, more than a decade before I arrived in Seward at age 10—in fact a year and a half before I was born—Byron Gillam stepped ashore in that same coastal community. Preempting his planned return to the States, the Japanese attacked Pearl Harbor, liquor was banned, martial law was established and no one was allowed to leave the Territory of Alaska.

After the war, Gillam made his stake of a little over $40,000 by diverting a ship bound for the Philippines with 8,800 cases of Hiram Walker aboard. He sold the whiskey to the 3,000 men and 50 women of Valdez. How do you like those odds, girls?

He put the entirety of that stake into purchasing the Nevada Bar, a Swedish bar on First Street in Fairbanks, happily discovering that there was a $50,000 inventory of booze in the basement.

I am missing some documented history here, but I am pretty sure the Nevada Bar burned down. I remember Mike James—husband of Pat James and father of my Anchorage High School classmate, Dr. Mike James, and his younger brother, attorney Pat James—telling me as a kid how as a member of the volunteer fire department in Fairbanks, he and his team of firefighters struggled mightily with pumps and hose to no avail, as the place went up in flames early on a cold, dark Fairbanks winter morning.

After rescuing some of that precious inventory from within the inferno, they would take a break to quench their thirst with a slug or two, salving their blistered egos while another team continued fighting the fire...and rescuing more inventory.

Having built a successful enterprise in Fairbanks, Gillam sold out to Larry Carr and moved his family to Anchorage in 1957 where he opened the Kut Rate Kid liquor store on East Fireweed Lane. He was the bane of the Seattle-based liquor wholesalers, importing forty-foot trailers loaded with beer and liquor directly to his store, bypassing the wholesalers and heavily discounting his prices to the public. He profited by selling a load of 5,000 cases of beer for two cents per case over his cost because his customers, while in the store, would buy a bottle of wine or liquor properly marked up or a bag of ice at nearly 100% profit.

In 1960 or 1961, Gillam was driving the freeway near Sacramento when he spotted a white four-story windmill, lit up, turning in the night, and had an epiphany. Soon, at a cost of approximately $13,000 including installation, there was a beautiful new windmill on East Fireweed Lane. Gillam advertised his Kut Rate Kid as being, "under the Windmill at Fireweed and Gambell."

Not everyone liked the windmill. Then, as now, there were those who did not like outdoor advertising, especially big, flashy stuff. In the very early 1960s, a municipal ordinance was passed that prohibited commercial signs, specifically targeting the windmill.

Byron responded with, "Where's the advertisement? Where's the verbiage? It's not a sign; it's a light. It's a windmill. Screw off!"

I would venture to say that if a bunch of local agitators tried to have that same windmill removed today from where it stands over the Chilkoot Charlie's parking lot, they would have a hell of a fight on their hands. It is a landmark. And it fits the character of Spenard better than where it used to sit on East Fireweed Lane, which is a little short on the elusive, legendary, and endearing character that defines Spenard. People in Spenard love it.

Byron's son Robert Gillam (1946-2018), having recently graduated from college, built a nice new facility further west on Fireweed Lane out of which they ran their liquor business until around 1978, the year Byron passed away. In 1980 the business and property were sold, and the new operator—not as adept at tracking those two cent profits—failed. The property fell into bankruptcy, which left the building and windmill sitting unattended for an extended period of time.

As the Anchorage economy boomed in the 1980s, fueled by the massive oil income from the newly-opened pipeline from Prudhoe Bay and Project 80s expenditures on infrastructure, Mafia Mike, who owned a pizza operation, was expanding. Mike was a local character who appeared in his own television ads sporting a black shirt, white tie and black fedora to support his namesake pizza operation. He even put his name on the ballot for mayor of Anchorage to garner more publicity. The flashy windmill, which he purchased out of bankruptcy, was a perfect fit for his personality. He was all set to open another location in Mid-town Anchorage and planning to move his newly-acquired windmill out there as his own landmark when the oil patch crisis hit Alaska. The price of oil spiraled downward by over fifty percent and ended many business dreams, including Mafia Mike's.

His expansion plans cancelled, Mafia Mike no longer had use for the windmill. But the owners of the property still wanted it removed. Mike asked around and, according to him, someone said, "Go see Mike Gordon. He'll buy anything," which was not entirely off-base because I had recently purchased that two-headed pig for Chilkoot Charlie's where it still sits in its jar of formaldehyde behind the South Long Bar. Word gets around.

Mike really did make me an offer I couldn't refuse. He said, "I'll give you the windmill if you move it off the property, re-erect it at the southeast corner of your parking lot, and put a plaque on it saying that it was donated to Spenard by Mafia Mike." So it was done, at a cost of $10,000. I also attached the plaque, which has long since disappeared.

Unfortunately, the cost of moving and re-erecting the windmill was only the beginning. Next we discovered what we might have anticipated in Spenard—loons who would want to climb the structure. There is a scruffy bar-inhabiting variety of loon in Spenard, *Gavia inebria,* whose only similarity to the common loon found in Alaskan waters is its red eyes. We had to build a six-foot fence around the structure topped off with barbed wire to protect these Spenard loons, strangely related to lemmings, from their suicidal proclivities.

Those *Gavia inebria* who are not interested in climbing the windmill still love it, many because its lights provide colorful targets at which to toss rocks. Normal Spenardians, like those who attend the neighborhood farmer's market right under the windmill, love it for its homey, reassuring presence.

The people who adore the windmill the absolute most, however, are the people who provide for its maintenance. We're talking job security here. Over the decades the total number of days during which all the lights on its support legs and on the spokes were lit up, and those spokes were rotating can be counted on the digits of your two hands.

If all the support leg lights are working, then the neon lights on the spokes or tail are totally or partially out. If by some chance all the lights everywhere are working, then the motor that turns the spokes has most likely died. It is a beautiful thing to behold though during those fleeting moments when the whole contraption is working. It's akin to witnessing a miracle.

Not long after the windmill was re-erected, we had a little celebration. As part of the festivities, we invited the public to bring items to put into a 55-gallon time capsule, which we then placed in a hole we had dug under the windmill. I hope the contents prove to be interesting to future residents of Spenard in, say, 2050, and this story will serve as a reminder to future archeologists that the capsule is there. Someone from the university system might write an intellectual treatise on the historic relics and perhaps even the fate of *Gavia inebria*.

Before I sold the business to my employees in 2015, I had a conversation in the Chilkoot Charlie's Swing Bar with Byron's son, Bob, founder and president of McKinley Capital Management, LLC, a highly successful investment institution and the first of its kind in Alaska. The family wanted to install the windmill on their property on Lake Clark as a family keepsake, so I investigated the cost of a metal replacement that would look enough like the original that no one in Spenard would feel short-changed. Bob agreed to pay reasonable expenses to make all this happen and I was perfectly happy to accommodate him and his family, but when it came to actually committing to spending the money, he demurred.

It would have been a win-win if the family had gotten the windmill they wanted for sentimental reasons and I had gotten one that kept the residents of Spenard happy and required less maintenance.

I told Bob that if we ever consummated a deal, he needed to consider investing some of his ample McKinley Capital money in a sign maintenance company and closed the conversation with "Be careful what you wish for, Bob."

Bob has since died and the folks from the Moose's Tooth now own the Chilkoot Charlie's property. So, any decisions regarding the future of the windmill will fall upon them—not, I hope, like loose parts from the sky high over Spenard.

The following poem hangs, framed, next to Shelli's bed:

"POEME"

Shelli, dearest, I am

reading in a

spellbound state about

your idyll in the

British Isles and your

remarriage in the kirk

where John Macaulay

once presided. Sheesh!

No wonder I've so often

brayed directly in the

face of Mountain Mike,

my admiration for your

grace, integrity and

style. Love, *Ruben Gaines,*

admirer stemming from

as far back as the

William Howard Taft

administration.

Ruben used to say to me loudly and forcefully in his inimitable style, over a half-eaten order of sushi, a tray of soy sauce and wasabi, and the umpteenth ceramic of sake, "She's got style, man! She's got style!"

Uncle Larry

Beyond a certain age, and given that we have figured out what an uncle actually is, we know uncles are not always real uncles. Families tend to be generous with the designation for close family friends who are not actually blood relatives. My wife Shelli's Uncle Larry was however an authentic, though very eccentric, uncle whom she discovered late in life due to her penchant for genealogical research. Larry's discovery was a mixed blessing. I said he was eccentric. To be more precise he was a flaming queen.

Larry was the chief blood banker at a hospital in San Francisco during the height of the AIDS epidemic. Not to worry. Larry had a life-long, monogamous relationship with George, so neither of them were ever exposed to the AIDS virus. They became acquainted while riding together on a military transport train during WWII. George put his hand on Larry's leg, and that was that. Larry was haughty, flighty, and emotional; George was unassuming, steady, and calm. They were a perfect match though I personally don't know how George managed it. Larry was such an emotional handful I will suggest there should be a larger-than-life effigy of George carried proudly along Market Street in the annual LBGTQ Pride Parade in San Francisco.

Larry had a right to be haughty. At a slim and fit six feet, two inches in height with brilliant blue eyes and wavy hair, he was an attractive man. He was not what I would call handsome because that description implies, I believe, at least a trace of ruggedness. Larry was more effeminate than rugged. George, on the other hand, was balding, with a little pot belly—rather ordinary in appearance.

George and Larry lived in San Rafael in a lovely Eichler home, with a pool and beautiful gardens that they fastidiously tended. Joseph Eichler (1900-1974) was one of the most prominent post WWII home builders in America. His company, Eichler Homes, built more than 11,000 of them in northern and southern California between 1949 and 1966. He was reportedly inspired by having lived for a short time in a Frank Lloyd Wright-designed home in Hillsborough.

Eichler developed inclusive, integrated planned communities for mostly middle-class Americans and was considered by many to be a social visionary. One of the unique features of the couple's Eichler home was a vine-festooned glass-enclosed conservatory that served as porch and entryway.

Before long, Shelli and Larry, excited to have found one another, had a trip to the Bay Area in the works for Shelli and me. This was the excursion, in 1984, when we also encountered "Clemmy" Mathis, brother of the famous singer, Johnny Mathis.

When I was attending college at the University of San Francisco in the early '60s, if you had a pretty girl, a bottle of cheap Chianti, and a Johnny Mathis album on the LP record player, you were as close to heaven as it got.

"Clemmy" was a toll collector on the Golden Gate Bridge. He was famous in his own right for working "in the lanes" with an undisputed flare.

"Where y'all from?"

"Alaska."

"Tell me the names of the captain and first mate of the Exxon Valdez and I'll wave your toll."

"Um…Joe Hazelwood and…Um…Um…."

"Jack Daniels and Jim Beam. That'll be three bucks, please."

"Clemmy" reportedly had female admirers who left him panties and bras, often with their phone numbers written on them. Brother Johnny would probably have been more interested in George.

At the end of a long day of travel we pushed the doorbell on the couple's front door. As we stood outside in the dark we could hear George and Larry inside talking and even see them walking around, but there was no response to our persistent pushing of the doorbell. We finally decided the doorbell was defective. This was before the cell phone became an extended body part, so we drove back down the valley to a gas station and called the house from a pay phone. Turns out the doorbell had been disconnected because their two parrots, Natasha and Nino, were fond of mimicking its sound, especially Natasha, a veritable avian operatic savant.

While most bowlers are not operatic savants, or even aficionados, Natasha was the exception and bowled regularly with Nino. A round rock sat on a book shelf next to the parrots' cages and they would either request it by saying, "B-o-w-l-i-n-g," or comply to a request to perform when the rock was placed on top of their cage. The birds would take turns tossing the rock onto the floor where it would roll across the oriental carpet as they enthusiastically strutted about, loudly proclaiming, "B-o-w-l-i-n-g! B-o-w-l-i-n-g!"

Once having gained entry to George and Larry's home, our Bay Area visit was thoroughly enjoyable. The four of us dined in San Francisco, at the Carnelian Room on the fifty-second floor, atop the Bank of America building. Needless to say, the views were spectacular. Fortunately, we were able to enjoy the experience before the restaurant was closed in 2010, the space being taken by a Finnish gaming company for $100 a square foot. The remodeling required the removal of 7,600 pounds of oak and mahogany paneling—a small forest.

On another evening they took us to Club Fugazi in the city to see Beach Blanket Babylon, the world's oldest musical revue. Created by Steve Silver (1944-1995), it's a campy production that follows Snow White around the world in search of her "Prince Charming." The performers wear over-sized decorative hats appropriate to the subject matter as they perform satirical songs and lampoon celebrities and political figures. BBB had replaced the female impersonation show at Finocchio's on Broadway Street—a must-see for tourists visiting San Francisco in the '60s while I was attending the university there. Finocchio's closed in 1999 after a run that stretched all the way back to the mid '30s.

After such a delightful beginning to the relationship between us and Larry and George, we all agreed a trip to Alaska should be next. Not only did Larry and George travel north to Alaska the next summer, they also brought Uncle Max along. Uncle Max was the aforementioned "honorary" type of uncle, not a real one, and lived in Hollywood.

Max was a longtime key grip and had worked on many a movie set— he knew a lot of Hollywood stars. He had also been a previous lover of George's and was older than either Larry or George. In appearance, compared to Larry and George, Max looked like a movie star prize fighter, and he had a deep, resonant voice. He was literally a man's man—and funny.

They all were met at the airport by Shelli, me and my sister Pat, who marched back and forth in her Scottish garb on the sidewalk outside the airport playing the bagpipes. It was an auspicious beginning to a grand but flawed Alaskan adventure.

I was regularly running long distances with a friend of mine, Glenn Cooper, and while we stretched under the second-story kitchen window of our condo in Woodside East in Anchorage before starting our runs, we would verbally spar with one another as sophomoric guys do. The less in the mood we were for the run, the worse it got, especially if we were hung over.

"You're ugly, Boy!"

"Eat me!

"Up yours!"

"Bend over!"

Shelli had heard us from the second story kitchen window on more than one occasion and warned us, "When my Uncle Larry and George get here, no bend over jokes! Promise me!"

Imagine her surprise when nearly the first thing out of Uncle Max's mouth was, "If you don't like my face, fuck it!"

He proudly claimed never to have had sex with a female explaining that what he did was fellate guys while masturbating himself.

Larry explained, "We're not going to put on an act for you. We're going to be ourselves and you should do likewise—no holds barred."

So, the rules were set. There were no rules, at least not on our end of the visits.

During a recent auction in support of industry initiatives to advance the culinary arts of young Alaskans, I had purchased an in-home dinner for eight prepared by UAA professor and master chef, Dieter Doppelfeld. We invited Don and Vivian MacInnes, our neighbors and parents of Shelli's best friend, Debbie, to join us. The meal was outstanding and accompanied by several bottles of first growth Burgundies and Bordeaux. In a photo of Vivian and Larry at the long wooden table in our dining room, Larry is obviously in his element. He had a taste for the finer things in life, including expensive French wines.

After a couple of nights in Anchorage we drove to Homer and crossed the bay to Halibut Cove. Glenn came along for the ride. Arrangements in Halibut Cove at the time, June of 1986, were rustic. We had no floating dock or stairway leading up to our wall tent, which was situated on a knoll overlooking the Halibut Cove narrows. Access was gained by anchoring the *Shelli Bird*, our 22-foot Boston Whaler Revenge, offshore. Then we rowed a rubber raft to our rocky beach and climbed up a steep, narrow trail through the woods to the wall tent. Larry derisively referred to the trail as "Goat Hill."

The wall tent was pretty cramped, with a homemade ¾ inch plywood bed, a sink, and a small table. There was, however, electricity, cold running water and an AstroTurf floor—even a small wine cellar. We had converted a smaller-size wall tent from a tool shed to a guest tent for George and Larry. Uncle Max and Cooper slept in a two-man tent between the guest tent and the outdoor shower, which was attached to the wall tent by a wooden walkway through the woods. This was before the spruce bark beetles had laid waste to the big trees so we were surrounded by an old-growth forest. It was a magical setting.

Of course, there was joking about Cooper and Max overnighting in the same tent.

"Coop. Sleep with your shorts on backwards?"

Max liked his morning coffee and he was an early riser. The coffee pot was in our wall tent, so Max would wander about outside early in the morning singing, "Good morning to you! Good morning to you! We're all in our places, with sun-shiny faces; Oh, this is the way we start a new day!" It was the "Good Morning" children's school song, written by Abbie Farwell Brown and Ernst Richter.

No matter. I would shout out from our tent, "Shut the fuck up, Max!"

Once Max was given control of the coffeepot, the Halibut Cove portion of the visitation went well in spite of the rugged accommodations. But Larry was definitely ready for a more civilized venue well before that part of the trip was over.

On the way to and from Halibut Cove, we visited with a friend of mine named Micki Koblyk (1952-2008) who lived near Soldotna. Micki was a first-class character and a queen in her own right. She had three retorts to just about everything: (1) "Life's a bitch and then you die." (2) "I'm not stupid, you know." And (3) I can't remember for the life of me. The guys were entranced by Micki and delighted in mimicking her retorts as Nino and Natasha might have done.

It used to take us three days to drive from Anchorage to Homer because we would overnight with Micki at her home on a little lake south of Soldotna, sometimes finishing up the previous night's game of Trivial Pursuit while sitting on her porch in the morning sunshine. Then we'd spend the remainder of that day recuperating and continue driving south the third day.

In the early '80s Micki owned a small bar named the Night Watch on the banks of the Kenai River. The place had all female bartenders and totally rocked. Local detractors called it the "Nit Witch." She also owned the only liquor store in Soldotna. Between the two operations, Micki was rolling in dough. Then she expanded the bar at great expense, making it into a larger, fancier operation that offered an upscale menu and live entertainment.

The economy soured, the business was trying to be too many things in a limited number of square feet, and it eventually ate her lunch. Safeway was finally successful in getting a package store license, despite years of Micki fighting their efforts, so she now had competition on that front.

After losing the Night Watch she operated in another, smaller location for a while, finally gave up, and returned to school to earn an accounting degree at the University of Alaska Fairbanks. She was really turning her life around when, at age 57, she was killed in a head-on collision with a sixteen-wheeler on the Sterling Highway.

In tribute to the "Great Race of Mercy," the delivery of serum to Nome to combat a diphtheria epidemic in 1925, the Iditarod Trail Sled Dog Race or "Last Great Race" was established in 1973. The diphtheria antitoxin was originally delivered to Nenana by train and thence to Nome by dogsled. Today, the entire 1,049 miles is run with a ceremonial start in Anchorage. Then they pack everything up and head 45 miles north to Wasilla, where the real race starts. That lifesaving epic delivery is commemorated by a statue of Balto—the lead sled dog during the last leg of the journey—which sits in, of all places, Central Park, New York City.

Nascent years of the Iditarod Race were dominated by Rick Swenson who at the time of our story lived between Manley Hot Springs and Fairbanks. Rick still, to this day, holds the record of five Iditarod wins—'77, '79, '81, '82 and '91. One of Rick's major race sponsors was Chilkoot Charlie's so he and I were well-acquainted.

Shelli had been hospitalized for an emotional and psychological breakdown in December 1985. She put on a brave face, but she was still in a fragile condition when Larry, George, and Max arrived in Alaska. No one in the group but I knew just how vulnerable she was, so there was a certain lack of understanding and empathy that prevailed when, after a few days in Halibut Cove, she and I, Larry, George, Max, Cooper, and my son, Michael, all headed north to Manley Hot Springs to do some pike fishing on the Tanana River. I drove the motor-home carrying Shelli, Larry, George, and Max while Cooper drove his pickup with Michael as a passenger.

Our very capable fishing guide was Frank Gurtler, who had taught school with my dad at Central Junior High School in Anchorage and would later guide our *Playboy* magazine friends. Frank and his wife, Diane, lived on the Tanana Slough and their home could be reached on one side by water or the other side by road. From Manley you drove along the right side of the gravel airstrip and passed a number of driveways before getting to Frank's log cabin.

I surmise, in order to protect his neighbors from clueless fishermen, he had posted crudely painted signs on the driveways encountered before reaching his own that read, one after the other: "Keep Driving to Frank's Place," "Not Frank's Place Yet," "You're Still Not There Yet," "Getting Close," and "You've Arrived!," with an arrow pointing to Frank's Place.

Everyone enjoyed catching big, ferocious pike—an underrated culinary delight—but after a week or so of fishing, sightseeing, rumbling over bumpy dirt roads, living in close quarters, conserving water in the motor-home shower, and basically fending for ourselves aside from a brief visit to the comforts of the Manley Roadhouse, relations became a little strained.

Shelli, in manic mode one morning, picked an abundance of bouquets of wild flowers for the motor-home, had a massive allergic reaction and became sick, incapacitated and ill-tempered, which in turn prompted Larry to become the easily-provoked, it's-all-about-me flaming queen, who did not handle deprivations of any sort very well and sorely needed a shower with lots of hot water. The relationship between Shelli and Larry never entirely overcame the series of events that unfolded. There was a lot of acting out—read drama—with some very unkind words expressed by Uncle Larry, and I was caught smack-dab in the middle of it.

Fortunately we were on the return end of the trip to Interior Alaska, and early on the morning of the drive from Manley back to Fairbanks, we stopped to visit with Rick Swenson at his homestead/placer mine/ dog racing kennel. It was totally off the grid, but with every accommodation including a shower with limitless hot water. There were six men in our party and one woman, Shelli, but there was no question who was going to have the first go at that shower. We all wanted "His Larryness" to have anything he/she desired in order to descend from his/her big black cloud, he/she having been, on top of everything else, complaining vociferously about the rationing of water in the motor-home shower.

The rest of us were all in the kitchen having coffee. Rick, a true Renaissance man, was reading his newspaper, having shown us around the quite impressive premises that included a well-stocked machine shop where the shower was located, when Larry literally burst upon the scene. He launched out of that machine shop and into the kitchen as if acting the lead role in a Steve Silver campy drama, rising to his full height in his bathrobe, glowing from ear-to-ear, and exclaimed in a loud voice, "Oh, Rick!" throwing one arm forcefully across his chest and then the other, proclaiming, "Your shower is *simply glorious!*"

Shelli and I had worried about Rick and Larry, that is, how Rick was going to react to having a flaming queen in his house. But we need not have been concerned. As we sat there aghast at Larry's performance, especially since we had warned him about acting out in front of our host, Rick just said, "I'm glad you enjoyed it," without even looking up from his paper.

The drive back to Anchorage was strained though uneventful, and the trio flew back to California after only another night or two. I do remember spending some time sitting in my car with Max out in front of our condo, receiving a fatherly dressing-down for not insisting that others "carry their own weight."

Max supported Larry's position and spoke on Larry's behalf. Larry wrote Shelli a letter from California in which, among other things, he called her a "CUNT." It was the closest thing I ever heard to the "pot calling the kettle black." Max died not many years after his trip to Alaska, and Shelli and I visited Larry and George one more time in Marin County.

On our last night together, the four of us dined at the couple's favorite Thai restaurant. We drove separate cars and when it was time to depart, Larry walked directly from the restaurant to the passenger side of their car, got in and closed the door. I saw it for the rudeness that it was and just walked over to our car without attempting to say goodbye. Shelli walked over to their car and, while George stood aside embarrassed, Larry rolled down the window just far enough to say goodbye to his niece.

Not long after that visit Larry and George moved to Palm Springs and Shelli visited them there once. I declined the invitation, having had enough of Larry for one lifetime. He and George have both been dead for years now. Larry went first, thankfully. I cannot even imagine him soldiering on without George. There would have been a dark cloud hanging over Palm Springs that could have been seen from San Francisco. Glenn Cooper is no longer with us and as previously mentioned, neither is Micki Koblyk.

If, however, Larry or George were still around, I'm sure either of them would promptly recall Micki's third retort that for the life of us, Shelli and I can no longer remember.

Dan Lowell

"I didn't think anything could possibly make me happy today," I said to Shelli.

We had just spent our worst night ever in Halibut Cove, after learning that the plane crash site of my friend, Dan Lowell, and his girlfriend, Maureen Sims, had been located in a pass near Cooper Landing. There had been a massive week-long search by the Civil Air Patrol and numerous friends of the Lowell family who owned planes. The few people who had actually seen the crash site were now scratching their heads trying to figure out why and how it had happened.

The weather had been beautiful on the Kenai Peninsula the day of the crash. The couple left Summit Lake at 1:25 p.m. for a flight-seeing trip to Seward. The Cessna 170 on floats had nosed straight into the ground and burned up in the middle of a seemingly tranquil mountain pass. Could they have been flying too low and been hit by a sudden powerful downdraft? Possibly. No one will ever know.

Few Alaskans have not had the experience of having a family member, a loved one or at least a friend or acquaintance killed in a general aviation incident. Commercial planes do not crash in Alaska any more than they do in other states, but there have been almost 1,200 private plane accidents in Alaska over the last decade compared with an average of 351 for each of the other states. The Federal Aviation Administration, focusing on Alaska in particular, has tried to keep the number of incidents under 100 per year. Alaska has 1.313 pilots per hundred residents, more than three times the percentage of the number-two ranked state, Montana. The national average is only 0.2. The combination of rugged terrain, harsh weather conditions and the sheer number of private pilots in the air over Alaska brings these numbers home to each of us on a regular basis. It's the price we pay for getting around the state we love.

I was totally devastated by Dan's death. I had never felt more anguish, even over the motorcycle death of my fourteen-year-old nephew, Curt, decades before. I simply could not believe it. I cried and cried. I howled all night and all morning. Shelli tried to comfort me but it was pointless. When we finally crawled out of bed the following day we discovered a message on our phone from Vivian MacInnes. Vivian knew we were looking for another piece of property in the Cove.

The message said, "I know you're not interested in our property on the bluff—that you want waterfront property—but you might be interested to know that the Perkins property is going on the market."

We were astonished. Dan and Birgit Perkins were locals. Birgit had been raised in Halibut Cove. We could see their place from ours and it was less than a minute to get there by skiff. Dan had a saw mill on the other side of us and had removed some trees for us, built our floating dock and porch complex, and installed our ramp. I had visited with the Perkins on a couple of occasions, sitting in their living room where they were home-schooling their two young children, so I was familiar with the substantial structure Dan had built, as well as the extensive landscaping he had done with his bulldozer. Shelli and I might finally have a real house in which we could contemplate retirement instead of the little wall tent we had upgraded to a one-room cabin with a sleeping loft.

After some years of living in the wall tent, we were discussing the purchase of another tent and raising the walls so we could fully stand up in it. That's when Ken Kennell, my property manager at Chilkoot Charlie's, said, "You know, Mike, for not a whole lot more money I could put a real roof on this place for you."

So it had been done, including the sleeping loft, which of course gave us a lot more living space on the ground floor. The cabin was cozy enough to hang out in during the summer months, but it fell way short of a year-round residence and there was absolutely no landscaping.

We called Dan Perkins, got dressed and were over there in less than half an hour. We took a tour of the property, including the dilapidated (full to overflowing) outhouse, the huge, five-foot-high pile of leftover building materials in front of the proposed guest house, which was essentially a crate with a busted-in roof, the rudimentary but excavated lawns; then the pond and the seven-hundred-gallon handmade wooden water tank with a plastic lining on the basement floor.

Shelli, unable to locate the plumbing down there, asked Dan, "How do you get the water from the tank to the upstairs sink?"

Dan looked at her like she'd given leave of her senses and said, "In a bucket."

As our soon-to-be new neighbor, a lawyer from Anchorage, explained, the Perkins lived a "nineteenth century lifestyle." The property was a diamond in the rough. A lot of work would still be required but the potential was clearly visible.

I asked Dan what he wanted for the place. He told me.

I said "Okay," and that was that.

I wasn't going to try to bargain with him and have someone else enter the picture. Besides, I thought he was asking a fair price. Elated, we returned to our little cabin. We decided our new home in Halibut Cove was a gift from Dan Lowell and it has had a special place in our hearts ever since. In fact, it is now the retirement home we had originally envisioned, though the work required on it has turned out to be a lot more than we ever imagined.

Dan Lowell had been a member of Anchorage South Rotary. We met one day when he was visiting Anchorage Downtown Rotary, that I belong to. He walked up to me after lunch, handed me his business card and said, "If you ever need any help with your insurance, give me a call."

His father, Dick Lowell, was an owner of Ribelin, Lowell and Company, a large and successful insurance brokerage in Anchorage, as well as a member of the Downtown Rotary Club—though I did not know him well at the time. Dan was the president of the firm. Dan's timing could not have been better when he handed me that business card because I was very pissed-off at my existing insurance agent. I owned seven little log cabins on some property adjacent to the Chilkoot Charlie's parking lot to the south and one of them had burned to the ground. In the aftermath, and to my utter dismay, the one that burned down had been the only one not on the list of insured buildings.

When confronted with the unaccountable absence of the cabin's listing my insurance agent had smiled at me and said, "That's why we have the small print."

I told Dick Lowell about the incident later and he said, "These things happen. We'd have just written a check."

When I moved my business and told the other broker why, the agent lost her job. Had I had the income from that cabin from then until now (approximately twenty-five years), my income from it would have been in the neighborhood of $150,000.00. I still own the other six.

Though Dan Lowell was in his early thirties—young enough to be my son—we became close friends. Raised in Alaska on hunting and fishing, I had not been hunting for many years, so I was keenly interested when Dan asked me if I wanted to go on a caribou hunt on the Egegik River.

Anyone who has hunted in Alaska knows that virtually every hunting trip in Alaska is an adventure. Something generally goes wrong. One's success is measured not just by whether game is procured, but by whether one survives the multiple ordeals and challenges that generally accompany the effort. Furthermore, common sense and experience dictate that you don't go big game hunting with just anyone in the Alaskan wilderness.

We did have some problems on that trip. I remember the wind blowing so hard one day the plane could have become airborne from a standing start. But we overcame the problems, shot some caribou and made it home alive and in one piece. I had missed all that.

Later, Dan invited me on a deer hunting trip to Afognak and another to Old Harbor. Both were real adventures and game was acquired on both. The latter involved a very rainy, drunken night in a Kodiak bar and a flight back to Anchorage on the Cook Inlet Regional Corporation jet. The former trip was an insight into the Native logging industry in Alaska.

We slept ensconced in a comfortable double-wide trailer at a logging camp, and early each morning we would enter the mess hall with all the loggers and drivers in what seemed to me to be an early 20th century operation. I would not have been surprised to see Dan Perkins, also a logger, waiting in the line in front of me.

Rugged-looking men doffed their hats and coats upon entering, treating the middle-aged lady running the place with the utmost respect. The food was more than fit for the last supper of a man on death row. The quality and assortment boggled the mind, and then there was an equally amazing selection of items you chose to go into a brown bag to take on the road or into the woods for lunch.

Afognak Island is just north of Kodiak Island, part of the Kodiak Archipelago. It is forty-three miles from east to west, twenty-three miles north to south, and the eighteenth largest island in the United States. It is crisscrossed with a maze of two-lane unpaved logging roads, and the truck drivers hauling the downed trees at remarkable speeds over those roads used a unique method—long since forgotten by me—of telegraphing their location by CB radio to anyone else on the road. The system works. As far as I know there have been no mishaps.

I have heard a lot of negative propaganda about clear-cutting, but I can tell you after driving all over Afognak for days that, perhaps aside from the unsettling view one might have from an airplane, it seems to work just fine. We drove through recently cut woods and woods that had been cut twenty years in the past and where the cutting had been done that long ago you would never have known it. What you saw was a beautiful, youthful, healthy forested area where there had been absolutely no rehabilitative effort expended. Just for the record, I'm not taking one side or the other; I'm just reporting what I saw.

Following those trips, Dan, his dad, a few friends and I traveled to Argentina and Uruguay to do some bird hunting. Buenos Aires was our gateway city. We spent most of our time at a very nice country lodge that was one hour out of Montevideo by small plane.

If you are ever in Montevideo, be careful. One of our group had his wallet pick-pocketed by a gang of kids while out for a walk one block from our hotel. Fortunately, the Uruguayan Coast Guard discovered his wallet and passport in a garbage can the next day—sans cash of course. It sounds hard to believe but another of our group had one of his suit-cases stolen at the airport while he waited with it in the check-in line.

But the bird hunting was fantastic. I had never hunted over dogs before and hunting perdiz, an upland game bird, was about as good as it gets. I can still hear the Uruguayan dog handlers calling "Hut, hut!" to the border collies as they chased the birds through six-inch-high ground cover. The calls restrained the dogs from flushing the birds too far out in front of us. Perdiz are very fast little birds and flush mostly in singles, doubles and triples. I got a lot of singles, and a few doubles, but never quite managed to bag the coveted triple.

Dan had Hollywood-actor good looks and bright eyes that flashed full of life: he captured the attention of anyone and everyone in a room of people. No one, least of all me, ever expected a life so exuberant and confident to be snuffed out so early. We all know that "only the good die young" is a bit of an overstated generalization, but in the case of Dan Lowell it struck a chord with everyone who knew him.

I got a call from my night manager at Chilkoot's at 1:00 a.m., the morning after the memorial was held in the Captain Cook Hotel. I was already in bed.

He said, "You need to come over to the club. There's a little group including Dan and Dan's dad over here in the Swing Bar having a toast and a cigar."

I said, "I'll be right there."

I found the group sitting at the bar having a drink and smoking cigars. Dan was there too. That is to say, his remains were in a box atop the bar with a shot of whiskey and a cigar next to it. It seemed kind of bizarre, but we had all cried our fill. It was time for a final tribute to a guy we all dearly loved.

Yearly hunting and fishing trips to South America continued with Dick and a core group of Dan's friends with the inevitable toasts to his remembrance. Dick and I became close friends and remained so until his death in 2015. South Rotary held an annual Dan Lowell Scholarship Fundraiser at Chilkoot Charlie's for many years. Some years they asked me to recite again the panegyric I had written for Dan's memorial.

Toast to Dan Lowell

Dan, my dear young friend, surely none of us thought we would ever be toasting you under these circumstances. Some fine achievement, yes, or some happy moment in your life, but never, ever, this.

You've shaken our sensibilities to the core. You've called upon us to gather here in your memory instead. We're barely up to the task but for knowing that in doing so we all share in your grace (becoming better human beings) more kind, more loving, more thoughtful, more understanding, as if borrowing from your extraordinary reservoir of these qualities.

You faced life head-on, Dan. You were never fearful—or even hesitant. You dealt with life's challenges with alacrity, as if you felt they were offered on a level playing field and you were just playing the game of life.

Quite simply, you were one of the finest human beings any of us here have ever known and we're going to miss you terribly. You were so handsome, magnetic, cheerful and energetic, whether dressed to go hunting or fishing or in your double-breasted suit taking care of business, those big bright eyes sparkling, just like a little kid.

We all have to go sometime and at least you left us on a beautiful Alaskan afternoon doing something you loved—flying. I know it'll be easier for me when my time comes knowing that I might get to go flying with you just one more time.

Here's to you, Dan. You were a good man and a wonderful friend. We all loved you dearly and you will never be forgotten. Whenever we see a rainbow, a beautiful sunset or moonlight shimmering across the water, we'll be reminded of that sparkle in your eyes.

September 7, 1999

Captain Cook Hotel

"Doctor Bob" Warren

I lived next to Dr. Bob, (Robert E. Warren, 1948-2015) for almost half my life. We both chose the convenient close-in urban condo lifestyle of Woodside East so when I say next door, I mean *right next door*, separated by a common wall.

Initially, we lived in spacious two-bedroom units that backed up to Lake Otis Boulevard. I was still married to my second wife, Tiffany, the ex-go-go dancer who had assured me the baby was mine, but that's another story already covered in *Learning the Ropes*.

Years later, in the mid-1980s, the developer, whose name I won't dignify by mentioning it, decided to improve on some bluff lots in our subdivision that overlooked the Chester Creek greenbelt, with a view of Denali to the north. Bob and I were both doing well financially, so we each bought one of these much larger units excited to be able to completely personalize the inside layout and décor. We were once again right next door to one another, with Bob on the right and me on the left, which was apropos, because although I'm not exactly what you'd call a "bleeding heart liberal," I was definitely to the left of Dr. Bob.

The developer was a jerk and the construction phase was a cluster. I can still hear Dr. Bob imitating him with, "But, Bob, you've got such a beautiful home," emphasis on Bob and beautiful, or "But, Bob, it's only a closet," emphasis on Bob and only.

Shelli, who was now living with me, and I heard the same lame excuses for screw-ups and poor workmanship over and over ourselves. The general manager on the job was a loser ex-banker who couldn't have successfully organized a cock fight in Port-au-Prince. The job site was a sloppy mess, with subcontractors coming and going in no particular order and stepping over each other every day. Lights were left on all night. We would stop on our way home, turn the lights out and try to clean up some of the ever-present mess. A lot of time and money was lost and quality sacrificed in the disarray and total lack of coordination.

Bob and I did end up with beautiful homes, but it was in spite of, rather than because of, the developer and his flunky. We had fun "borrowing" ideas from one another. Most of the "borrowing" was done by Bob so it was fun to have something to needle him about. Of course he could not devote his full time to the construction site like Shelli, who could operate her own construction company or walk into her own interior decorating business overnight. And she misses *nothing, ever.*

You would think a guy that owned a rowdy bar in Spenard would be more likely to be a problem neighbor than a gay dentist. Not so, and it starts with Bob owning the sweetest female golden retriever for years. She moved down the street with Bob when we both rebuilt. Her name was Samantha and she died, as dogs tend to do, so Bob replaced her with a black Labrador retriever he named Pinot. I never saw the pedigree paperwork, but I assume that name was short for Pinot Noir.

Bob was an oenophile. He taught an informative, interesting wine class on the University of Alaska campus. I know this because I took it. Bob was an expert in and on anything he took a fancy to, including stamp collecting and golf.

David, Bob's "nephew," was now living next door with Bob and they were a couple of very busy guys, which meant Bob's young, energetic dog was alone a lot, penned up in a tiny chain-fenced kennel behind their condo. Bob would place the dog back there in the morning and head off to work. I worked until 3 a.m., so right about the time I was about to get some meaningful sleep the dog would start crying and barking—non-stop, right under my bedroom window.

I complained a couple of times, but dog owners you may have noticed, have selective hearing when it comes to their beloved four-legged household members. I wrote a reproving note to Bob and stuck it in his mailbox. One could not have mistaken my feelings, and I warned I was going to just start letting the dog loose if the annoyance continued.

Nothing changed. The routine continued—and the annoyance. Now feeling totally ignored and abused, I followed through with my threat. I could not figure out why Bob was ignoring my plight, much less Pinot's, and Bob could not figure out how his dog kept getting out of its confinement under my window. It no doubt would have helped if we were communicating, but we were not.

We all dined and socialized at Jens' Restaurant and Bodega a lot at the time and Jens Hansen, the Danish proprietor, delighted in hearing the latest tidbits from each side. To him the whole conflict was hilarious. When I would walk in it was the first thing he wanted to know: "How is Pinot?" he would inquire with a devilish twinkle in his eyes as he peered at me over his multi-colored reading glasses.

Although by no means an exoneration, it came to light that the letter had fallen between the mailbox and the wall and Bob had never actually received it. Eventually the dog got hit by a car, fortunately not seriously injured, and I admitted letting it loose. Receiving the, "Nice going, Gordon" routine, I responded that I had been left no choice. Fortunately the unopened letter was soon discovered, Bob apologized, and we all got over the affair and on with our lives.

The other problem we had, and there were only two—that I know of—was that Bob installed his gigantic living room speakers on the wall adjoining my unit. I had to call him on occasion because the head of my bed was right up against that wall and the bass would be literally moving my bed covers.

There was an even bigger offender than Bob who used to house-sit or get his hands on the volume control during a visit. I would call over to ask for the music to be turned down expecting Bob to answer, and the person who picked up the phone would be none other than Van Hale, one of the owners of the Marx Brothers Café, an Anchorage dining institution. I never knew Van had such a penchant for loud music. Van, incidentally, had also been the "preacher" who had married Shelli and me in a hot air balloon over Anchorage on a beautiful autumn day in 1983.

One night, Bob and David had a "coming out" party next door. A lot of our mutual friends were there, so I joined in. It was no surprise. Everyone knew Bob and David were a couple—everyone except Shelli—that is. Bob had told Shelli that David was his nephew, so she believed him.

When I told her about the party she was practically in tears, saying, "I feel so naïve. Am I the only person in town who thought David was actually Bob's nephew?"

"Pretty much," I said.

Van and his wife, Nicki, have done a lot more traveling with Bob and David than Shelli and I have, but we did take a trip with them to the Central Coast wine country a few years ago. We all stayed at the Turley House and flipped a coin for the larger of the two bedrooms. Fortunately Bob won because if Bob's not happy, nobody is going to be happy.

It was a great trip. We had some excellent meals, and one notably bad one. We toured a lot of wineries, visited the amazing Hearst Castle and watched the sea lions basking in the open air on the long stretch of Pacific Coast sandy beach. At Bob's insistence we ate in one night with him cooking. He was the only one who wanted to eat in. It would have been cheaper to eat out at the French Laundry Restaurant, and it most certainly would have been less time-consuming and stressful.

Bob loved his wine and he loved his food. He was a gourmand who was not about to settle for second best, and he was one of the few people I have ever known who liked buttermilk as much as I do. I drink it every day. He told me about, and we purchased, his favorite brand with chunks of butter floating in it—the kind that is impossible to find these days. Now I am the only one in my house who *ever* drinks the stuff, so I'm used to just grabbing the carton and drinking right from it. Well, Bob caught me drinking from the carton.

"Nice...Gordon. Hey David, Shelli Bird—Gordo's drinking buttermilk straight out of the carton. Guess he couldn't find a glass." Oops.

Shelli and I have held an annual Labor Day weekend barbecue for the Homer/Kachemak Bay Rotary Club for twenty years. Club members, along with wives, husbands, special others and kids, pile into boats and come across the bay for a few hours to soak up the ambience of Halibut Cove and Shelli's gardens. I take little credit for the gardens, but I will take credit for the centrally-located rock garden and water features which, as I write, have been waterless due to the unlimited thirst of Mother Nature's porous bedrock and my inability to quench it with either cement or sealant.

Homer is a gardening community and Shelli is a well-known and respected gardener. In fact, she is more than a gardener—as I've said, she's a farmer. Dr. Bob felt as if he sat at the feet of the master each year as he and David came down to help put on the event, manning the barbecues so I was able to do some socializing instead of being tied to the grill. Bob would follow Shelli around like a docile puppy dog, looking at flowers, shrubs and compost piles while peppering her with questions and taking notes. Not surprisingly, Dr. Bob was an excellent gardener. His and David's new spacious home and grounds in Anchorage, again overlooking the greenbelt, are beautiful—worthy of a painting.

Hanging out with the best chefs in town for decades has had a similarly salutary effect on my cooking skills. I do virtually all the cooking in our home, and I am particular, but I will bend a rule once in a while, especially in Halibut Cove, where there is no store close at hand. You had to be careful with that when Dr. Bob was in the compound. I was making something that required Parmesan cheese and had the temerity to employ the use of the *pre-grated, pre-packaged* variety. Caught, red-handed, I was openly chastised before all for my wanton behavior. I felt like I'd been caught cheating on an exam or drinking buttermilk from the carton.

"Come now, Gordo, you're not going to use *that*, are you?!"

Neither David nor Bob, of course, have visited us on Labor Day weekends since Bob's death. Though I now am able to use packaged Parmesan or drink out of the buttermilk carton without fear of reprimand, you can bet whenever I do I am looking over my shoulder to make sure Dr. Bob isn't watching.

I will never forget the time I was having dinner with a young bar owner in Jens', and Dr. Bob and David approached our table on the way out. Bob was obviously drunk and I am not at all sure what prompted it, but he said something like, "Blah, blah, blah, Gordon, you cocksucker!"

David, shocked, turned on him and said, "Who are you to be talking!"

The young bar owner, also shocked, had never seen Mr. Gordon talked to like that.

I just looked at Bob, recognized that he was drunk, took no offense and continued eating my meal.

David told me later he thought, "Well, that's the last time we'll ever visit Halibut Cove."

It was not, and in spite of Dr. Bob's eccentricities he was a wonderful, fun, intelligent, and caring human being whose last act was trying to help another person who had fallen ill while on a trip with David to view manta rays at night in Hawaii.

"Sealskin" Charlie McAlpine

A Brahmin is a member of the highest caste in Hinduism. They are the caste from which Hindu priests are drawn. They teach and maintain sacred knowledge. Charlie was an Alaskan Brahmin. He was also one of the most self-assured, shameless, interesting, funny, entertaining, magnanimous, intelligent, endearing, frustrating, unscrupulous and contradictory people I have ever known. He was a bit of a hustler and con man: a lovable scoundrel, a breed of Alaskan passing into history with the speed of WW II soldiers, women who blush, and bankers who make loans based on the character of the borrower.

We used to dine out together all the time. Charlie thought Jens' Restaurant was "a good place to be seen." He always sat at the table by the front door, to the right as you enter. One night as we sat down at Jens' I said to Charlie, "Intelligent, charming, sensitive, gracious, humble, generous... Well, enough about me. Let's talk about you for a while, Charlie." He liked that.

"Good one, Gordon!" It wasn't often that you got one over on Charlie, and he had a high-pitched giggle when something delighted him.

The female staff in the restaurants loved Charlie. A totally bald septuagenarian with a glass eye and a limp, from childhood polio, he could charm any female in any establishment. He also always graciously allowed them to take his coat, hat and scarf when he came in and tipped generously upon leaving. They generally knew who I was also, but I was with Charlie; he wasn't with me.

Charles Frederick McAlpine (1932-2019), was born in Aitkin, Minnesota to Stanley and Irene (Duross) McAlpine. He was raised in Flint, Michigan, where his parents were friends with many owners of General Motors Company. After graduating from the University of Michigan, Charlie worked for General Motors Company's overseas operation until his wanderlust took him out west.

Charlie first traveled to California where he met Glenn Yarborough, lead singer of The Limelighters. Being a naturally gifted singer himself, Charlie managed the group while living in the Bay Area. Next, he went to Aspen, Colorado, living the life of a ski bum, residing at the ski-in/ski-out Little Nell Resort.

Charlie's zest for an adventuresome life naturally drew him to Alaska. Arriving in 1963, he first worked at Alyeska Resort and Crow Creek Mine under Arnie Erickson. He bought a Cessna Super Cub and quickly taught himself how to fly. Then he headed for the Arctic. Operating out of his home base of Nome, where he owned and operated the Anchor Bar, Charlie flew his Super Cub to the many Native villages to trade modern tools, clothing, and equipment for Native art and artifacts. He developed a deep, lifelong respect for the Elders in many of the villages.

Dr. David Beal, who was at the same time examining the eardrums of Native children in the same villages to ascertain the type and amount of ear diseases, spent a bit of time with Charlie at his Anchor Bar in Nome. Dr. Beal recently told me how Charlie got the moniker "Sealskin" Charlie, a story I had never heard before.

According to Dr. Beal, as Charlie flew in and out of the villages, he noticed that walrus and seal skins were being left on the ground to rot. When he made inquiries as to why, he discovered that all the older women who knew how to prepare the pelts for clothing or other uses had died off without passing on this vital information.

Charlie soon visited an Athabaskan village in the Yukon Delta, found a lady who knew how to do the job, and flew her to the northern villages to teach their women how to tan the skins and turn them into gloves and footwear. The undertaking was a win/win for Charlie and the villages. One can only imagine the impact it must have had on the village economies. Some villages that had been patriarchal became matriarchal. Dr. Beal ascertained that there was a great love for Charlie, who treated the Natives fairly and would loan them money at no interest in their times of need.

I do not remember exactly when Charlie and I met. It was probably in 1968, when I was part-owner of the Bird House Bar in Bird, on the Seward Highway on the way to Girdwood. I operated the bar, which was cobbled together out of buildings left over from railroad construction, with my partners Norman Rokeberg and Johnny Tegstrom. We ran the place from December 1967 to December 1968 at which point we sold it to Dick Delak.

I certainly knew Charlie in the early years of my Chilkoot Charlie's operation which I opened on January 1, 1970. By that time Charlie was well-established in his trading operations in the Arctic, and in the process of relocating to Anchorage.

Charlie had a concrete block building which I believe had previously been a church on the north side of 15th Avenue just east of Gambell

Street. He took me in there one day and showed me a bedroom-size room that was full to capacity with oosiks. That is when I first comprehended the scale of his trading operation.

At the time Charlie was probably doing more trading with the Arctic Natives than anyone else, which is doubtless what brought him to the attention of the feds. Once you get into their crosshairs they will use any means, legal or otherwise, to bring you down. If they cannot put you behind bars they will break you financially. They have unlimited resources and there are never any consequences for them it seems, no matter how egregious their own behavior.

As far as I know they never got a conviction on Charlie, but they spared no effort and dragged him through the bowels of hell. They did the same thing to Joe Hendricks, Alaska's senior big game guide, who was also a friend of mine.

I had my own run-in with the feds when one of our bartenders married a waitress of ours from New Zealand. My business partner at the time, Doran Powell, officiated the event on the north side of Chilkoot Charlie's.

A customs and immigration investigator threatened to charge me and Doran with defrauding the United States government. He contended that the girl had married the guy just to stay in the country and that we had been co-conspirators. I didn't take the matter very seriously at first because it seemed so silly and inconsequential.

I will never forget the look on the guy's face. He was dead serious. He spent days digging through every one of our employee files, and we were fined for any that were incomplete in any minute way. Admittedly, the girl had not crossed the water in a flimsy boat from Haiti, or swum across the Rio Grande, but she certainly had as much right to be in this country as those who did.

Good grief. A bar in Spenard, Alaska? A New Zealander? Defrauding the United States government? What the hell for? It's not like we were looking for cheap labor to pick fruit or even to wash dishes. And the bartender and girl were in love as far as I knew. In any event she was taken into custody and deported. Smacks of a bizarre plot in a Tom Robbins novel.

Charlie was a hustler and a natural entrepreneur. Even during his last days, suffering from dementia, he would talk enthusiastically to our mutual friend, Tony Lewkowski, and me about going to Nome. He was back in the day.

Sitting in the daylight basement apartment of his caregiver's home, in his pajamas Charlie would say, "I'm going to Nome. You guys should come with me. We'll buy a bar and make a ton of money!"

Tony would ask, "When are you leaving, Charlie?"

Charlie would reply, "As soon as possible. Tomorrow morning. Pack your bags!"

"Alright, Charlie. What should I bring?"

It was so amusing, because it was so like Charlie, and it was so sad, because he was so excited and energized. But Charlie wasn't going anywhere.

For the longest time my wife Shelli lived full-time in Homer or Halibut Cove and I spent half my time in Anchorage taking care of business, so I was always looking for someone to go out with. Charlie and I became pretty much constant companions—for years. Our friendship became more than just a casual one and it meant a lot to me.

When I still operated Chilkoot Charlie's, the club sponsored the weekly Thursday Night Fights that took place at the downtown Egan Convention Center during the winter months. I would get free ringside seats for myself and whomever I might want to bring along. Charlie and I were regulars. We would have a nice dinner at Ginger—a half block to the east on Fifth Avenue—and then walk over during the warm-up fights. Sometimes we would be accompanied by Tony Lewkowski or another close friend, Joe Columbus. Those were fun guys' nights out.

I hung in there with Charlie during an awful period when he suffered from an eye infection inflicted upon him by a dentist who punctured his nasal cavity during a dental procedure. The subsequent infection cost Charlie his eye. It was the only time I had ever seen Charlie when he was suicidal. He suffered terribly with that eye infection. I insisted that he had a legal case against the dentist, but he never would pursue it, not that he couldn't have used the money.

For a while Charlie managed, and lived in, a low-end trailer court in Spenard where the tenants were renters, not owners, so he had his hands full collecting rents and combating illicit activities. He was up to the task. He would answer the door with a pistol in his hand. When Tony Lewkowski and I would visit, we would holler, "It's Mike and Tony. Don't shoot!" as we rang the doorbell. Tony got so worried that Charlie was going to do something regrettable with that pistol that he took the bullets out of it and hid them, even at the risk that if Charlie ever found out he might never talk to him again.

Then there was "Charlie's Coffee Shop," downtown in the old Club 25. Charlie had the best-looking female baristas in Anchorage, mostly ring girls he had conscripted from the Thursday Night Fights. Charlie invested the usual level of enthusiasm into the enterprise and, of course, a codependent relationship with the girls. Charlie also sold art pieces out of the coffee shop, and it was fun watching him interact with his girls and the public.

Charlie used to say, "I'm a river to my friends." He certainly was to me. He used to actually promote me. He introduced me to all of his most wealthy friends and he had a lot of them. "Mike Gordon is not your average bar owner," he would announce with his high-pitched giggle.

I appreciated his vocal sentiment because I have never liked being pigeon-holed. What I do, or did for a living is not nearly the entirety of who or what I am.

Charlie saw me for who I am. He talked about the "giants" he knew (he knew a lot of them) as a passing breed. Many were members of the very exclusive San Francisco Bohemian Club and Rancheros Visitadores. Elmer Rasmuson, founder of National Bank of Alaska, was another of Charlie's best friends. Charlie included me in that group.

He would say, "There aren't many of us left, Gordon. People like you and me; we're a dying breed."

I would probably have been a little uncomfortable hanging out with the likes of Charlie's "giants," but it felt good to be told that I should. Charlie pestered me relentlessly for years to join The Bohemian Club and Rancheros. I probably should have, but I was busy doing my own thing and I just wasn't that interested. Charlie did, however, sponsor my membership in the prestigious New York Explorers Club.

Charlie's number one devotion in life was to his son, Cullen. For Cullen no effort was spared. Charlie made sure that Cullen got the best grade school education available in Anchorage by enrolling him in Holy Rosary Academy. Charlie then got Cullen into St. Paul's Academy, one of the best and most prestigious college prep schools in the nation and finally, he made sure that he got Cullen into Harvard, from which Cullen graduated in 2011, the same year I finally graduated (46 years late) from the University of San Francisco.

Charlie used to harp on Cullen about the same clubs he wanted me to join, and finally did get Cullen to join the San Francisco Yacht Club which, of great importance to Charlie, gave you access to the New York Yacht Club.

Not an ounce of the effort or a dollar expended on Cullen was wasted. I have often described Cullen as "the finest young man I've ever met." My wife, Shelli, agrees wholeheartedly.

Shelli, a genealogy sleuth, advised Cullen to preserve Charlie's DNA and provided him with a sample kit for which he reimbursed her during the next sale by purchasing a replacement kit. Cullen administered the kit to his father a few days later and when the results were in Cullen and Shelli determined that Charlie had another son no one knew about. His name is Jamie Nachinson and he lives in Jerusalem, Israel.

When I first saw his picture I said, "Wow! There's no doubt about who his father is!" Jamie was able to travel to Alaska and meet Charlie before Charlie's death, and Cullen was able to meet his half-brother, both of whom were only children.

Charlie had three long-lasting avocations. First was his extensive trading with the Natives in the Arctic. Another was his real estate brokerage business, and lastly, he was a curator and appraiser of fine art.

Charlie was the middle-man in a lot of art transactions involving mostly Alaskan masters like Laurence, Ziegler, Lambert, Machetanz, Heurlin, Dahlager, and the like. He was also an appraiser for the Anchorage Museum. I always owed Charlie money for years. It went like this:

Charlie would pull up in front of my office and start laying pieces of art on my lawn from the trunk of his car.

"Gordon, look at these nice pictures."

"Those are nice, Charlie. I particularly like that Lambert, but I don't have any money."

"That's okay, pal. Just pay me when you feel like it."

Charlie described these transactions as "a dollar down and the chase is on!"

Of course Charlie knew I would always pay him, and I always did. Shelli and I have a very nice collection of paintings by Alaskan masters, many purchased from Charlie.

Once, while walking behind me on the way into a restaurant, Charlie noticed that my legs are short. He thought that was pretty funny. No one had ever said anything to me about it, but it is true. I explained that it might be the result of having survived scarlet fever as a child. I would get into the car and he would start chuckling.

I'd say, "Shut the fuck up, Charlie. At least I'm not a bald-headed old Cyclops. And I don't limp."

Charlie was homophobic and anti-Semitic; he would make off-color embarrassing jokes about both. He would frequently suggest that I or other male friends wear their best dress or their pink underwear, or that he would do so, for a dinner date. I would criticize Charlie for his sophomoric attempts at humor and he admitted that Elmer (Rasmuson) had not liked them either, but he just couldn't help himself. He made the pink panty suggestion to me in front of Shelli one time, though, and that was the last time he did that.

It was so perfect that Charlie ended up having a son who is a practicing Jew in Israel. It would have been even more perfect had he turned out to be gay, but he didn't.

Charlie's jokes were not always funny. His businesses did not make millions like many of his friends. He did not always play by the same rule book as the rest of us, and he perhaps had a higher opinion of himself than was appropriate. But Charlie always paid his own way if he could and was generous to a fault. He was mostly charming and good company, he lived a life of adventure few can parallel, he rubbed shoulders with "giants," and he was truly a river to his friends.

Some of those friends returned the favor by generously, and with alacrity, supporting Charlie financially in his later years. Charlie wasn't embarrassed by that. He was proud of it.

"Polka Dan" Zantek

Dan Zantek (1935-2019), aka "Polka Dan," aka "Poke Her Dan," was my pal. To him I was "Mountain Man." We had a brotherly relationship that was intimate but respectful. It was fun but serious, but not too much of either; and it was seasoned with years of growth rings like a couple of old-growth spruce trees from Girdwood. At a certain point our trunks joined. It was Dan's initiative. He sort of adopted me, and I enjoyed his company.

Dan was the genuine article—24 karat. He was no "fair weather" friend. If Dan was your friend you could count on him. That big heart of his was pure gold. He truly cared about people and had little patience for those who did not. He was worldly and could spot a phony or a con man from a mile off. He could smell bullshit before it hit the ground.

When Charlie McAlpine had his real estate brokerage operation in Anchorage on Fireweed Lane Dan hung his license there. He and Charlie were friends also, but they were too much alike to be close friends. Charlie thought Dan didn't work hard enough, that he spent all of his time doing things for no money. As the broker, I guess Charlie might be forgiven to have felt that way. On the other hand, Dan didn't need to make a lot of money, having earned multiple pensions. He enjoyed his lifestyle, and thought Charlie was a sometimes annoying, but useful, putz.

I have a foggy remembrance of the real old days in Girdwood—the mid to late '60s and early '70s. Being an owner of the Bird House Bar I spent most of my time sloshing cocktails over the slanted bar, placing them gently on slightly wetted "skid-proof" toilet paper napkins in Bird Creek.

But I did find time to party at the Double Musky Inn in the early days when Julian Maule operated it and he and Dan played concertinas together. Julian, the original owner of the Double Musky, was a big, fun man like Dan. Another friend and character from those early days, John Trautner, was on the scene to accompany Dan with his one-string gutbucket.

Dan had graduated from Northland College in Ashland, Wisconsin. He majored in social studies and minored in piano. He traveled north to Alaska after the 1964 Great Alaskan Earthquake in search of job opportunities, soon settled in Girdwood and began regularly playing his concertina at the Double Musky Inn. Dan had lived in Girdwood for fifteen years when he at last moved to Anchorage.

The man was a master at the concertina and never went anywhere without one. He had played from the age of seven. When his older brother, Louie, left for military service he told Dan, "Don't touch my concertina!" Of course Dan immediately picked it up, started playing and never stopped. On September 16, 2017, Dan was inducted into the World Concertina Congress Hall of Fame.

"For me, it's quite an honor," he said.

Dan was fluent in Russian and Polish and honked "kordeen", his concertina, all over the world, mostly in Russia and Europe. We enjoyed talking about our travels; Russia travels in particular.

You have to envy the way Dan died. He went to sleep at age 83 and never woke up. His friend Joyce (Lu) Haugstead found him the next day. He always said the way he wanted to go was "in the saddle." Though he wasn't that lucky, he took the next best thing.

Not long before Dan died he showed up at a book signing for my memoir, *Learning the Ropes*, at Writer's Block Café on Spenard Road. Dan was part of a small group that had read my working manuscript. He played for the little crowd that had formed while a trio from Nashville, fronted by Tim Easton, was setting up.

Dan had also brought a couple of new friends with him, Ralph Chancy and Barry Haught who were visiting from Tampa, Florida. I am still in contact with Ralph. I'm not sure how they all met, but the two men had been to Denali and elsewhere, and Dan had taken it upon himself to be their guide while they were in Anchorage. The trio from Nashville that had come up to play the Salmonfest Alaska Music Festival in Ninilchik, was fantastic. We all stayed for their entire performance that night.

After the book signing and entertainment I followed Dan and his two new friends to the Imperial Palace Restaurant, across the street from the small plane airport of Merrill Field. I hadn't even known the place was there, but Dan knew the proprietress and had been a patron since they had moved from a downtown location. The restaurant has since permanently closed its doors. Probably nobody but Dan could find it.

Dan loved to entertain at "Koot's," always placing a heavy nasal emphasis on those two "o"s. He even held his 70th and 80th birthday celebrations there. He would pack the South Side bar on an off night with elderly patrons that still liked to party and dance the polka. His memorial at the Moose Club on Arctic Boulevard was packed as well and provided a polka band in which his girlfriend, Lu, played concertina and ukulele. Shelli and I attended, and I saw people there I hadn't seen in many years.

Though best known for playing his concertina, Dan had held a variety of jobs during his long life. He boasted he had never held a job for more than five years. He worked as a welder, a lineman, an electrician, a teacher, a bricklayer, a counselor and a car salesman. He also worked as a real estate salesman during my last years running Chilkoot Charlie's.

Dan knew I was struggling with the business and wanted to sell, so he worked at putting together a deal with Carlos' n Charlie's, a big restaurant chain out of Cancun, Mexico that owns and operates casual restaurants mostly in Mexico and the Caribbean. They typically have rustic atmospheres and fun environments, so it seemed like it might be a good fit. Unfortunately, nothing came of it.

When I still operated Chilkoot Charlie's, Dan and Lu used to come in pretty regularly for a beer in the afternoon. Dan would sometimes bring an old friend with him. Dan and Lu were always a very close couple and fun to be around. I didn't get to see them as much, of course, after I sold the place and moved full-time to Halibut Cove.

When I did see them we talked about the two of them visiting Shelli and me in the Cove and Dan playing his concertina at The Saltry Restaurant. I pestered them to do it while Dan could still manage the 105 steps from the dock up to the house. In retrospect, I should have been more insistent. Dan would have been a big hit at The Saltry or the Halibut Cove Experience Gallery, and he would have loved the Cove and the people who inhabit it.

Wicked Wanda

Of all the characters over the decades that have bartended at Chilkoot Charlie's, Wanda Prince is certainly one of them. She, along with her partner in crime, Anne, held down the day shift in the Bird House Bar until the new management of the place closed down daytime operations.

The original Bird House burned to the ground in 1996, but I repurchased the "Bird House Bar" name and replicated it in precise detail as part of Chilkoot Charlie's. Wanda, aka "Wicked Wanda," is also nominally the mayor of Spenard. Orion, a local musician who competed with Wanda for the dubious title, recently said to me, "She runs a wicked campaign!"

Dynamite comes in small packages. Wanda was the bouncer at Blues Central before becoming the lead day bartender at the Bird House Bar. Short of stature but tall in the saddle, Wanda's charming southern accent and wry, in-your-face humor made her far better at defusing barroom altercations than any guy could have been. Even so, she can out-party seasoned Spenard imbibers half her age and at present shows no signs of slowing down, much less the need to.

When Girls Gone Wild visited Anchorage and filmed partying ladies in the Bird House Bar, Wanda—then in her eighties—showed off what spunky ladies do in those circumstances. The response was a universal, "Wow! Not bad!"

Wanda is a charter member of the Red Hat Society, Spenard Chapter. I have witnessed her and her red-hatted, purple-dressed friends gallivanting around town on more than one occasion. The society, formed in 1998 and headquartered in Fullerton, California, with the motto "Red Hatters Matter," is an international organization. Its original membership was of women fifty years and over but it now allows younger women who wear pink and lavender. There are purportedly 70,000-plus members in 20,000 chapters in over 30 different countries. I suspect someday soon Wanda will be selected as the international "Top Hat," or at least "Red Hatter of the Year," a position held by Floretta Gaines in 2015.

Red Hat Society activities focus on gathering in large or small groups to have fun and support one another. Events vary depending upon the proclivities of individual chapters, but common activities are hosting tea parties, going to movies or to the theater, playing games and going on excursions to RHS conventions.

The society is dedicated to encouraging a positive outlook on life through the sisterhood of local chapters. Offhand, I cannot think of anyone with a more positive outlook on life than Wanda. Her portrait should be plastered on one end of batteries in place of the plus sign. No one who knows Wanda would be confused.

Wanda traveled a lot when I was running Chilkoot Charlie's and still holds court in the Bird House Bar, though I have heard present management is not as lenient as I was. Her soul mate and fellow traveler was Sandy Barker, who held down the day shift on the South Long Bar. When they took off, which was frequently, and usually for a week or two weeks at a time, I had to scramble to cover their shifts with back-up bartenders who were not usually as good behind their bars or as popular with our clientele. This was not an insignificant management challenge.

But, one might ask, "What is management for?"

I used to complain that Wanda and Sandy traveled more than I did; that I had the wrong job. They would travel to Las Vegas, Nashville, or some other fun destination, their notoriety no doubt preceding them, and noticeably enliven the nightlife thereabouts.

Fun begets fun and craziness begets craziness. Wanda is the one who recruited Anne as the other day shift bartender for the Bird House Bar. If any one female in the world is as suited for the craziness of that particular bar as Wanda, it is Anne, Annie Git Yer Gun, Anne Fannie, Zany Anne, you name it. She is a hoot. Both are dedicated employees who absolutely loved working in the Bird House Bar. I am certain they were devastated when the day shift came to an end. Closing the bar during the day was discussed during my reign, but I could never bring myself to do it.

Now I have to tell you a story on Wanda. She is unquestionably a wonderful bartender and draws people to the bar like salmon to their spawning grounds, but she cannot make a drinkable margarita. I make a very good margarita and was determined, since I liked to drink one once in a while, to teach Wanda how to do it right. It was a dedicated effort, but after laboring at it patiently I decided to throw in the tequila, the limes, and the towel. It would have been a lot easier to put up a sign that announced, "This is not a Mexican Restaurant, so don't order margaritas here!"

As previously noted, I am a Rotarian and my wife, Shelli, and I have hosted many Rotarians at our home across Kachemak Bay in Halibut

Cove over the years. We've donated the place for up to eight Rotarians and their spouses for a weekend, food and wine included, to raise money for the Rotary Foundation annual gala. For twenty years we have also held a Labor Day barbecue for the Homer/Kachemak Bay Rotary Club.

One year, a fellow member of Anchorage Rotary and past District Governor, Lloyd Morris, bought two nights at our place during an auction but wasn't able to make the trip. Three years later he asked if he could use his purchase by bringing a group of six visiting Russian Rotarians over for a couple of nights. Calling in your purchase three years late is not supposed to happen, but what are you going to say to a friend and fellow Rotarian who had donated serious money for the experience?

We had a ball with Lloyd, his wife Joan, and the Russians, during which time they heard all about the Russian memorabilia collection at Chilkoot Charlie's and the Bird House Bar, so they insisted that I meet them there following their visit to the Cove.

The tour was well-received. Our Russian guests were impressed with the collection, though there was one awkward moment.

Among the collection in the Soviet Walk is a large Pillars of America poster announcing a presentation to Anchorage middle and high school students by Viktor Belenko, who had absconded with his Mig-25 "Foxbat" jet fighter in 1976, landing in Japan and offering the West what George H. W. Bush, then Director of the CIA, called, "an intelligence bonanza."

One of our guests pointed at the poster and said forcefully, "This is bad man!"

After touring the Russian Rooms and the Soviet Walk we all settled into the Bird House Bar, with Wanda Prince bartending. She was in rare form.

Wanda pulled out every trick in the Bird House book of tricks. She fulfilled their selections of draft beers from the one and only keg by simply changing the pour handle to the beer they had requested. She proffered eye-watering Bird House pickles I had made myself, soaked in "hormone of wolverine" that even a seasoned Siberian flinched at the smell of. She had one of the guys call the ptarmigan with the ptarmigan whistle and sign—with the exploding pen—the book of previous ptarmigan callers, his face covered with flour from the ptarmigan whistle.

Wanda also walked them through the bumper stickers behind the bar beginning with WYOOSYOOB, "When you're out of Schlitz you're out of beer." She hoodwinked one into pushing the AOOOGA! "timber bell" button and buying a round for the house. She told stories about both the bar and me, some true and some fanciful.

Wanda even demonstrated, then sold to the Russians, several of the world-famous Bird House aprons which sport a huge, undercover male appendage that pops out when the apron is lifted up. I hear Siberian barbecues are now livelier events than ever before.

I sat across the bar from my new Russian friends and laughed until my sides ached and tears were running down my cheeks. If Shelli and I ever make it to Eastern Russia, we'll be well taken care of. That visit to Chilkoot Charlie's was the highlight of their trip to Alaska.

After Lloyd and Joan ushered the Russians, who are no doubt still talking about their two hours in Chilkoot Charlie's and the Bird House Bar, into a couple of cars to return them to the airport, Wanda turned to me, put her hands on her hips, and said loudly in her southern twang, "Now, Mr. Gordon, do you think it really matters whether I can make a margarita or not?"

I said, "No, Wanda, it certainly does not."

When my mother died, she bequeathed her gold Chilkoot Charlie ring to my wife, Shelli, who already owned one—the first ever made for a woman. Since Shelli did not need two rings, and the one from my mother was special, Shelli decided to give it to Wanda, who wears it proudly to this day.

Dale & Sherri

Dale was smarter than the average guy and one of the best bartenders I had at the time, but boy was he a handful. It was somewhere around the late '70s or early '80s. I don't believe I had yet added the Spenard Bingo Hall building to the north side of Chilkoot Charlie's, doubling the size of the club.

One of my persistent security and management problems in those days, in addition to theft, shrinkage, absenteeism, drug sales, drug usage, on premise sex, over-imbibing on the job, and workers' compensation claims, was making sure that my employees didn't use the place as a private after-hours club when we officially closed down at 5:00 a.m.

Dale Prairie, aka Prairie Dog, was as likely as anyone on the payroll to take advantage of any kind of breach in club security in order to indulge in such activity, and our security staff made sure he exited the building after he'd finished counting his banks. One morning, however, still in the mood to party and dissatisfied with being ushered outside, Dale decided to take matters into his own hands.

We had a shoulder-high Lexan window at the security station next to the main entrance. Dale pried it open and crawled in through it. The security staff was having a meeting, discussing the events of the previous evening, and here comes Dale again, a little disheveled from his creative reentry but ready to party nonetheless. He was caught and held hostage until a cab could be directed to take him home. Lots of people at the time, not just my employees, had difficulty recognizing when the party was over. Many never did figure it out and are probably still partying in their graves. The pervasiveness of cocaine was a large part of the problem.

There was a pretty Alaska Native woman named JoAnne who worked as an exotic dancer. JoAnne was not only very good-looking, she was also a contortionist, so you can imagine her popularity at the Bush Company, a strip joint on International Airport Road that was doing a land office business at the time. JoAnne was high-spirited and liked to party every bit as much as Dale Prairie and they dated for a while.

I still had my condo on the top floor of the Royal Kahana on Maui and arranged for Dale and JoAnne to use it for a vacation. I was to occupy the unit immediately after them and arrived the day they were vacating.

They had gotten into a big brawl and Dale had thrown JoAnne's suitcase from my tenth-floor lanai. Bras, panties and makeup bags were strewn all over the lawn and Joanne was in banshee mode.

One time we had Herbert Butros Khaury (1932-1996) entertain on the north side of the club. You might know him as Tiny Tim. Tiny Tim had made "Tiptoe Through the Tulips" a novelty hit in 1968 with his quavery falsetto voice and ukulele. I personally remember him appearing on the Steve Allen Show and Steve telling him he had better save his money, the implication being that he was destined to be a momentary celebrity.

Tiny Tim's celebrity lasted longer than Steve Allen's prediction. He played in nightclubs all over the country singing songs like "Take Me Out to the Ball Game" accompanied by the ukulele he carried in a brown paper shopping bag. When he married Vicki Budinger, a 17-year-old fan he referred to as Miss Vicki, on the "Tonight Show" in 1969, it was watched by 21.4 million households—that show's largest ever audience.

During Tiny Tim's celebrity period women would shower him with tulips during his performances and, true to form, they packed the north side of Koot's and brought armloads of tulips for him. In the lead-up to Tiny Tim's performance, we held a variety show with customer participation called *Stupid People Tricks*, a take-off on the television show, *Stupid Pet Tricks*. He appeared on our stage with Tommy Rocker on one side, him on the other, and JoAnne in the middle.

Tommy Rocker played guitar and emceed and Tiny Tim played ukulele while JoAnne, practically naked, turned herself inside out and backwards while balanced upside down on one hand like a tantric yogini. Poor Tiny Tim could not take his eyes off of her. He looked like he was witnessing the birth of the universe or the "second coming."

Following his performance, Tiny Tim stayed on the stage for at least an hour, signing autographs and receiving armloads of tulips. Afterwards, Shelli and I took him to dinner, where he talked a lot about JoAnne, calling her "pretzel girl."

Tiny Tim cut quite the figure: He was dressed in a white sort of loose-fitting tuxedo outfit with purple lapels and black musical notes all over it, a tie, and his dyed, black, scraggly hair at shoulder length. His face was highlighted with mascara and lipstick and he wore more than a stack of pancake makeup. He was very polite and rather withdrawn. He told us that when he wasn't on the road, he lived in a hotel room by himself. He asked for a wrapped straw to drink his beer and wrapped plastic tableware to eat his meal. He's the only entertainer I ever took to dinner who asked me, "Mr. Gordon, may I have dessert?"

One time, "Prairie Dog" and I and a few other guys traveled to Thailand together. We partied hard before boarding our China Airlines flight. Dale and I were properly "tooted up" and could have probably partied the entire lengthy flight but at a certain point, when all the lights on the plane but ours were turned off, the Chinese stewardess, when we ordered yet another round of drinks, bent down to our level and said forcefully, "We got no mo likka!"

We were in Thailand for about a week, but from the time we got to our hotel to the time we left, I never saw Dale once. I was told he had spent the entire week in an opium den. That was a bridge too far, even for me.

Dale was well regarded in spite of his craziness. I'm not sure if he got fired for one or more of his shenanigans or just decided to move on, but I was told he wound up in Florida, where he was killed in a motorcycle accident.

Which reminds me. The best employee I EVER had was in the early '80s. Her name was Sherri A. Jaussaud (1960-1983). She was barely old enough to legally consume, much less bartend, but she was dedicated to her job and thanks to her purity and honest dedication, she literally held a whole clientele and workforce of people together better than I could do on my own. She was everyone's good example, and, heaven knows, we all needed one. Everyone loved Sherri, from the loser who usually could have cared less to the hardened biker who generally shunned exhibitions of emotion that didn't involve the loud rumble of a Harley Davidson motorcycle.

Incidentally, on vacation in Hawaii, Sherri had an affair with Guy Maynard, the Okinawan bartender at the Chart House Restaurant who had let me use his registration to run the Honolulu Marathon. Sherri was in love and Guy was planning to travel to Alaska to spend some time with her.

I haven't cried much writing this sequel but I'm crying now. I just googled Sherri. That's all it took. There was her lovely young face. She was so beautiful. It may seem a stretch but in my mind she was Spenard's "maiden," Spenard's Joan of Arc, sent by God as an inspirational gift. France needed a "maiden" to save Orleans during the medieval Hundred Years War with England, and like Joan of Arc, Sherri was our fearless guiding light and, like Joan, she came to a tragic end.

I am not casting aspersion, holding anyone responsible or making any moral judgments, but I did not like it or approve of it when I learned that Sherri was buying a motorcycle and that key personalities and employees around the bar were encouraging, tutoring and helping to equip her with appropriate riding gear and apparel. I let my feelings be known. I had a foreboding. I just did not feel she had the physical strength to handle a big, heavy Harley Davidson cycle. But she was so excited. Friends and employees assured me she'd be fine. Sometimes I hate it when I'm right.

One afternoon Sherri was out riding with some of those friends. I don't remember who the friends were, but I'm sure I knew them all. Sherri got sucked under the sixteen wheels of a truck and trailer. Her shocking, grizzly departure left each and every one of us who knew and loved her indelibly imprinted with a lifelong commitment to being a better person.

Sherri was survived by her daughter, Renee, who was raised by Sherri's mother, who brought her as a young girl into the bar to show her the memorial display we hung on the wall, which, to the best of my knowledge, is still there. I personally promised Renee and her mother I would never remove it.

Michael Thomson

It was a chance meeting and Michael Thomson was the unlikeliest of friends.

The year was 1983. Shelli and I were on our honeymoon, which began in London. A few days later we took a London taxi to Cardiff, Wales.

We had hailed the driver to take us to the train station. But when he saw our luggage, he said, "You'll never be able to manage all that luggage on and off the train. It's not a real choo-choo train like you're thinking. It's a commuter train."

"Listen," he continued, "I'll drive you to Cardiff for what you would have paid for an airplane ticket, and you can stop wherever you want along the way."

How could we beat that? So we agreed. It was a very pleasant journey and the cabbie was good to his word, obliging us whenever we wanted to stop and tour a castle or whatever we fancied.

When we got to Cardiff everyone we met said, "Everything's going to be just fine. Don't worry about a thing."

"Well," we wondered. "What the devil could go wrong?" It was especially worrisome because we heard the same thing from the bellman, the woman at the front desk, room service personnel—literally everyone we met.

The next day was a Sunday, but the Cardiff Castle was open, so we took a taxi to tour it. The first thing the cabbie said was, "Everything's going to be just fine. Don't worry about a thing." We started looking over our shoulders. We felt as if we had suddenly walked into Rod Serling's *Twilight Zone*.

There was a marathon in progress and part of our taxi ride to the castle was on the marathon route, which was restricted to slow, one-way traffic. I wished I had known about the race in advance. I was on my way to run the original marathon in Athens, Greece, and could just as easily have run the one in Cardiff as a warm-up.

Cardiff Castle was home to the Royal Welsh regiment, whose slogan, "Gwell angau na Chywilydd," translates to, "Death before Dishonor." Those guys laid down their lives all over the world for the British Empire and after only a day and a half of eating Welsh food we decided the slogan might more aptly have been, "Death Before Mom's Cooking."

Pork and beans came with every meal and the breakfast bread was deep-fried in a skillet with pork fat. The English must have gotten their bad rap on cooking from the Welsh. I have had plenty of excellent meals in England. It has been awhile, but I used to find myself in London frequently, and I always made a point of dining at the five-star Capital Hotel Restaurant on Basil Street, Knightsbridge. I took Shelli there for dinner on our honeymoon and they remembered me from my last visit, a year before. The food, the service, and the wine list were all first class. Googling it, I discovered the restaurant is now called Outlaw's. Specializing in fresh local seafood, the current operation is Michelin starred and gets wonderful reviews.

But back in Wales it was, "Everything will be just fine. Don't worry about a thing!"

Next stop on the journey was Dublin, Ireland. We met two people there who would become friends. One was a young medical school student who served us in a local pub. He was so engaging that I invited him to visit Alaska to work for me. His name was Carl Birthistle and he worked two summers bartending at Chilkoot Charlie's. We brought him to Halibut Cove while he was in Anchorage, introducing him to Alaskan fishing, shrimping and crabbing. Pulling a live Dungeness crab from our pots, we would lay the crab on its back, split it down the middle with the flat end of an oar, pull it apart and splash out the guts into the saltwater. Whenever it was time to clean the crabs, Carl was so distraught with the process we nicknamed him "Dr. Queasy."

The main restaurant in our Dublin hotel required a coat and tie, so Shelli and I decided to dine in the room set aside for those who preferred casual attire.

There was only one other person dining in our area. He looked over at us and said, motioning with his hands, something like, "There's no sense in us eating at separate tables. Come join me."

He was an older gray-haired gentleman wearing a sporting coat with those leather patches on the elbows; attire he obviously considered casual. His name was Michael Thomson.

We explained to Michael that we were on our honeymoon, that we were on our way to Paris and then Athens and beyond, and that I was going to run the original marathon from Marathon to Athens. Michael told us he collected the works of lesser-known British impressionist painters and had traveled to Dublin to attend an auction, which had not been very productive for him. Now that got our interest. Shelli and I, avid art collectors, had just purchased in London some paintings by Alan Davie (1920-2014), Scotland's greatest living painter at the time, and Paul Jenkins (1923-2012), the American abstract expressionist.

Michael said he owned an estate called Phesdo House in a very rural area of Scotland near Crieff, and that he and his wife enjoyed having guests but had not had many lately because they no longer hosted bird hunters. We exchanged contact information and Michael asked us to please visit him and his wife Anne the next time we were in the area. It took a while—about eight years—during which time Shelli faithfully kept in touch with Michael and Anne by exchanging Christmas cards.

After those intervening years, Shelli and I returned to the U.K. in 1990 to do some genealogy research on her family. It took us about a week in and around London and Edinburgh to complete the research, then we headed for Phesdo House, which turned out to be located near Fettercairn, in southern Aberdeenshire. I had begun my attempt to climb the Seven Summits, though I do not believe this particular trip to London involved a climb.

We were prepared for Phesdo House to be pretty nice, since instead of having an address, it had a name. It was a place—like a castle or a museum. From the main two-lane country road, we followed a quarter-mile of crushed gravel driveway lined with tall deciduous trees. Between the trees we could glimpse pastureland with horses grazing. Toward the end of the drive we passed a long, rectangular pond with black and white swans gliding through it, before finally reaching the pillared entrance of the huge, two-story Georgian-style country house made of quarried rock.

Michael and Anne came out to meet us. After some pleasantries we were ushered into an elevator to reach our comfortable quarters on the second floor and informed of the time for cocktails in the library to be followed by a formal dinner.

The four of us convened in the library, which was just off the dining room, where we were served sherry sitting next to the fireplace. One of Michael and Anne's two Burmese mountain dogs was also on hand.

As the dog, named Jane, or lovingly referred to as "Ugly Jane," approached Michael's chair he said, "Watch this."

Jane had a well-practiced routine. First, she gingerly placed a paw upon Michael's leg and then, slowly, stealthily, paw-by-paw and inch-by-inch, she ascended until her sixty-five pound body was entirely upon him. In the end, it was as if Jane had magically just appeared upon Michael's lap, having not disturbed his attire in the least.

We enjoyed a wonderful meal in the dining room, prepared and served by Anne, and accompanied by appropriate French wines and followed by Portuguese vintage port. Since we had met Michael on our honeymoon, he and Anne entertained us with their personal story.

Michael had been married, but in love with another woman—Anne. They explained that it was tough to get a divorce in the U.K. and that Michael's wife was not cooperating. Due to archaic, convoluted British law, the process sometimes took years. He was not getting any younger, and the most expedient means of getting a divorce was to create a scandal. Just saying you wanted a divorce would not get it done. Someone had to have "done somebody wrong," and gotten caught at it. So they hired a private detective to catch, and photograph, Anne and him having an intimate assignation in a hotel room. That got the job done.

The next day, Michael gave us a tour of the estate. First we visited the horses. I had just walked incautiously around the corner of a barn building when a monstrous head appeared out of nowhere. It belonged to a giant Clydesdale horse. I just about leapt out of my skin. I have never been comfortable around horses, and this one was twice as big as any other horse I had ever encountered. I know when a dog is about to bite me, but I do not have a clue about when a horse might, so I was intensely pleased to learn Clydesdales are known for their gentle nature.

Clydesdales are draft horses, originally from the county of Clydesdale in Scotland. They literally weigh a ton and stand an average of roughly 16.5 to 18 hands tall at the shoulder. The one towering over me was definitely larger than average.

These gentle giants have traditionally been used in plowing fields and hauling freight over long distances, and Michael told us how he'd discovered that one of his farmhands, on his own time, had been employing one of the farm's Clydesdales in local plowing competitions. He'd been winning, too, but the farmhand had kept the activity to himself because he thought Michael might not approve. When Michael did find out about it he started backing the guy financially, placing his own bets, winning, and becoming fully and actively engaged in the enterprise.

In the top floor of one of his barns, Michael showed us his Clydesdale museum, which contained a large room full of antique bridles, harnesses, various accessories and trophies. Lots of trophies. The trophies were all for a single show horse, a mare, which had won best of show in every imaginable category.

Next we visited Anne's aviary which contained her collection of rare bird species, the recently acquired interest why they no longer hosted bird hunters. It was a marvelous glass aviary the size of a normal house with a state of the art security system and held quite an assortment of rare and exotic birds—but not quite as many birds as that mare had trophies. There were climate-controlled rooms and flight spaces for different species of birds complete with trees and water features.

Shelli and I continued on our merry way, doing more genealogical research on her family in Scotland and on mine in Ireland. In Ireland we drove to Monaghan County in the province of Ulster, in the Border Region, where my father's family came from. We spent part of our time digging through census records kept in a basement locker by a local civil authority.

I was unprepared for how beautiful the countryside was, with its verdant rolling hills and pastoral settings. It struck me how the people who migrated during the "Hard Times" must have been facing very hard times, indeed, to leave such a lovely place.

Our next visit with Michael and Anne was in 1993. I had climbed to the top of six of the Seven Summits and was about to embark on my third attempt of Mount Everest. Shelli and I had just celebrated our tenth anniversary by renewing our vows in the beautiful old St. Oswald's Church in Malpas, England, on the border with Wales, where her 5th great-grandfather, the John Macaulay of Ruben's "Poeme" to Shelli had been vicar.

There was a sizeable group in attendance including some of Shelli's English relatives; her aunt Gwen; Gwen's daughter Linell; her great-aunt Ferne; her favorite uncle, Joe; her best friend's parents, Don and Vivian MacInnes; Carl Birthistle, whom we had met in the Dublin pub on our honeymoon; John Evans, my friend and assistant guide on Denali, who lived in Wales; Jim McCartin, one of my roommates from the University of San Francisco, and his wife Maureen; and last but not least, my mother, Ruth.

After the ceremony Shelli and I, with my mother in the back seat, drove to Phesdo House. Don and Vivian MacInnes followed in their own vehicle. Traveling with my mother was a real eye-opener. When I was growing up she used to make fun of people chewing gum.

"Look at her! She looks like a cow chewing her cud," she'd say.

Now she sat in the back seat for mile after mile, not only chewing gum but cracking it as loud as she could. It was so annoying to me that I complained.

"That's not my mother cracking her gum back there, is it?"

"Crack, crack...CRACK!"

I eventually left my car window open in an attempt to drown out the sound, which could be why she caught a cold.

Whenever we stopped, she would buy candy.

Once I said, "Mom, you don't need that candy." I was worried about her expanding girth.

"Well," she said, "you don't need that wine you drink with your dinner every night either."

When we arrived at Phesdo House mom had a pretty bad cough, so Anne took her to a doctor in a nearby town. She received excellent, professional treatment and medication at no cost whatsoever.

Michael and Anne were every bit as hospitable as on our first visit. After freshening up and dressing up, we all sat down to another formal dinner accompanied by an excellent Bordeaux prepared and served by Anne. After dinner we were all escorted to the drawing room which boasted a blazing coal fireplace. There, Michael served us fine, vintage Portuguese port and used a special pair of scissors to ceremoniously unwrap a large, wax-papered bundle of Cuban cigars. There was another couple in attendance: a very large woman with a very small one-legged man, both friends of the Thomsons. She smoked a cigar with the guys. I had never seen a woman do that.

Now if I was ever going to slip and smoke tobacco again in my entire life, it would have been then and there. But I demurred. I well-remembered a friend of mine, Jim Hickel, who used to be the headmaster at Holy Rosary Academy—a wonderful private Catholic K through 12 school near Chilkoot Charlie's—telling me how he had quit smoking for six years when he was offered a cigar in a pink wrapper at a friend's house. His friend had just become father to a baby girl so Jim smoked the celebratory cigar, thinking it wouldn't hurt to have just one. Then he stopped at a store on his way home to buy a pack of cigarettes. By the time he told me that story, he had been smoking again for several years.

After our overnight visit with Michael and Anne, Don and Vivian went their own way while Shelli, mom, and I drove to Edinburgh where we saw a production of the Andrew Lloyd Webber musical, *Aspects of Love*, famous for its song, "Love Changes Everything," and which had been first performed only in 1989. The book, *Aspects of Love,* based on the autobiography of David Garrett, Virginia Woolf's nephew, was written by Andrew Lloyd Webber, himself, and the song was a big hit for Michael Ball. We purchased last-minute tickets so we were seated in the "nose bleed" section, high in the theatre, up a very steep and narrow staircase. Mom, understandably, remained in her seat throughout, even during intermission.

She said, "I got up here. I'm staying here!"

Shelli and I never saw Michael and Anne again, and they have both since passed away. But we were able to somewhat repay their peerless hospitality, years later, by hosting Anne's ex-son-in-law, Michael Aldridge, an estate agent in Scotland and his wife Claire in Anchorage and Halibut Cove for a week.

Nick Fuller

Michael and Anne weren't the only beautiful people who have walked into my life, offered their hand in friendship, and freely shared their bounties. Another such was Nick Fuller.

Nick drank Heineken for breakfast—every day—at least when he was at his Callaloo Beach Resort on the Caribbean island of Antigua in the West Indies. It's pronounced AN-TEE-GA, as if someone stole the "u" and tried to hide it by heavily accenting the sharp "i".

He sent me a post card from down there that showed a beautiful beach with bungalows. On it he had written, "I've got a little resort smack on a white sandy beach with gin-clear water. I'll trade you straight across for free drinks at Chilkoot Charlie's. Stay as long as you want." Now that was an offer that got my immediate attention, though I had never met the guy and it took me a couple of years to act upon it.

The namesake of the resort—callaloo—is a popular dish that originated in West Africa and is served across the Caribbean, although its definition varies. In some countries, callaloo is a type of soup. In others, it is a sort of vegetable stew. Different countries, depending on their culture and available ingredients, favor their own national recipes. Some even make a callaloo juice.

In any case, the main ingredient is a leafy vegetable, generally either amaranth or taro or xanthosoma, and variously referred to as callaloo, coco, tannia, dasheen bush, or bhaaji. Callaloo is also the name used to describe spinach, sometimes called *bhajgee* (bah-gee).

Antigua is hot pretty much the year around. Essentially there is only one season: summer. So when Nick took a vacation he liked to head north, especially in the winter to escape the heat, and it so happened he had a West Point pal, retired Brigadier General Bruce Ingle "Rock" Staser (1919—2010) who lived just up the street from Chilkoot Charlie's.

Rock was born in Anchorage to Harry I. and Barbara (De Pencier) Staser and graduated from Anchorage High School in 1936. He attended the University of Alaska Fairbanks and took his nickname while attending West Point, when he won the East Coast heavyweight boxing title. He served in the U.S. Army's 13th and 82nd Airborne Divisions during World War II and is interred at the U.S. Military Academy Cemetery at

West Point. He served as chief of staff for the Alaskan Command and under Governor Bill Egan as commander of the Alaska National Guard in the early 70s. He also served as Anchorage's civil defense director under Mayor George Sullivan.

During one of Nick's visits to Alaska to visit Rock, the two walked to Chilkoot Charlie's for a beer. Nick was a natural-born Spenardian. It was love at first sight. He was so delighted with my slogan, "We cheat the Other guy and pass the savings on to You!" he had a photo of himself standing under the sign tacked to his office wall in Antigua.

Nicholas A. "Nick" Fuller (1919-1998), was born in Toledo, Ohio, and graduated from West Point in 1944. But he was not commissioned with his 1944 classmates because of poor eyesight. Nick sat for the Foreign Service exams instead, and the State Department first placed him in charge of the American Consulate in Antigua. After an assignment in war-torn Columbia, Nick moved his family to New York and joined an advertising firm, but he wasn't able to get the sand out of his shoes. He returned to Antigua where he opened a small hotel named The Lord Nelson, the first commercial lodging on the island. Nick operated the Lord Nelson until 1980, when he moved across the island to build Callaloo Beach Resort, a low-profile operation next to Curtain Bluff, the most expensive resort on the island, which was fondly referred to by him and his guests as "Cretin Bluff."

Nick's wife, Adele, took over management of the Lord Nelson, which Nick referred to as a "real business." Nick's Callaloo Beach Resort was run for the camaraderie of his friends, who were legion, from all over the world and all walks of life.

There was only one paying couple during our entire stay at Callaloo. It was a young couple. She was gorgeous and exotic looking, from Namibia. He was a talent manager. One of his clients was Chris de Burgh, the singer of "Lady in Red," as well as other great songs. Non-paying friends of Nick's did take on responsibilities and assist with chores, generally between a leisurely breakfast and the 1 p.m. onset of the extended cocktail hour.

Nick knew everybody who was anybody, and anybody who was nobody, in the Caribbean. During the war years if you needed a passport, a visa or anything of that nature, you needed to see Nick. He was a legendary character. He traveled light without suitcase or wallet, with only an open canvas shopping bag containing underwear, Glenlivet Scotch and Cuban cigars. He did not own a credit card. His only card was an Antigua driver's license with a photo of him holding a glass of Scotch. In his pocket he carried a wad of $100 bills.

When I finally found the time to take Nick up on his offer to stay at Callaloo, I arranged for Shelli and me to stay for a week, returning right after Christmas. We were having so much fun we extended our stay until well after the New Year; we were lodged in a little tin-roofed bungalow a leisurely stroll from the main building, kitchen, office, sundeck and clubhouse with an open-air bar. Across the dirt road behind us was a pasture with donkeys. We didn't need an alarm because early each morning the donkeys would wander over behind our building and serenade us with a chorus of, "Heehaw! Heehaw! Heehaw!"

One of Nick's more memorable guests at Callaloo during our stay was the Honorable Gerald David Lascelles (1924-1998), who was accompanied by his second wife, former actress Elizabeth Collingwood. Gerald was the younger son of Henry Lascelles, 6th Earl of Harewood, and Mary, the Princess Royal, and only daughter of King George V.

Gerald had attended Eton College and served as a captain in the Rifle Brigade (Prince Consort's Own), an infantry regiment of the British Army. Gerald was a jazz enthusiast, and in the '50s he collaborated with jazz critic Sinclair Traill on a compilation of jazz yearbooks. He was also a race car driver, served as president of the British Racing Drivers' Club, and was a director of the Silverstone Circuit race car track in Northamptonshire, England.

The Honorable Gerald could be seen mid-morning in his XXXL swimsuit, on hands and knees making his contribution to the chores of the day, scrubbing tiles around the clubhouse with a bucket of bleach water. Following that chore, he would assist me in the opening of the bar for the day. We became pals and enjoyed sparring with one another. One day I got him good.

I had made a comment about our schedule, pronouncing it the way we Americans do and Gerald corrected me by pronouncing it the way the Brits do, to which I replied, "Gerald, if you say 'shedule' instead of 'skedule,' why don't you say 'shool' instead of 'skool'?" He was stumped. It was the one and only time he failed to retort.

About halfway through our stay, a woman named Doone Beal from the prestigious Conde Nast *Gourmet* magazine stopped by Callaloo, ostensibly we thought to write a story about the food at the resort. The food there was good, but really didn't seem to inspire an article in a food magazine. Doone and her husband, Pelham, also known as Lord and Lady Marley, were very old friends of Nick's. She insisted that she be referred to as Lady Marley and we thought it was amusing, especially Gerald, who was actually, factually, royalty.

Once, when Shelli and I were lounging by the clubhouse visiting with Gerald and Elizabeth, the subject of Lady Marley came up. Gerald, stretched out like a beached beluga whale on his lounge chair, his usual Dewar's Scotch and water in hand, dramatically announced, "I don't care what anyone thinks. I'm not speaking to someone who hasn't a first name!" Heavy emphasis on the words *anyone, first* and *name,* with no "r" in *first,* the word *name* followed by one of those loud British sniffs up both nostrils. Shelli and I laughed so hard we practically fell off our lounges.

One day while walking along the beach, Shelli and I turned a corner and there was an expanse of white sand covered with a huge mound of conch shells that had, apparently, been harvested for serving in the restaurant. It was literally a conch graveyard, beautiful in a bizarre sort of way, and mildly upsetting. We nicknamed it Conchwich.

Hugh Stancliffe was a regular guest of Nick's who produced brochures for the resort. Shelli and I were having some personal issues at the time, which were not aided any by the fact that she was more strikingly beautiful than usual walking around the resort in the pink jumpsuit I had bought her in Honolulu. Hugh was divorced from his first wife and he and Shelli became quite friendly. I'm afraid, in my insecure frame of mind, I took it the wrong way and became jealous. I didn't say anything to Shelli or Hugh at the time but expressed my feelings in a previous rendition of this story printed in the *Anchorage* Press. A friend of Hugh's in Antigua forwarded the article to him in the U.K. and in subsequent communications he explained that he was only being a friend, which Shelli sorely needed. He also kindly pointed out some other inaccuracies in my original story.

As if the diversity of guests needed pollinating, there was "Fat Jack," visiting with his wife, Hillary. Fat Jack was a West Point classmate of Nick's whose claim to fame was that he had piloted one of the P-51 fighters that escorted the B-29 Superfortress, Bockscar on its mission to and from Nagasaki to drop off the atom bomb, "Fat Man."

There was also a guy I will simply describe as "The Walker." He was some sort of big-shot construction guy who was really into walking long distances. He and whoever he could recruit would walk 20 to 25 miles a day. I was running marathons at the time and would put in my 5-to 10-mile run each morning, which I deemed more time-efficient, but then I didn't see as much of the island as "The Walker" and his entourage did.

Another West Pointer was Renee Lopez-Duprey, who was accompanied by his wife, Ada. They were an aristocratic couple from Old San Juan, Puerto Rico. Ada wore a lot of expensive jewelry and kept her hair coiffed up in a bee hive. Delightful and genteel, they owned a rattan furniture factory in Puerto Rico with a branch in the Philippines, and we enjoyed a visit with them in Old San Juan on our way back to Alaska.

Finally, there was Ray Dunster aka "Rotten Ray" and his wife, Isabel, who hailed from Ontario, Canada. According to Hugh Stancliffe, they were lifelong friends of fellow Canadians, George and Joan Ledingham, friends and supporters of Nick from the early days of his Bucket of Blood nightclub over by the Lord Nelson.

One day Shelli and I drove into town to watch the horse races at the Cassada Gardens Race Track, a feature of the Antigua Turf Club. It was the second day of what was billed the Christmas Meeting. The date was January 3, 1988. It was a colorful affair that boasted enthusiastic spectators seated on rickety bleachers, one of which collapsed under the weight of the crowd. Fortunately it was not our bleacher and no one was injured, but the red, volcanic earth was wet and muddy from recent rain, so you can imagine the effect on one's attire.

The race track brochure advertised "BREED YOURSELF A TRACK RECORD BREAKER! IF YOU HAVE THE MARE WE HAVE THE STALLION, CALIBI. BREED FOR SPEED AND BREED FOR STAMINA TOO."

It was while attending the races that I discovered they sold a marvelous bottle of Guinness beer with lemon juice in it. It was packaged as a throwback to the British navy days when they provided grog and lemon juice to prevent scurvy, and there was a nifty British navy pattern on the label. Unfortunately, I have never seen it served anywhere else. Chilkoot Charlie's was the first bar in Alaska to serve Guinness on tap but, though I did inquire, I could never locate the bottled stuff with lemon juice in it.

On the way to and from the races we spotted the town's "RUDE BOY STAND" and stopped to take a photo of four local boys clowning around on what is the local version of the dunce hat. It is a simple concrete roadside platform used for publicly humiliating young miscreants who are required to stand on it for all to see for prescribed periods of time.

Our extended vacation time finally came to an end. Shelli and I returned to Anchorage and never revisited Antigua, though I was able to arrange for a one-week honeymoon at Callaloo for my daughter Michele and her husband Jerry. The last time I saw Nick was when he was once again visiting Rock in Anchorage.

I was counting the bar banks one afternoon in the office at Chilkoot Charlie's when the bartender rang me and said, "Mike, there are two old geezers out here who say they drink at Koot's for free."

Knowing exactly of whom he spoke, I said, "Yep. Set 'em up."

"I'll be right out."

Shelli and I brought Ruben to Halibut Cove for a visit in the early eighties. It was before The Saltry restaurant opened its doors in the spring of 1984. We had installed steel pilings, a floating dock and stairs up to our recently purchased property and little canvass wall tent in the woods. Ruben was ensconced in an even smaller wall tent we had rearranged for him that was generally used for storage.

There was only one phone in the Cove then, a short distance away by skiff. We all had CB radios and "handles," ours being *Shelli Bird*, the name of our boat. We were in the woods, so there were no lawns or gardens to tend. I spent a lot of time fishing for salmon, Dungeness crab and shrimp. We read a lot and sometimes didn't get out of bed for several days. Occasionally I think about those days longingly, especially as I'm mowing our rolling lawn that now takes me three days to complete in sections.

Ruben was thrilled to be able to visit Clem and Diana Tillion, the patriarch and matriarch of Halibut Cove, since it was Diana who pressed the legislature to name Ruben as Alaska Poet Laureate. He was rightfully proud of that position, which he held from 1973 to 1978.

The most fun we had with Ruben in the Cove, however, was visiting with Tom Larson (1899-1994), aka Old Tom, who lived in a shack on the water a short distance from our property by trail through the *oplopanax horridus*, aka devil's club and alders. I remember weed-whacking the trail that fall, flashlight in one hand, machete in the other, with Shelli and Ruben in tow carrying a couple of bottles of wine and four wine glasses for a night of festivities with Old Tom.

Shelli and I always, after the first time, carried our own glasses to Old Tom's. That first time he offered glasses from his sink that he thoughtfully wiped off with the filthiest dish rag either of us had ever seen. Pathogenic organisms come in five main types: viruses, bacteria, fungi, protozoa and worms. We felt certain that all five were present and accounted for on that greasy rag. Tom was a bachelor and he lived like one. There was a pile of newspapers stacked in one corner, and on one visit Shelli discovered the pile was smoldering atop an electric hot plate evidently in the operating mode. The place probably would have burned down had she not noticed it and helped Tom clean it up.

Old Tom was Norwegian and had a big, booming voice. He had lived in Southeast Alaska and came "out west" to "teach the women how to dance," as he described it. He had worked on the construction of the Richardson Highway from Valdez to Fairbanks and loved telling stories about the experience. He had also lived in Halibut Cove since the '30s, when there was a vibrant herring fishery, a real saltry, and more residents than there are currently.

Of course, Old Tom knew of Ruben. Everyone knew of Ruben in those days. Here were two old codgers that were made for an evening of trading yarns, and a grand evening it was. Tom got to visit with his radio idol, and Ruben was equally charmed to hear one of his longtime admirers relating tales of the madams that operated roadhouses every twenty miles or so along the nascent Richardson Highway.

Thomas Ween Larson was laid to rest in the Tillion Cemetery in Halibut Cove.

Venezuela

It all started with Nick's devastating fall—another Nick—Nick Coltman. He was the co-founder and publisher of the *Anchorage Press* and being the owner of the largest nightclub in Alaska, I had a longstanding relationship with that local alternative newspaper.

Nick was also one of the more capable of my alpinist friends. But around mid-day of November 11, 2000, while climbing with his dog Boozer, Nick fell victim to a slab of unconsolidated snow in a narrow gully on Flattop Mountain just outside Anchorage. That moment changed his life forever.

The short story is that Nick was lucky to have survived at all. He severely injured his back in the fall, and he has been confined to a wheelchair ever since. Nick was able to reach his cell phone to call 911, then endured a three-hour wait during which he struggled desperately to stay warm with the help of Boozer's body heat. It took two helicopters to rescue him because the first was not equipped with a harness that could lift him up. Finally, he was whisked to the hospital.

Nick was a positive, can-do, athletic man of 36 years at the time of the accident. With the help of his loving, sturdy wife, Maggie, he made a remarkable—even inspirational—recovery and adjustment to his new life after an extended period of rehabilitation in the state of Georgia.

The one thing everyone in such circumstances can use is money. We raised the cover charge at Chilkoot Charlie's by a dollar each weekend night after Nick returned to Anchorage, and like the AFLAC duck, I would deliver the cash to the *Anchorage Press* office on East 5th Avenue each Monday in a brown paper bag. We kept it up until we reached a total of $20,000.

Nick was so grateful that he later arranged for a travel agent friend of his in Florida to put together a trip for me to Venezuela. I had long been fascinated by the tepuis, or soaring mesas, of that country. I even had fantasies about climbing one. I brought along my club manager, Doran Powell, and good friend Dick Lowell (1941-2015), with both of whom I had done a lot of previous traveling in South and Central America.

Tepui translates into "house of the gods" in the language of the Pemon, the indigenous people of the Gran Sabana. The tepuis themselves are remarkable geologic creations. One of them, Mt. Roraima, at 9,219 feet elevation, is said to have inspired Arthur Conan Doyle's 1912 blockbuster book, *Lost World*, in which living dinosaurs still inhabit South America. On a perfect day the columns of the tepuis will protrude right up out of the jungle through the cloud cover and in stark contrast to it. Because of their composition, location, elevation, and individual isolation each tepui supports flora and fauna unknown elsewhere in the world, even on other tepuis in the same general locale.

The tepuis are situated on the Guyana Shield made up of igneous and metamorphic rocks, mostly granites and gneisses. They are some of the oldest rocks on the earth's surface formed 3.6 billion years ago in the western area of the supercontinent of Gondwana which began to separate late in the Jurassic Period (150 million years ago) when the South American and African plates were drifting apart allowing the formation of the Atlantic Ocean. The Roraima Formation making up the tepuis is comprised of layers of sand deposited from Gondwana subsequently compressed and solidified by silica to form, after erosion of their surroundings, the towering, unearthly sentinels we see today.

We got in and out of Caracas, one of the most dangerous cities in the world, as quickly as we could. From there we flew south to the Rio Orinoco for a few days of peacock bass fishing while the drug-laden boats plying their way between Venezuela and Columbia cruised past us, the inhabitants carrying barely-concealed weapons and menacing dispositions. Peacock bass are one of the world's best game fish and make excellent eating. We would jerk a balsam top-lure with dangling treble hooks and a spinning prop on its butt across the surface of the water. When the big bass hit, it was akin to an explosion.

We were not equipped, nor did we have the time, to climb one of the tepuis, so we flew in a small plane between, around, and amongst them on our way to overnight in a remote lodge on a river near Auyantepui, a massive tepui which reaches 8,040 feet of elevation and has a surface area on its plateau of 260 square miles.

The next day, we landed at an airport near Canaima and a short distance from Mirador Laime and Angel Falls, which drops from the cleft near the summit of Auyantepui. It was not the rainy season, so we could barely see the falls, but we walked and waded through waist-high water into an open area reminiscent of a cathedral that had been carved out by the falls. There we found a quantity of water still falling down as we basked in the downpour and the cool, clear pools. It was a magical experience.

As the tallest falls in the entire world, nineteen times the height of Niagra Falls, one would think that Angel Falls might be named after a deity or at least an acknowledged angel. Instead, it is named after an American pilot and adventurer, James "Jimmie" Crawford Angel (1899-1956) of Cedar Valley, Missouri, who is credited with discovering that natural wonder.

Jimmie flew over the falls in November of 1933 in search of mineral deposits, namely gold. He returned to the remote Gran Sabana region in October of 1937, in his Flamingo monoplane, *El Rio Caroni,* with his wife, Marie; his friend, Gustavo Henry; and Miguel Delgado, Henry's gardener to attempt a landing on top of Auyantepui.

The landing was only marginally successful since the plane's wheels got stuck in the mud, preventing a takeoff. It then took eleven days for the group to descend the tepui and return to civilization. News of the adventure stimulated interest in the area, and years of scientific exploration ensued. Jimmie's plane remained atop Auyantepui until 1970 when the Venezuelan military disassembled, removed, and reassembled it for posterity. It is presently on display at the Ciudad Bolivar Airport Aviation Museum, while a replica sits atop the falls themselves.

Though the falls were named after Jimmie, others were reported to have discovered them much earlier. Sir Walter Raleigh is said to have discovered the falls as early as 1594 on an expedition to locate El Dorado. Also, a Venezuelan explorer named Ernesto Sanchez La Cruz reportedly discovered the falls in 1910 or 1912. Finally, Aleksandrs Laime, a Latvian, was the first to reach the falls on foot.

There was one other person who had committed to going on the trip to Venezuela with Doran, Dick and me: Carl Marrs, onetime president of Cook Inlet Regional Corporation and a bar-hopping pal of mine from the Wild West days of Anchorage in the '70s. It so happens that Carl had been a U.S. Marine, and a fellow Marine friend of his, now with a position in the State Department, discovered Carl's plan. His friend told Carl he was not going and cancelled his passport. We were soon to discover why.

Visiting Venezuela and the tepuis was a bucket list item for me, and I was grateful for the gift extended from Nick and his travel agent friend. But every single connection on the entire trip was problematic, as when we arrived back at the airport in Caracas to fly out to Los Roques, north of the city in the Caribbean Sea, for some bonefish action. It turned out the flight had already departed. Dick Lowell, a no-nonsense, fastidious, and demanding man with high expectations and a low tolerance level for snafus, stood on the simmering tarmac, bag in hand, feet apart, glaring at me. It wasn't my fault, but...no matter.

We finally arrived on the island early that evening, where we ensconced ourselves in a comfortable bed-and-breakfast operation run by a middle-aged widow with joint U.S. and Venezuelan passports. I sat up with her until late at night, after Doran and Dick had gone to bed, discussing her situation. Hugo Chavez had recently been elected the 45th president of Venezuela. She was preparing for the worst, packing her precious belongings and getting ready to move to the States.

We all awoke the next morning, barely after daybreak, to the sound of troops marching and counting cadence, their boots rhythmically pounding the dirt roads of that quiet little fishing village. It was a disturbing sound, especially in such a remote, idyllic corner of the country. One could only imagine what was happening elsewhere. But not sensing any imminent danger to ourselves, we decided to stick to our itinerary.

None of us had ever before caught a bonefish. They reside in shallow tropical waters where they grub on the bottom for food and can grow up to 30 inches long and weigh as much as 14 pounds. The grubbing also clouds the water which protects the bonefish from predators like barracuda as they feed.

We used wet flies for lures and simply dragged them slowly through the areas of cloudy water that marred the otherwise crystal-clear sea. Our guide, a big black fellow with huge, gnarled and muscular bare feet that would have broken out of shoes like a pair of recalcitrant inmates, spoke no English but was very accommodating.

He was removing a bonefish from one of our lines over the side of our small wooden boat, perhaps a foot above the water-line when— WHAM!—a barracuda shot out of the water like a bullet. The only thing left on the hook was part of the bonefish's head, dangling there with blood dripping from it, less than an inch from the guide's fingers. The guy was sweating from the brow and his eyes were like big, white, round saucers, though he managed a toothy grin.

If barracuda like bonefish that much, Doran and I suggested, using sign language and broken Spanish as our guide gathered his wits, let's use them as live bait. What a great idea that was. Use one fish to catch another, like turning one class against another. Just cloud the water. The fate of the bonefish was sealed as tightly it turns out as the fate of the people of Venezuela. Socialism seemed like a good idea to the hapless population that elected Hugo Chavez and his United Socialist Party with 56% of the vote. We soon reeled in several barracuda whose fate was no better than that of the bonefish. After all, no one wins with socialism, except those tugging on the lines.

When Chavez took over Venezuela, it had the strongest economy in Latin America. It still has the largest proven reserves of oil in the world. He was able to get away with following the path of the Castro brothers—nationalizing businesses, handing out money and costly social programs to the poor, and taking care of his military cronies—when oil was at $100 a barrel. He even offered a discount on the price of oil to indigenous bush village residents of Alaska.

But the price of oil crashed in late 2014, and Venezuela's economy crashed with it, traveling down the road of more and more government control of the economy, and the populace, until Chavez's death in 2013. His replacement by the hand-picked and far less capable ex-bus driver, Nicolas Maduro, has ultimately led to a worthless currency, over 83,000% inflation, double-digit unemployment, and severe shortages of food and basic necessities, including prescription drugs.

Since 2015 some 2.3 million Venezuelans have left the country, straining the ability of neighboring South American countries to absorb them. For the first time, Venezuelans are the largest national group seeking refuge in the U.S. One half the children of Venezuela are suffering from malnutrition and the average resident of the country has lost nearly 20 pounds at a time when the rest of the hemisphere is suffering from obesity.

Half the economy of Venezuela has literally disappeared in the last decade, and Maduro has become a virtual dictator. He is no socialist dreamer like Chavez was. He is just a thug and all too ready to rig elections, dismantle the country's remaining institutions, murder his opponents, and use the heavy hand of the military as he sees fit.

Circumstances are bad enough for Venezuelans themselves, but they are rife with nightmarish possibilities for the rest of the hemisphere as well. The Russians, the Chinese, even the Iranians and of course the Cubans, have all loaned money and given assistance, or both, to the regime as a means of infiltrating and manipulating it to their own advantage. Hezbollah Venezuela, a branch of the Shia Islamist militant political party based in Lebanon and financed by Iran, is a reality and should send shivers up the spines of people from Punta Arenas to Barrow.

Given the history of U.S. heavy-handedness south of the border, we should be careful not to overplay our hand, but we should continue to stand strongly behind democratic forces in the country and let it be very clear that Venezuelan instability is a Monroe Doctrine matter and a table stakes game in which the U.S. is all in.

Chavez used Venezuela's democratic institutions to take over the country by appealing to the poor. Venezuela is a beautiful country with enormous natural resources, but it is home to an all-too-common South and Latin American ruling elitist minority, undersized middle class, and oversized poor population. Such is a demographic formula ripe for the promises of a socialist "dream" from the likes of a Hugo Chavez.

Socialist panderers are popping up in increasing numbers in the new far-left version of the Democrat party, while our ever-increasing number of elites grows ever richer by shipping jobs overseas, undermining our institutions, and creating an unequal and unfair system under the law.

The Great Recession of 2008, created by corrupt Wall Street elites, hand-in-hand with corrupt political elites of both parties, dealt a severe body blow to middle class America from which it still has not recovered. If we lose the middle class, we lose the bulwark against this most destructive political philosophy of the twentieth century.

Back on the boat, our guide happily kept a few of the barracuda for himself and we returned to the bed-and-breakfast where our hostess was still packing. I hope she got out of there in time. Doran, Dick, and I went on our merry way to Aruba where we lounged on the beach and took a raucous party bus around town one night. We then headed back to the States and Anchorage after yet another airport connection snafu.

No matter where I've been, no matter what I've seen, experienced, or learned it always feels good to have American soil again under foot.

More from "Conversations Emeritus," by Mike Dunham

Gaines' popularity was so widespread by 1960 that the new state's legislature made him Alaska's poet laureate.

Traditionally, the laureate-ship is for life; but in attention-deficient Alaska the title has since shifted to other people through means not necessarily legislative. While purists might consider this an insult, it appears not to bother the original office holder of the title.

In fact, he has sought out assistance from another laureate, Joanne Townsend, and attends her weekly writing class at the Anchorage Senior Center, which he calls Gaffersville. 'Sometimes I have to drag myself into the class. Joanne is continually goosing us to get a writing regimen under way, but I haven't come up with a system. All the same, I'm much in her debt,' he said.

Without the daily deadline of a radio show, Gaines admitted, he can fall into 'a long sere period.' (That's a dry spell, students.) Part of the difficulty is an acknowledged lack of sympathy for many well-known contemporary poets. 'I can't help but keep looking for meaning, and poetry doesn't have to mean anything. It should be an explosion, raising hell with the language.' He shook his head, 'I'm in trouble; a poet who can't read poetry.'

Except his own. While his early rhymes may look silly and the later verse shaky, they take on heft, clarity and potency when he reads them aloud. This is, to some extent, true for most poets, but few have his gift of sonority or the luxury of eight decades of reflection and refinement.

Jo Gordon, a prize-winning poet in her own right, said, 'He's grown every year that I've known

him, until now he's a real intellectual philosopher. Ruben can read a nursery rhyme and we think it's marvelous, but when he reads his poetry and we listen to his written words we begin to hear what he's saying.'

'The changes to Alaska have been horrific,' Gaines said. 'In '46 it was free and easy. Handshake time. Oil brought many people up here who, unfortunately, did not go back and schlepped all their prejudices and distress and insidiously made Anchorage something other than Alaska. (Territorial governor and U.S. Sen. Ernest) Gruening once prophesied that Cook Inlet basin would hold millions. It's beginning to show signs of it now. The Alaska frame of mind is gradually thinning out. I don't draw any moral conclusions. I do regret that you have to lock the door.

'There wasn't much talk about hardship in those times. You didn't feel underprivileged. You appreciated what you had!'" He briefly clinched his teeth at the thought of the wildness of the scene. 'We did a hell of a lot of drinking. It was interesting, drinking in Alaska. The bartenders were performers. I got a lot of material out of the bars. Ed (Stevens) died an alcoholic. I'm not sure why I didn't.'

I could not agree more with the sentiments expressed here by Ruben, and the changes have only accelerated since his passing. Maybe it's spending so much more time in Halibut Cove—or maybe not—but I almost feel like a stranger in Anchorage, the city I grew up in. I'm inclined to think that Ruben would be disheartened by the current state of affairs and it occurs to me that there is a time for all of us to go gracefully on.

Russia and Mount Elbrus

Ever since Marco Polo's epic thirteenth century journey to the orient from Venice, the value of travel has been undisputed. I have tried to squeeze as much of it into my life as possible and do not regret a single trip I ever took. There is a lot to be said for a "world view" with the ultimate vista being that of astronauts. It changes their outlook and perspective as roaming around earth's surface does for those of us bound to it by gravity.

Some of my trips have been well-chronicled in *Learning the Ropes*, but my three trips to Russia, due to the conciseness required of the memoir, could not be properly detailed. They were amazing experiences, so I will attempt to better tell of them here, sans the climbing details. The main focus is on the third trip that was as they say, "the charm."

It took me three attempts to make it to the summit of Mt. Elbrus, hence the three trips to Russia. Our 1989 Genet Expeditions group, led by Mike Howerton, was strong. We got close to our goal but ultimately turned back on the summit ridge because of deep, unstable snow and strong winds.

My second attempt in 1990 was also with a Genet Expeditions group which could have made it had we been fully committed. I was furious as I watched the members of a Rainier Mountain expedition walking into the saddle between the two peaks on their way to the summit in beautiful weather. Meanwhile, we sat inside the Pruitt Hut, the starting point of the climb that looked like a massive Airstream trailer and has since burned to the ground, packing our bags and preparing to leave. It meant another dreary trip to Russia.

My 1989 trip had been during the painfully bleak, forlorn Soviet Union days. The 1990 trip was during *Peristroika* and *Glasnost* when Russia had become somewhat more open, but it was still a wretched, banal netherworld.

The last thing in the world I wanted to do was return to that god-forsaken country a third time. The people were oppressed, sad and withdrawn, the accommodations were worse than third-rate, and the food was awful.

But I had to get to the top of that mountain. As previously mentioned, I carried cachets to the top of each mountain I summited. The cachet for Mt. Elbrus was dedicated to my father, and I kept telling myself that was why it was so difficult for me. I had never had a chance to reconcile with him during his lifetime and here I was still sorting things out more than ten years after his death.

My third trip was in August 1991. Though having been to Russia twice before, amazingly, I had never heard of the Armory Museum located under the Kremlin walls. If you're ever in Moscow, do not miss it.

During our tour of the museum, our Russian guide stopped, pointed over to our right and asked, "Can anyone tell me about that throne over there?"

I said, "Yes, that's the double throne made for young Peter the First (in Russia they don't refer to him as Peter the Great) and his older brother, Ivan, while Sophia ruled Russia as regent."

She was suitably impressed. I had been a student of Russian history and a big fan of Peter the Great for many years, and I was astonished that the Soviets still had all those priceless articles from the Romanov dynasty hidden away down there under the walls of the Kremlin. I said as much to the guide and she replied, "Well, the Communists were Russians too."

Okay. Even so. I knew those same Russian Communists had destroyed just about everything else in the country, including the entire royal family, so I was still impressed that this absolutely priceless cornucopia of regal clothes, carriages, thrones, Fabergé eggs, snuff boxes, crystal, jewelry, crowns and other incredible, hand-crafted articles of all sorts was miraculously saved from the ravages of the revolution. The Romanovs were, after all, the richest family in the world before the revolution.

At 18,510 feet, Mt. Elbrus, the tallest mountain on the European geographic continent, is located in the Caucasus mountain range of southeastern Russia near the border with Georgia in a tourist area known as the Baksan Valley. The highest mountain in the confines of political Europe, and the Alps, is Mt. Blanc, which straddles France, Italy, and Switzerland, but rises to just 15,781 feet.

In the late 1980s and early 1990s the Baksan Valley was one of the few tourist areas in the world that could have advertised itself as *au natural*, meaning no toilet seats and no toilet paper.

The food served at the lodges was horrible beyond description. When you were served chicken, you could never discern from what part of the bird's body it came. It was as if they had turned the birds loose in a room with a drunken maniac wielding a dull meat cleaver. It did taste like chicken, but then a lot of things taste like chicken.

One of the standard meals served to us was meatballs, of questionable origin. We nicknamed them sinkers (think fishing) and used them mostly as projectiles. I usually walked into the cafeteria, looked over the selection of fly-covered culinary delights, grimaced, picked up an apple, polished it on my sleeve and walked out.

In Moscow, we were lodged in a rather nice hotel by Russian standards of the day, though my buddy from previous climbs, Bob John, had complained about mosquitoes the previous night. Todd Burleson, the leader of our little expedition, and I shared a room. We had gotten somewhat inebriated, gone to bed, passed out, and taken no notice of the pesky critters. In retrospect it's a wonder we had the strength to get up in the morning. Perhaps the mosquitoes stole our hangovers. That's a pleasant thought.

I did not feel like I had gotten a good night of sleep since leaving Anchorage and I was determined to get one the next night. Our plane was due to depart for Mineral Vody the following afternoon, so I went to bed at 9:30 p.m. But after an hour of trying to sleep beneath squadrons of the little buzzing bastards, I decided to go on the offensive. I checked to make sure the windows were secure, and determined to kill every mosquito in the room, went on a bloody rampage with my t-shirt. After an entire hour of pitched battle I began to realize the utter futility of the melee.

Todd returned from another night of partying with a pretty good buzz on (no pun intended) again. He crawled into bed and went to sleep immediately, once again oblivious to the horde feasting on him. But I lay there for hours with a small towel in my hand, swatting mosquitoes—and myself—until my head rang from the pounding it got.

Finally, at 3:30 a.m., I got up and staggered into the bathroom. I killed what I thought were all the mosquitoes in that small room, stuffed towels under the door, put a couple of blankets on the tile floor, and tried again to get some sleep. They must have been coming in through the vent, so I got all of about an hour of sleep between 4:00 a.m. and 5:00 a.m. I probably just passed out from loss of blood. It was the worst night ever.

The next day our little expedition—Todd Burleson, who looked and acted like he'd had a perfectly normal night's sleep, plus Bob and Jan John and I—took a rather long bus ride to another airport. Todd's mother, Ann, and his cousin, Lorraine, who were traveling with us, remained in Moscow and were to meet us in Leningrad after the climb.

As we drove I thought about the mountain and the forthcoming climb. While so musing I took note of the tanks being transported on railcars traveling on tracks right next to us. The sight of them rolling along did not seem incongruous or startling. After all, we were in the Soviet Union. How could we possibly have been able to guess the reason for their movement? But something momentous was, in fact, transpiring.

We spent the next couple of weeks somewhat isolated in the Baksan Valley, and while on Mt. Elbrus we were completely out of touch with current events. I had made a point of making my third visit in August, hoping the weather would be better than my previous attempts in September, and my choice was rewarded. Bob, Todd, our Russian guide, Arsentiev Sergei, and I all stood on the summit in beautiful shirtsleeve weather, a major contrast with the weather I'd experienced on both previous climbs.

Descending the mountain on the tram, we heard that Gorbachev had been ousted. Later, at the hotel we heard he had resigned. It was hard to understand what the Russians thought about it. For all their complaining about Gorbachev, I thought they were not too keen to see him go. They were all glued to the black-and-white television in the lobby but according to Alexis, our interpreter, there was very little hard information. He reported that they were playing a lot of classical music and repeating the same vague story over and over.

"Such is our way," he said.

The Russians expected there would be a slowdown in political and economic reforms, though it had been mentioned in the broadcasts that "private businesses" would not be affected. I personally thought Gorbachev was an extraordinary man—impossible to replace—but from the Russian perspective he had dismantled their empire and ruined their economy.

The fact is, no one in Russia knew the first thing about how or why an economy or a business, for that matter, worked. They were absolutely clueless. We were in the nicest hotel I had experienced in the Baksan Valley, but the maid had not touched my room since my arrival. The elevators only worked half the time. I pulled on the window handle to open my window and it came off in my hand. You could not get a hot shower until 7:30 a.m. They played moronic, obnoxious disco music from breakfast until bedtime, inside and outside the building, so loud you could hardly talk at the dinner table. One could scarcely blame all that on Gorbachev.

The next day we went for a hike and visited the headquarters of the area's mountain rescue team, then went into Elbrus Village to get my cachets stamped and postmarked. It went smoothly with all three Russians helping out. They would not allow me to pay for the stamps saying, "It's not very much money."

On the last day in the valley we were taken to a small man-made lake by a stream in the middle of a cow pasture. We took an upright portable barbecue with us, along with watermelon, pears, plums, apples and tomatoes; caviar; bottles of sherry-like wine; brandy; *Piva*, the Russian equivalent of beer, which tasted more like what the name sounds like; cheese and a freshly killed lamb. We gathered wood from the hillside and Abdul, our bus driver, who lived in Elbrus Village, did the honors.

As we ate and ate, and drank and drank toast after toast, a young bull joined us. He became friendly enough to eat a tomato out of my hand.

When it was my turn to toast, I said I had not had such a good time on previous trips to Russia and that I had thought I would never want to return, but they had changed my mind.

Oleg, one of our Russian guides, said, "If you think this has been good, wait until we get through with you in Leningrad!"

We had an interesting drive back to Mineral Vody. When we stopped at a major intersection to replenish our fuel, Bob got out of the bus to take some photos of the broken-down pumps and the long lines of vehicles which pissed off the station attendant who hurled insults at him and appeared ready to physically attack him. He also refused to sell us gas, though we had waited in line for a long time.

Not knowing what else to do, we pulled over by the interchange and stood for about a half hour with a bucket and siphon hose, waving currency, trying to attract someone who might sell us or get us some gas. No one stopped, so we drove on toward Mineral Vody slowly, coasting down the hills to conserve fuel until we finally came to another smaller interchange that boasted several pumps. As usual only one of the pumps worked, with long lines of vehicles approaching from both sides. After about a half-hour, with Bob and his camera confined to the bus, we were able to refill our tank and continue happily on our way.

We arrived in Mineral Vody around 2:30 p.m. for a flight that was scheduled to leave at 6:30 p.m. and said goodbye to Abdul. I gave him a Chilkoot Charlie's t-shirt, with which he was visibly pleased, and we began hauling our gear into the overcrowded, smoke-filled, filthy, smelly airport.

When we eventually entered the In-Tourist area, the first thing we learned was that the flight had been rescheduled for 9:30 p.m. Bob bought three Heinekens in the lounge for himself, Todd, and me. It was a nice gesture, but the only thing working in the beer cooler was the light bulb, so the beer was not just warm—it was hot.

While we waited for the flight, Gorbachev held a long live press conference. Alexis had gone to another airport with Oleg, and Sergei was struggling to explain what was being said, but it was apparent that whatever had happened was over—a major relief.

Sergei left about an hour before the rest of us and took fully half of the bags with him. Finally, we were ushered onto the tarmac separately. I took a photo of Bob sitting on the steps leading up to the huge Aeroflot plane, proudly displaying the remains of his boiled Heineken.

When we arrived in Leningrad late that evening, we were met by Todd's mother, Ann; his cousin, Lorraine; Oleg's wife, Irena; and Igor and Sergei. The girls had champagne and roses, were in a high state of excitement, and had quite a story to tell. Ann and Lorraine had taken an overnight train to Leningrad where they decided to treat themselves by staying at the Astoria Hotel instead of at the hostel where they had reservations. As the political and social upheaval unfolded, the Astoria, adjacent to a large square, became the focal point of activity during the attempted coup. Lorraine sounded like Christiane Amanpour as she described the events of the previous few days.

The conspirators, in a feeble attempt to forestall further reforms, had kept Gorbachev under house arrest at his holiday retreat in Foros, Crimea. At first, they gave him the option of joining them, which he declined to do. As we all know, they were unable to get Boris Yeltsin, the recently elected president of the Russian federation, or Anatoly Sobchak, the mayor of Leningrad to join them either.

Sobchak and Yeltsin were in contact with one another and Sobchak actually faced down the KGB, the police and the military, convincing the military not to attack the city and preventing the spread of unrest. Conspirators had taken control of the radio and television stations, but Yeltsin and Sobchak managed to get their message to the people that the actions being taken by the conspirators were illegal and that they did not support them.

Yeltsin stood on a tank in Moscow to get his message to the people and Sobchak stood on a balcony of the Astoria Hotel and exhorted the people to turn out *en masse*, which they did, surrounding the hotel and barricading the streets. The Astoria became an anti-coup headquarters, with young men making Molotov cocktails in the lobby in preparation for a confrontation with the military. Fortunately, that confrontation never transpired. The conspirators, finally realizing they were not going to be able to consolidate power, gave in and attempted to flee the country.

We pulled up to the Astoria Hotel at 2:00 a.m. and found the place practically deserted. Fearful of the outcome of the attempted coup, most of the guests had left the country. Had the coup been successful, the new leadership, it was assumed, would not have been particularly friendly to Westerners. During the frantic swirl of events, Ann and Lorraine had gone to the American Embassy and registered all of us. Then, wanting to let our families know we were safe, they tried unsuccessfully to phone or fax Todd's office in Seattle from the Astoria.

Resourceful women that they were, they boarded a Swedish ship in the harbor and, when told the facilities were for guests only, they bought a room for the night for $150 and faxed away. For some reason my family was never contacted, and there were only three American families involved in the expedition, so who was faxed or called is a mystery to me. Shelli was calling the U.S. State Department daily to listen to the report on Americans stranded in Russia and passed the information on to my mother, who was nearly hysterical in Honolulu.

Copious amounts of champagne were consumed in the wee hours of that first night in the Astoria. I did not get out of bed until 1:00 p.m. the next day. Todd, Lorraine, Ann, and I had brunch in the hotel lobby and were waited on by an incredibly inept and obnoxious waiter. I picked up the tab and stiffed him, drawing a line through the area on the American Express voucher set aside for gratuities.

He brought it back to the table and demanded my copy, saying that I had ruined it. I told him to go fuck himself, that I had done it on purpose and would not return it to him under any circumstances, whereupon he stormed off and never returned. There was an absolute disconnect between service and gratuity for that waiter and most others in the Soviet Union. To them the tip was an entitlement.

After brunch we took a taxi to an area just off Nevsky Prospect where a lot of vendors had moved. We did some shopping but returned to the Astoria before long because our guides had promised us an adventure involving a boat ride.

Our complete complement of guides and interpreters joined us on a diesel-powered boat that looked like a war surplus launch or PT boat, where they told us they were all now involved in an exciting new capitalist enterprise known as Qwest. It was primarily an adventure expedition company, but they were also preparing to deliver titanium oxygen tanks to Todd's company for use on Mt. Everest.

The boat cruised through canals for about half an hour before ending up on the Neva River. Cruising down the river past the Hermitage Museum we viewed the imposing bronze statue of Peter the Great on his rearing horse atop a huge stone.

The statue's history is as interesting as the statue itself. Commissioned in Peter's honor by Catherine the Great and generally known as the Bronze Horseman, the statue was sculpted by a Frenchman named Etienne Maurice Falconet. He never got to see the finished work because he fell out with Catherine, who sent him packing back to France before the unveiling.

The stone that serves as the base of the statue, known as the Thunder Stone, originally weighed fifteen hundred tons and is the largest stone ever moved. It was moved by men alone—there were no machines or animals employed in the massive undertaking. A Greek named Marinos Carburis, who was serving in the Russian army as a lieutenant colonel and who had studied engineering in Vienna, volunteered for the job. He is considered the first Greek to hold a diploma in engineering and employed new techniques that foreran the development of ball bearings.

It took four hundred men nine months to relocate the stone from near the Gulf of Finland to its present location, with the stone cutters fashioning it during the journey. Engraved on the side of the Thunder Stone is the message, "From Catherine the Second to Peter the First." An almost equally epic, $40,000 replication of the statue presently overlooks the dance floor on the Russian-themed south side of Chilkoot Charlie's.

Next, we turned around and cruised past the Peter and Paul Fortress, up the river to where the old cruiser *Aurora* is parked. Shelli and I had visited the fortress and the Peter and Paul Cathedral, which is inside the fort, on our visit to Leningrad in 1989. She had learned to pronounce the Cyrillic alphabet before traveling to Russia, which had come in pretty handy because a lot of Russian words are the same as French and English.

She was voicing out loud the writing on the tombstones with a whole knot of other tourists behind her, intently listening. Buried there are Peter the Great, Nicholas II, Catherine the Great, Alexander II and III, Nicholas I and Paul I, among others. During our taxi rides in Moscow Shelli would read aloud the names of restaurants and pharmacies, which always impressed the taxi drivers.

After a tour of the *Aurora*, which is both a Communist Party and a Russian Navy museum, we met the deputy commander of the ship, Alexander Goroshko, in a tastefully appointed conference room. Sitting around a big beautiful conference table under the watchful eyes of a bust of Vladimir Lenin, which dominated the room from the far end, we listened intently while our host explained the operations of the ship and proceeded to very candidly describe what he knew of the attempted coup and how he felt about it.

I was amazed because in my experiences in the Soviet Union, no one spoke their minds about anything. I told him we were very pleased that democracy, and law and order had prevailed, and felt the Russian people had acted heroically.

The deputy commander indicated that the Russian Navy, for its part, was not at all involved in any of the action, and had been concerned mainly with maintaining order and protecting lives and property. Goroshko was extremely professional, gracious and charming—a handsome man in uniform with whom the girls were obviously taken. He left the room several times for what appeared to be official reasons, and on one of these occasions was gone for nearly half an hour.

Oleg was wearing a Chilkoot Charlie t-shirt and sitting at a piano with his back to the room, facing the prominent bust of the serious-looking Vladimir Lenin. Todd observed that a great photo could be had since the back of the t-shirt sported our slogan, "We cheat the *Other* Guy and Pass the Savings on to *You!*

Oleg was also conveniently wearing a Chilkoot Charlie hat with our logo on it, so when it was turned stylishly backwards on his head the logo and the slogan were both nicely displayed beneath the bust of V. I. Lenin. The photograph was duly taken and, never one to pass up a good promotional opportunity, I decided an even better photograph would be with the hat on Lenin, himself. We pursued this activity as quickly as possible for fear our splendid host would return and terminate our welcome, if not us.

In the almost tangible, comic but anxious relief of the aftermath of the photo session, Alexi said, "Of course, in Russia this would be sacrilege, but to me is very funny!"

I believe that photo still hangs in Koot's. What I find ironic about the juxtaposition of Lenin and our slogan is that we thought of it as a joke, but to the Communists it was an operating socialist philosophy. I do not know how you could better describe Soviet communism, or socialism, for that matter.

In due course our host returned and we all relaxed with more questions and answers, while I personally felt relieved not to be shunted off to a gulag for my politically incorrect behavior. At the end of our interview, though thoroughly entertained, I was tired and hungry. So, when we were told we were to have tea in the captain's quarters, I was not in the least excited to hear it. I don't know whether the mention of tea was a joke or whether it was a problem of translation, but what we saw upon entering the captain's quarters was not a tea setting. It was a feast.

We gathered around a large table covered with caviar, assorted meats, vegetables, fish and what looked like enough champagne and vodka to float the ship itself, and the inevitable toasts began. I was cajoled into making one earlier than I was prepared because Alexi, Sergei, and Oleg wanted to down another tumbler of vodka.

I had wanted to wait until Deputy Commander Goroshko had returned, but Alexi said he was busy and might not be able to return at all. So I stood up and reminded everyone what I had said in the Baksan Valley and what Oleg had said about how my mind would really be changed about Russia when they got through with me in Leningrad, to which I replied, "No shit!"

As soon as I sat down the deputy commander returned and took his place at the head of the table. Bob, who had been in the U.S. Navy for three years and who had been chomping at the bit to get up and toast the deputy commander, stood up and did so, explaining that when he had been in the U.S. Navy, the Russian navy was the enemy and how incredible it was that he was now being treated with such civility by an officer of that same navy. Past American naval officer and current Russian naval officer warmly embraced and more tumblers of vodka were downed all around.

Soon we were told that an entertainer of some reputation had stopped by and, though it had not been planned, we would return to the conference room, scene of the recent photographic crime of the century.

The entertainer was a large man, a Ukrainian accompanied by his wife, both in their forties.

Their son had graduated from the naval academy along with the son of another naval officer, who was also present. The couple had just returned from a tour of Mexico and the man said he was going to sing us a ballad—I believe he said it was by Tolstoy. He stood at the head of the table and sang the ballad *a cappella* in a beautiful baritone voice. For the next hour he and his wife sang one beautiful piece after another, both solo and as a duet. We all had tears in our eyes.

Following that remarkable musical performance, Deputy Commander Goroshko took Sergei and me into his office, proudly showed us his guest book, and asked us to sign it for him. He then paged through it, showing us a signature and comments by American astronaut Buzz Aldrin. He told us how pleased he was to meet some famous alpinists and how he had done a small amount of climbing in his youth. He also talked about some of the parallels of climbing and being at sea.

Sergei told him of my Seven Summits quest and explained to him that I had only one left, Mt. Everest, which I was going to attempt the following spring. Sergei himself was famous in Russia for being the first Russian to summit Everest without oxygen.

By now the Ukrainian, his wife, and the other naval officer had left, so we returned to the captain's quarters to resume our feasting and toasting. After another short absence, the deputy commander stood up and made a presentation to Bob.

We were all astonished. He gave Bob a nail that had been in the hull of the ship and was now attached to a book about the ship, with the description, in his own handwriting, of the events which the ship had been through while the nail was still in its hull. Bob was visibly overwhelmed and the two naval officers embraced again. More vodka.

Soon Goroshko stood up again and said, "Now I have a gift for my friend, Michael."

He presented me with a shard of glass from the bottle of champagne that had been used to re-commission the *Aurora* after repairs in 1987, along with his card, upon which he had hand-written a description of the gift. His card and the bottle shard are among my most cherished possessions.

At the onset of the twentieth century, when the *Aurora* was first built, she was one of the finest cruisers in the world. More importantly, she is also the ship from which the shot was fired that announced the beginning of the Russian Revolution. Lenin made the announcement himself, and his message is on the wall next to the transmitter into which he spoke.

During the earlier tour of the ship, Oleg had pointed to a gun on the bow and said, "That is the most powerful and destructive gun on earth, having caused seventy-five years of destruction with the firing of a single shot—a blank."

After the presentations and hugs and official toasts there was a lot more eating—and drinking. I cannot remember having a better time in my entire life. I felt so privileged.

I told Sergei, "I don't know how you pulled off this party, but I am truly impressed."

It was late in the evening when we departed, cruising up the river in the opposite direction from the Hermitage Museum past huge civilian and military vessels under a clear sky with a full moon. Turning back in the other direction we pulled into a canal, stopping long enough for our driver to step off on the bank and throw up. None of us were in much better condition and though some continued to party when we returned to the Astoria, I went directly to bed.

The next morning Bob and Jan and I were up early making entries in our journals over a breakfast of hard-boiled eggs, caviar and yogurt in the empty hotel restaurant. The first stop on a tour of the city was a beautiful blue and white, dome-topped cathedral that had once been a monastery. There was a small group of musicians out in front conducting a memorial service for the several people killed in Moscow defending the parliament building.

Next we drove to the Great Patriotic War Cemetery, walking through the mass burial area with its huge grassy mounds identified only by brass markers with a hammer and sickle and the year of internment of the occupants, then up to the enormous statue of Mother Russia, and back through the individual plot areas.

All these people, mostly civilian men, women and children, had died of starvation and disease in the nine-hundred-day German siege of Leningrad in World War II. Two thousand people are buried in each mass grave, and they go on and on, row after row, under the gaze of Mother Russia. The sound of funeral music being broadcast over speakers hanging from tall evergreen trees makes for a weighty atmosphere as the sorrow floats down around your head and settles upon your shoulders. One cannot help but be moved.

Though I had previously visited the cemetery with Shelli, it had no less of an impact on me the second time. Oleg said his mother and grandmother had been trapped in Leningrad for the first year of the siege, but had luckily been able to escape before they, too, surely would have perished.

Shelli and I had not exactly gotten off to a good start during that previous visit. Following my second failed attempt to summit Mt. Elbrus, I arrived at the hotel in the middle of the night. When Shelli opened the door, instead of the loving embrace I had anticipated, she started pounding on my chest with both fists.

Shelli, not part of a group like our expedition, had to make all her own arrangements for getting to Leningrad—not an easy thing to do at the time. She was not only worried about me being on the mountain, but had been ill at ease wandering around a depressing Leningrad by herself for a couple of days before I arrived. Shelli had no idea how I was even going to find her. Such was the Communist travel agency's communication that her official Russian itinerary was devoid of information between her arrival at the Leningrad airport and our departure to Helsinki by train.

The next day, things were better. We bought caviar, vodka and bread, and strolled the grounds of the Summer Palace until we found a suitable place to have the perfect lunch. We visited the Hermitage, masterpieces on display and the building itself being in shocking disrepair, and during our departure we witnessed a chilling scene of real life behind the "iron curtain."

At the depot, while awaiting our train to Helsinki, we watched the touching but sad departure of a couple of middle-aged Russian-American brothers. On the platform was a small band and festive gathering of family and friends, but it was obvious the men had been visiting and were saying goodbye to their mother for the last time.

Coincidentally, we later shared the same train compartment with those same two men, watching in absolute horror as two KGB officers interrogated, searched, and harassed them all the way to the Finish boarder. With mean-spirited efficiency the officers went through every single item of luggage and clothing, gleefully confiscating any little keepsake or photo they could find.

Shelli and I were also forced to leave the compartment for an extended period, presumably so the KGB officers could make an even more thorough, intimate search. We were not supposed to take rubles out of the country and I had a wad of them in my pocket that I planned on returning with the next year. Not knowing whether Shelli and I might be searched next, I took the opportunity to flush the whole wad down the toilet, which I could see emptied straight onto the tracks. I am sure I made somebody's day. After crossing into Finland, the KGB officers gone, the two men retrieved and proudly showed us a few precious family articles the government thugs had missed.

After a night in Helsinki, Shelli and I took an overnight cruise to Stockholm, where we had dinner with the two young Swedes I had ridden with on the way out of the Tibetan Mt. Everest Base Camp to Kathmandu back in 1989.

Shelli and I had acquired a taste for vodka, bread and caviar, so before flying out of Stockholm on our way back to the States, we stopped in a caviar store and bought some of each. We were not seated in first class, but we were in the row directly behind it eating our caviar and drinking our Stoli when the first class stewardess saw what we were doing.

I hadn't seen a single black person in a month and I was immediately charmed by her. She said, "Where'd y'all git that? I swear, y'all are eatin' better than these folks up here in first class!" It was so great to hear an American southern accent.

Back to the third trip to Russia in 2001, it was decided to take the guides and interpreters out to dinner at a hard-currency restaurant as a treat before we left. They made the reservations at a Swedish joint-venture establishment. It had a modern Scandinavian atmosphere and turned out to be more of a nightclub and casino, with slot machines, blackjack, and dancing.

When we arrived we were practically the only people in the place. The wine was almost undrinkable and the food was terrible, but at least the portions were small. Worst of all, the bill was $1,000 U.S. It was outrageous. I thought Todd was going to get into a fistfight with the waiter and then the manager, but in the end we paid, putting all the charges on Todd's Visa card in $150 increments because that was their floor limit.

There was also a loud argument over the exchange rate because they charged in dollars but then converted to rubles on vouchers and were using a rate of conversion significantly higher than the official rate, which was already much higher than the street rate. It was a disastrous evening. We could have given our Russian friends $1,000 U.S. and they could have arranged a banquet fit for royalty.

My last day of that 1991 visit to Russia I awoke at 5:00 a.m., packed my gear, and joined Ann in the restaurant for a pot of coffee—it was ground on the spot and cost $16. We took some group photos out front, and Oleg drove Bob and Jan to the railroad station. They were taking the train to Helsinki and an overnight cruise to Stockholm, as Shelli and I had done.

The rest of us were taken to the airport which was a total disaster area. It was small, dirty, disorganized, and over-crowded—a virtual nightmare of unruly squeezing, shoving, pushing, shouting and thick cigarette smoke. We would never have managed it without our Russian guides.

At one point a woman with a fist-full of tickets tried to push her way to the counter in front of us. We, and everyone behind us, screamed at her until she retreated. Once we got checked in we waited another hour in the main lobby, not so crowded but where *everyone* was smoking. I had had more smoke blown in my face in the previous week than ever before in my life, and I owned a night club. In Russia, everyone smoked.

The modern Finnair plane was full of happy campers. The flight to Helsinki was only forty minutes, and every passenger on it cheered when the wheels squeaked on the tarmac. We had an hour-long layover there before we boarded the flight to New York, so I bought some news magazines to catch up on world events. The next plane contained another load of happy campers who all, again, cheered when we touched down in New York City.

The next day I boarded my flight to Anchorage. It was only half full, leaving plenty of room to stretch out in an aisle. Writing in my journal, I reflected on what a successful, wonderful, exciting trip it had been. I had also purchased some nice things with which to remember the journey and I wasn't surrounded by cigarette smoke anymore.

I had finally stood on the summit of Mt. Elbrus. With six of the seven summits down and one to go I could devote my full attention to a third attempt on Mt. Everest, a story that is told in full in my memoir, *Learning the Ropes*.

When Ruben lived in a trailer in East Anchorage Shelli and I would arrange for our housekeeper to clean his place once a month or so. When he got to where he couldn't drive anymore because of failing eyesight, we set up an account for him with Alaska Cab. All he had to do was call them, and they billed me on a monthly basis along with the club's regular billing. Ruben's idea of hydration was coffee in the morning and boxed wine from noon on, so we got him a water dispenser and pestered him to drink water regularly.

We helped organize his seventieth and eightieth birthday galas—grand affairs at the Captain Cook Hotel. At one of them I got a kick out of giving him a cane with an air-squeeze horn and rearview mirror attached to it.

Ruben suffered some of the standard health issues of the elderly, but the end was precipitated while living in his ex-wife's condominium off of Tudor Road. He fell in the kitchen and could not get up off of the floor. No one, including Ruben, knew exactly how long he was on the floor without food or water until his young, attractive female neighbor and admirer discovered him. She took Ruben's garbage out for him and in return he took her to Sunday brunch weekly, though he would certainly have taken her out anyway.

When Ruben did not answer his door, which turned out to be unlocked, the neighbor called me at Chilkoot Charlie's. My manager, Doran, and I drove directly to the condominium to find paramedics on the scene as well as Ruben's daughter, Christine, who had flown up from California because he was not answering his phone. Between the two of us, Christine and I were able to convince Ruben to visit the ER at Providence Hospital—something she had not been able to convince him to do on her own.

Art

Who knows what it is about art and me? I've definitely got a thing for it. Our condo on the end of the spit in Homer was built in large part to display our art. Shelli and I busted the budget on everything, especially lighting, sparing nothing in order to properly display our collection.

I was collecting art long before I met Shelli. Fortunately, having a degree in art and art history, she has a love for it also. We even have a similar appreciation for most kinds of art, though we do have disagreements, most notably regarding my small collection of original German Neo-expressionist paintings by Bazelitz, Penck, Immendorff, and Rauch.

I am the only person in my household who appreciates art that makes a statement even if the statement is disturbing. The art of the post-World War II German Neo-expressionists is reflective of the tortured conscience of an entire nation. I find it powerful and evocative. Shelli finds it unsettling so the collection was long ago consigned to a storeroom, along with a lot of the rest of our art, until we can build an addition to our Halibut Cove home.

We had quite the honeymoon. We went to London, Cardiff, Dublin, Paris and Athens; on an eastern Mediterranean cruise to the Greek Islands; then on to Rhodes, Alexandria, Cairo, Kusadasi (Ephesus), Tel Aviv, Jerusalem and Haifa. Then we flew to Corfu and spent a week in Istanbul before returning to London and back to Anchorage.

I purchased some art during our first stop, London, and my young bride wondered how we were going to afford to get home. My purchase included three original watercolors by Paul Jenkins (1923-2012) whose large oil painting was featured in the 1978 movie *An Unmarried Woman* starring Jill Clayburgh and Alan Bates.

Parts of the movie were filmed in Jenkins' studio, and feature a cameo performance by the artist himself. Jenkins taught Bates how to look like a real artist on screen, producing the kind of paintings Jenkins actually made. We also purchased three original oil paintings and one watercolor by Alan Davie (1920-2014), Scotland's greatest living artist at the time.

One oil painting, a large one called *Flap Your Wings and Fly,* is a very early work from the 1960s. The other two are from the 1980s, smaller and from a series called *Bird Magic*. The small watercolor is from the same time period as the two smaller oils and is called *Disappearing Act*.

Years later, we purchased a couple more of Davie's paintings. One is very large, called *Village Myths*, from the late-middle age of the painter's career. The other is titled *Moon Mover* and is from the early-middle age of his career. Davie, also a jazz musician, traveled widely in the Third World and used a lot of symbolism in his works. His readily recognizable paintings are found in many museums of modern art around the world and, though expensive today, are not nearly as expensive as they will be someday.

I started out purchasing prints over forty years ago, and as I became more affluent, I began to purchase original works. Over time I replaced just about all of the prints by using them to decorate rentals or donating them to fundraisers.

I've always been astonished by wealthy people I know who build big, beautiful homes only to hang tasteless junk on their walls. I know I've got an "art problem," but I'd rather have mine than theirs.

Our collection is an eclectic one featuring multiple paintings by all the Alaskan masters and an international collection that includes works by Joan Miro, Alexander Calder, Paul Jenkins, Alan Davie, Leroy Neiman, Robert Motherwell, Haitian painter, Arijac (Harry Jacques)—our poodle's namesake—as well as paintings I've purchased during my travels in Africa, South America, Europe, Russia, India, Bali, Thailand, Australia and China.

Our original paintings by Alaskan artists include Sydney Laurence, Mangus Colcord "Rusty" Heurlin, Ted Lambert, Fred Machetanz, Eustace Ziegler, Jules Dahlager and many others, but my personal favorite Alaskan artist is Ted Lambert, Zeigler's protégé. I like Lambert's works the best for their impressionist qualities and because they are emotionally evocative. In Lew Freedman's book ***Ted Lambert, The Man Behind the Paintings***, Lew quotes Lambert's contemporary, Alaska journalist Kay Kennedy, as saying, "Ted's paintings have guts."

Almost twenty years ago I had cataract surgery. I had my right eye done one week and my left one done the next. After my first operation, I went home in the afternoon with orders to leave the patch over my eye and remain in a prone position. But as soon as my time was up, I started walking around our home looking at our paintings with my left eye, then both eyes, and then just my newly un-fogged right eye. It was like seeing our collection for the first time. Shelli got home and wanted to know what I was doing.

I said, "I'm looking at our art and I can hardly believe my *eye*."

The clarity, brightness, and colors had been so glacially covered over by my cataracts that I had never noticed how much I was missing. It was as if I had been seeing the world through a thin, muddy, yellow veil.

Shelli and I both delight in reading books about art and artists—fiction and non-fiction—and there are some notable ones out there. One of my favorites is *The Lost Painting: the Quest for a Caravaggio Masterpiece,* the true story of the discovery and authentication of a lost Caravaggio painting, by Jonathan Harr. Irving Stone's *The Agony and the Ecstasy*—a historic novel about Michelangelo—and a non-fiction biography of the great artist by Gilles Neret, titled simply *Michelangelo*, are both fascinating in their own ways. *Lust for Life*, also by Irving Stone, is about the life of the great Dutch painter, Van Gogh.

Art theft is also an interesting reading genre. I avidly read Matthew Bogdanos' appalling story, *Thieves of Bagdad,* about the theft of thousands of priceless art objects from the National Museum of Iraq—after our military took over the city—and our attempt to recover them. *Stealing Rembrandts,* by Anthony M. Amore and Tom Mashberg, is a fast-paced thriller about some of the most famous art thefts ever, and *The Art of the Heist,* by Myles J. Connor, Jr. with Jenny Siler, is the fascinating memoir of the promising genius-IQ rock star, a member of Mensa and son of a Boston policeman, of whom you've probably never heard, but who became one of the most notorious art thieves in history.

I like to purchase art objects and/or paintings while traveling, as mementoes of the places I've visited. On a trip to China, Nepal and Thailand a few years ago, while in Beijing, Shelli and I spotted a large oil painting by a Chinese artist. It's a world-class piece that depicts two Buddhist women on a pilgrimage to Lhasa. One, a beautiful young woman in traditional Tibetan garb, faces straight on with her hands held high in prayer fashion, partially covering her face, with a rough road and mountains in the background.

The second pilgrim portrayed is elderly—presumably the young woman's grandmother—depicted with her head to the ground, her remarkably detailed hands stretching into the foreground in prayer. The painting was not inexpensive, so we took a card from the store with us to think it over for a few days and ended up consummating the deal by phone from Chengdu, before we entered Tibet.

We have a collection of the works of Arijac, a Haitian painter, who was born in Gonaives, Haiti in 1937, and is widely considered to be one of the best of the Haitian artists. All our works of his are oils, a couple being of kids playing with kites on a beach alongside beached fishing boats. One is a female nude in repose, in the Modigliani style. Another is of elegantly-dressed people in a salon setting.

My favorite is a blue and green impressionistic work of two starkly nude female figures standing naturally on the beach chatting with each other, with three other women seated behind them, lakeside.

I have had a few experiences in my life of passing up the purchase of art, usually due to my errant Scottish frugality, and regretting the decision. The piece of art I most regret not buying was by Arijac. I saw it in a gallery in Port au Prince. It was Picasso-like, of a woman looking into a mirror with one of her eyes coming out of it toward her. I suppose it doesn't sound that desirable as described here, but it was a stirring painting and it has haunted me for forty-five years.

Although no great work of art, one of my favorite pieces from my travels is the portrait of Peter the Great that hung in my office in Homer. I love Russian history and particularly the part Peter played in it. He was the first tsar to leave Russia. At the same time he was building St. Petersburg, his new capital city, he also created the Russian navy and conquered the littoral lands needed to launch that navy through the Gulf of Finland to the Baltic and North Seas.

Peter was an intellectual sponge. He visited with Isaac Newton in London and learned ship building in Holland. He fought the Swedish army of Charles XII, the best army on the continent at the time, off and on for twenty years. And when Charles invaded Russia, long before Napoleon or Hitler, Peter was ready and beat him at the battle of Poltava. Peter literally dragged the Russian people, kicking and screaming, into the modern world.

I also have several small pieces I purchased at an outdoor fair in Soviet-era Moscow: a landscape painting, one Soviet-era watercolor depicting the fall of the church, and a lovely little impressionistic oil of an old lady, cane in hand, walking on a winter trail toward a cabin in the woods. It cost more to frame them than I paid for them, which is no reflection on their quality.

On my trip to Africa to climb Mt. Kilimanjaro, I purchased an original watercolor of the mountain by a European artist along with another painting, an oil of a curious warthog looking out at you from the underbrush. I also purchased a couple of ebony carvings, one being of a witch doctor and the other of a giraffe in repose. The former carving might have meant the end of our Bengal cat Tsering had she damaged it on one of her wild romps around the house.

Marshall Arisman (b. 1937) is an urbane New York illustrator and painter. He's been on the cover of *Time, Penthouse, Newsweek, Mother Jones* and *The Nation*, frequently portraying violence and predation. He performs one-man shows in the United States, Europe, and Japan, and his show *Sacred Monkeys* was the first American exhibit in China.

I happened upon a large classic oil of his when visiting a gallery near Union Square in San Francisco on a band trip with Don Fritz, my long-time manager at Koot's. *Facial Marks* is a portrait of a transmogrified male human form—one of the better, I discovered—from a whole series of such works by the artist. I had no idea who Arisman was, but I was struck by the painting and its noticeable influences of Francis Bacon and Lucian Freud. I bought it on the spot. The painting is so good that Shelli likes it, despite her aversion to disturbing subject matter.

My good friend Charlie McAlpine, a major dealer in Alaskan Native artifacts, was also a serious fine art dealer. Charlie was best friends with Elmer and Mary Louise Rasmuson before they passed away, and was the middleman in many of the art purchases by the extremely wealthy—by Alaskan standards—couple. Charlie also acquired a lot of art, mostly by Alaskan masters, and resold the pieces to other Alaskan art collectors, including yours truly. Until he gave it up, I always owed Charlie money. Notably, he sold me a beautiful oil of a lively alpine stream with mountains in the background by Belmore Browne.

Asa Martin was an old-time Alaskan physician who liked to party and was one of my earliest customers at Chilkoot Charlie's. I remember a tipsy Asa wearing a toilet plunger on his head, getting it snarled in the fishnet that decorated the low ceiling. Asa also liked to collect art by Alaskan masters and had a significant collection.

I became friends with Asa's daughter, Alice, a talented ceramist, and over the years, while visiting at the Martin's home I would admire the paintings—especially one depicting a fall scene, probably in the Fairbanks area. It was a beauty—the finest Lambert I had ever seen, with yellow and orange birch trees, a brilliant blue sky and a log cabin. Asa died, Alice inherited the paintings, and I would stop by the house on occasion for the parties she liked to throw. I always reminded Alice that if she ever wanted to unload that Lambert, she had a ready buyer.

One day, many years later, Alice called me from Washington State and told me that she was having some health issues, needed money and remembered my interest in the Lambert painting. I gave her the asking price. It's sad that Alice had to sell the painting under such circumstances, but she got the money she badly needed and I got the painting I had coveted for perhaps thirty years.

John Young was a long-established Chinese painter who lived and painted in Hawaii until his death in 1997. His large abstracts adorn the walls of fancy hotel lobbies in Honolulu. Until Young began painting only abstracts, he painted stylized horses. My first sighting of his horses was the large triptych hanging on the back wall of the bar at the Hana Hotel on Maui. I wanted one, so when Shelli and I returned to Honolulu I inquired at the gallery that carried his works. I was told that John Young's paintings of horses were simply unavailable and, even if one came up, there was a long line of people ahead of me.

A day or two later on the same trip, Shelli and I were to dine at the Maile Room in the Kahala Hilton Hotel. We arrived early and, while waiting for our table, wandered around the premises. There were paintings on the walls with gallery names and prices affixed and—lo and behold—down one remote passageway hung a John Young original painting of a couple of horses. It was lovely, and the price was within our range. The next day, I called the gallery and told them I knew where there was a painting of horses by John Young and wanted to purchase it. They didn't believe me.

I said, "If I tell you where it is and I'm right, you have to promise to sell it to me for the price that's on it."

They readily agreed, thinking I must be hallucinating, so I told them where it was. They were dumbfounded to discover I was right. They had completely lost track of the work but, true to their word, sold it to me for the price on it at the time of discovery.

One of the worst investments I ever made was at the behest of a young stockbroker in the early 1980s. The investment was in a limited partnership in a shopping mall in Denver and when the oil patch crisis hit in the mid-1980s, property values and the economies of Alaska, Texas, Louisiana, Colorado and other oil-dependent states all collapsed like folding tents. Not only did the value of my investment disappear, but I was still on the hook for partner contributions. Worst of all, because of new tax legislation passed during the Reagan administration, I got stuck with taxes on the mortgage write-down. Essentially, I had to pay taxes on money I had lost.

The young stockbroker had a sister who was an art professor at Wellesley College in Massachusetts, universally recognized as one of the top women's liberal arts colleges in America. He showed Shelli and me photos of some of her works and we were impressed. The sister, Bunny

Harvey, also does guest lectures and has been a visiting professor at Harvard University. Bunny's interests include particle physics, the cosmos and archeology, and she has done extensive archeological research in Egypt.

Her interests are reflected in her paintings, three of which Shelli and I purchased, and unlike the investment in the Denver shopping mall, we've never regretted purchasing the paintings. All three paintings are rather large. Two reflect her interest in the cosmos and quantum physics—*Measuring the Ages* and *Vertical Insight*, and the third reflects her interest in Egyptian archeology—*Imhoptep's Dream*.

Call me a curmudgeon if you will, but I've never been a big fan of the Alaska State Fair. To me it smacks of that "big sucking sound" Ross Perot squawked about when President Clinton signed the North American Free Trade Agreement that took effect at the start of 1994. From my perspective the fair is unfair, just like NAFTA was, but on a smaller scale.

The fair is subsidized by money from our state coffers, so they can throw "stupid money" at popular bands to play there. For years they have had a full schedule of bands, making it nearly impossible for local promoters and Chilkoot Charlie's to find bands to play in Anchorage during that time for reasonable fees.

We were preempted from holding any concerts in the parking lot during the second half of the summer because, even if we could find a band that the fair hadn't already contracted with for a price that wasn't artificially high because of the "stupid money" the fair throws around, we couldn't advertise it because all the air time had already been scooped up by the fair to promote their shows.

The fair just sucks a lot of people out of Anchorage for a couple of weeks, spending their money in the Mat-Su Valley instead of in town.

The last time I was daft enough to fight the traffic and attend the fair was sometime in the late 1980s, and I happened upon a booth occupied by an artist selling prints of an oil painting. The painting was called *Final Journey*, and I loved it. It is a simple but perfect representation of a couple of spawning salmon. The artist sitting in front of the booth was Gary Kremen (1950-2001), whom I was meeting for the first time. Gary was affable and charming, and we formed a lasting friendship.

At the fair that day, I told Gary I wasn't interested in any of the prints, but would gladly purchase the original, which was hanging inside the booth. He thought about it for a while, tendered a price and the painting was mine, though I allowed him to keep possession of it until the fair ended.

I saw Gary around town for a number of years after the purchase of *Final Journey* and visited him in his studio, which was located where Snow City Café is today. Gary painted a series of vintage bush planes in flight over Alaskan topography, some of which were selected for U. S. postage stamps. He also painted wildlife, some realistically rendered and some somewhat surreal. *Final Journey* is more impressionistic than any of his other works, which is why I liked it, and I urged him to concentrate more on that style, but to no avail. I think *Final Journey* is the finest painting Gary ever did and I'm proud to own it.

Gary was best known for a continuous sixty-two-foot-long painting of Alaska's natural wonders and wildlife, titled *Tribute to Prince William Sound*, which was painted after the Exxon Valdez spill. He began painting the work in March of 1990 and worked on it all day, every day, for nine months. It toured for two years under the sponsorship of the Exxon Corporation. *The Guinness Book of Records* was interested in the painting because of its length, and Gary was quoted as saying, "They don't have a category for the longest continuous painting, but they're thinking about starting one because of mine."

Gary closed his studio, moved to the Lower 48, and I lost track of him, so I was shocked and dismayed when I learned that Gary had died at age fifty-one in Scottsdale, Arizona.

Over the years we have acquired a collection of works by Halibut Cove artists, including several by Alex Combs, a patron artist of the community; Marion Beck, daughter of Clem and Diana Tillion, the patriarch and matriarch of the community; Sydney Bishop; Annette Bellamy; and Jan Thurston. We also have a number of paintings by matriarch Diana Tillion, who was widely known for painting with octopus ink.

Steve Gordon (no relation) is one of the most successful artists in Alaska today, if not the most successful, and a good friend of ours. He and his wife, Karen, and their four wonderful, adopted children have been visiting us in Halibut Cove for many years. The Gordon family originally visited us in Halibut Cove when I learned Steve did commission work and asked if he would paint our home there.

Steve is an avid gardener and can do more yard work in a day than a family of groundhogs. Over the years he has been a tremendous help with various gardening and landscaping efforts. We have a large collection of Steve's paintings. One of our rental units on the end of the Spit, since sold, is a virtual tribute to his artistry.

One of our most prized paintings—an original oil by Fred Machetanz—has traveled extensively around the state as part of a collection of Fred's works sponsored by the Anchorage Museum. As mentioned earlier, we were fortunate enough to get to know Fred and Sara before they passed away, thanks to Charlie McAlpine, who took us to their beautifully located home overlooking a lake in the Mat-Su Valley.

Our painting, *Crucial Moment,* is a close-up of a group of Eskimo hunters in an umiak, the harpooner having just unleashed his harpoon. It is a beauty—I believe it is one of Fred's finest paintings. We own another smaller pastel by Fred titled *Across Kachemak.* Our friend, Ken Flynn, who has a nice collection of Alaskan art himself and a good eye for it, spotted the painting online and brought it to our attention because it was the view from our living room window in Homer when we lived on the end of the Spit.

Shelli and I also own a sizeable Sydney Laurence painting of a mountain in winter, its slopes alight with alpenglow. The mountain isn't Denali. It's Mt. Logan (19,551), the tallest mountain in Canada, situated in the St. Elias Range in the Yukon. I bought it in Coeur d'Alene, Idaho, while there for my sister's wedding.

We own a number of Laurence oils, among them one of a cache in a fall scene, another of the northern lights over a cabin in the woods, a couple of small ones of Denali with quite different perspectives, and one of a fishing boat on Cook Inlet that was originally a birthday gift to a little neighbor boy with whom the artist shared a birthday. We also own an early painting by Sydney, done while he still lived in England, of a haunting derelict ship on the beach in fading light. It is signed Sydney Mortimer Laurence. Shelli has a dozen small paintings of Alaskan flowers done by Jeanne (Kunath) Laurence, a French-born artist who immigrated to the United States in 1920 and whom Sydney married in 1927.

Our Alaska collection, in addition to Alaskan masters and Halibut Cove locals, includes a beautiful sub-zero winter scene of the Interior by Frank Rademacher; a portrait of a Tlingit-Haida Indian chief in full regalia and a working fishing boat, both by Goodale; a couple of lovely oils by Marvin Mangus; one of Pioneer Peak with a Mat-Su farm in the foreground; and one of a of a lively stream in winter. We have a number of paintings by Scott McDaniel who used to live in a house only a couple of blocks from our Anchorage condo. Some adorned our rental units on the end of the Spit, now sold, and some have been retained. Also included in our Alaska collection are works by James Belcher, Leon Anderson, Kesler Woodward, Norman Lowell, Theodore Richardson, Rod Weagant, Earnest Robertson and Shane Lamb among others.

Shelli and I recently spent an afternoon in La Conner, Washington, with my son Michael and my first wife, Lilla. We went our separate ways in an antique store and I found myself upstairs looking at paintings, both hung and stacked against the walls. I spotted a nice little oil by Scott McDaniel for $245, which I considered briefly, then continued looking around.

Most of the paintings had prices either stuck to their frames or hanging on a price tag. Leafing through a stack of four paintings leaning against a wall, I found a roughly 12" x 18" oil of a cache in a fall sunset, orange sky and yellow reflection on a pond in the foreground, with a wedge of geese high in the sky. The painting had been done by James Belcher and was dated 1968—very early in his life—before he actually became a career painter. Belcher is right on the edge of being considered an Alaskan master painter. His works are sought after and expensive. There was no price tag affixed.

I presented the painting to the young lady at the counter downstairs, walking on egg shells and hardly able to breathe, but managing to say, "There's no price on this painting."

She said, "Oh, I'll call 'so-and-so.'"

When the phone rang for the last time before the recording—with me still holding my breath—she left a message about a guy wanting to buy an, "um (looking closely at the bottom right of the piece) James Belcher painting. Please call me back."

Turning around, she said to me, "How much will you give me for it?"

I said, being as casual as I could be, "I'll give you a couple hundred dollars for it."

She replied, "That sounds like a pretty fair offer."

I said, "I believe so."

She said, "Okay."

I could hear the clock ticking at the far end of the building.

I paid her with two crisp one-hundred-dollar bills, heart beating like a bass drum, dreading the sound of the phone ringing. She took what seemed like an eon to ring up the purchase, put the painting in a bag and give me a receipt.

I headed straight for the door and took an immediate left down the sidewalk and around the corner, where I called Shelli, still in the store, to tell her where I was. I've read many stories of people finding unrecognized and underpriced objects d'art at flea markets, auctions and second-hand stores, but until my trip to La Conner, it had never happened to me.

Right on cue after Michael and the girls met me on the sidewalk, Shelli said, "How come you didn't offer her $100?", and Lilla said, "You probably could have gotten it for $25."

Tough crowd.

I have yet to have the painting appraised, but I'm reasonably certain it is worth between $1,000 and $2,000.

One of my favorite Alaskan works, *The Happy Splasher*, is by the highly accomplished Aleut artist, Alvin Amanson, who served as director of Native Art at the University of Alaska Fairbanks. He grew up in Kodiak and has works on display in the Ted Stevens International Airport and in the Federal Building in Anchorage. *The Happy Splasher* is a saltwater scene on canvas with a larger-than-life three-dimensional papier-mâche' puffin attached to and in front of the painting, landing with wings outspread and feet akimbo. The piece hung in the perfect location in our Homer condo—over one end of the Endless Pool. Shelli and I nicknamed it *Everybody out of the Pool!*

I spotted *The Happy Splasher* in a gallery downtown one day and had to have it. We had no more wall space in our condo on Sorbus Way, but I sneaked it home anyway, and it sat on my bedroom couch for ages. I arranged for it to be displayed at the Alaska Native Heritage Center where it hung for several years, and I was convinced it would probably hang there forever because the staff loved it. Though I now had a place to hang it, I didn't want to ask for it back.

Then, one day I got a call from a staff member of the Heritage Center saying they needed me to remove the painting because they were doing some repairs to the building, and I said, "I'll be right over!"

Other Alaska Native artists included in our collection are Robert Mayokok, George Ahgupuk, James Schoppert, Ken Lisbourne, and James Kivitoruk Moses.

Perusing a catalog I used to get in the mail from Christie's Auction House one day, I came across a painting by George Marston, Ernest Shackleton's official painter on the *Endurance* trip. You may recall that ship got stuck in the Antarctic ice, was crushed and sank, requiring a two-year survival effort for the expedition members to make their way back to civilization.

The painting, done after the fact in the artist's studio, portrays the *Endurance* stuck in the ice with a dog team heading toward it. I put in a successful bid for it, and it hung on our library wall over a framed letter to Shackleton, written by a young female admirer who asks a lot of silly questions about his likes and dislikes, and to which the great adventurer answers with polite stoicism.

In his later years, the actor Anthony Quinn made a splash into the art gallery world with his paintings and sculptures, especially the kind of galleries I've learned to stay away from—the flashy hyped-up galleries that sell, among other things, expensive prints by artists like Salvador Dali, Leroy Neiman, and Marc Chagall, along with painted clowns by Red Skelton—accompanied by "Certificates of Authenticity."

We do have a few prints by some of these artists, used mostly to decorate rentals. I also have a modernistic pink marble sculpture by Anthony Quinn, *Pink Lady,* that has been appraised for as much as $30,000 and though I liked it enough to purchase it many years ago I certainly wouldn't give anyone that much money for it.

When in the Orient, Shelli and I love to stay in the Oriental Hotel in Bangkok. Once, while walking down the busy street outside the grounds of the hotel, I spotted a beautiful antique statue of a standing Buddha in the window of an antique store. We walked past the store window several times, and the more I looked at that Buddha the more entranced I became, to the point I began singing, "How much is that Buddha in the window?" to the tune of "How much is that doggie in the window?"

Finally we entered the store, looked at the Buddha more closely, talked with the proprietor and ascertained a price. We learned that the statue was a 19th century Burmese Buddha in the Mandalay style. His colors had faded due to his age, but I think he is probably more beautiful today than when he was new to the world. We agreed we had to have him. The question was, how we were going to pay for him?

Shelli came up with the idea for raising the money. She suggested we sell Michael's truck, the third vehicle I had bought for him.

My son, Michael, had recently become mentally ill with schizophrenia, was in no condition to drive the vehicle, nor was he likely to be for the foreseeable future. So Michael, in a sense, purchased "Burmie the Buddha," who has been another family member ever since and now resides in our library in Halibut Cove. Unfortunately, the packers in Thailand damaged one of Burmie's hands with a hammer while preparing him for shipment to Alaska. But he is still a beautiful, serene, stately presence. The story of my son, Michael, is fully described in my memoir, *Learning the Ropes*.

We own one other sculpture worthy of mention. It's the one created by Alaskan artist A. E. "Betty" Park, who painted the large figures of Chilkoot Charlie and Six-Toed Mordecai as well as the centerpiece and all the inserts for the back bar in Chilkoot Charlie's. She was a good friend of Ruben Gaines and illustrated a couple of Chilkoot Charlie books for him, as well as the cover for his two LPs of Chilkoot Charlie tales: *Vat I* and *Vat II*.

Now if I could only locate that painting by Arijac...

Ruben never fully recovered from that fall in his kitchen. Shelli and I visited him on his death bed at Providence Hospital. He was cheerful. Accepting his fate without remorse and with his ever-present wry sense of humor, he said, "If I'd known I was going to live this long I'd have taken care of myself."

As we held his hand, reminiscing for the last time, he said, "You guys have made a difference." It was a wonderful sentiment and Shelli and I were heartened to hear it.

Ruben made a difference also—a big one. Over time I'm sure the people of Alaska will return the love he showered upon them by remembering his creative genius and his contribution to Alaska's ethos. No one has ever been more Alaskan than Ruben, nor contributed more to what that means.

India

My friends who had traveled more than I, and there were not that many, had always assured me that India is the ultimate travel destination. They were right.

This adventure was the result of a dinner party at Chez Columbus, the name affectionately given to the home of Joe and Gena Columbus. Joe is a very good chef and Gena is a very good sous-chef, as well as both being wonderful people. Joe and Gena, Leonard and Tannie Hyde, and Shelli and I have travelled as a group on several occasions to the wine country in Oregon and California. We travel well together.

On the occasion in question during the winter of 2011-2012, as we were all sitting around the dinner table I mentioned that traveling to India was at the top of my bucket list. I was fishing for a response from the group and Leonard, who was sitting directly across the table from me, looked at me and nodded agreement.

Tannie announced in no uncertain terms that she was not interested in the least, followed immediately by Gena and Shelli. Joe was silent, which is not uncommon. I once found the perfect gift for Joe in Lhasa, Tibet. It was a t-shirt with five yaks embroidered on the front of it, and "Yak, Yak, Yak, Yak, Yak" stitched underneath them.

After affirming that no one else at the table besides the two of us had any interest whatsoever in visiting India, Leonard and I made a pact to do it together and worked up a five-week itinerary with Bespoke India Holidays. We flew on separate planes with somewhat different itineraries, but both of us arrived in New Dehli on April 11, 2012.

We were ensconced in the beautiful modern Oberoi Hotel in New Dehli, which sported a lovely elevated outdoor pool in which I swam for an hour on our first morning while Leonard found a place to practice yoga. This routine continued unabated for the rest of the journey, except for the next segment, which was mountainous Kashmir. After our individual exercise routines, we would meet for breakfast or lunch. Then we would begin our scheduled tours for the day together, generally wrapping it up with a shared dinner.

During our one full day in New Dehli we boarded a rickshaw and visited Old Dehli, Jama Masjid (the largest mosque in India), the massive

Red Fort, Chandni Chowk, and Raj Ghat, which is the cremation site of Mahatma Gandhi. For less historically educational entertainment, we sat with an elderly gentleman and his snakes in a downtown park. The old guy, with his coiffured white beard and mustache surmounted by an orange turban, removed his reptiles from a little round woven basket and placed them lovingly around our necks while a group of amused young Indian men looked on from the sidelines.

Bespoke India Holidays had initially left out our request to visit Leh in the predominately Buddhist area of the country. When confronted with the oversight, they inserted it at the front instead of at the end of our travels. If we'd gotten to go a month later it would have been an entirely different experience. Instead, we arrived in Leh, the largest city in Ladakh, in the far north Himachal Pradesh, just below where it borders with Pakistan, China, and the disputed area of Jammu and Kashmir, early in the season. Too early.

It was not even spring yet. It was barren and cold, and most of the hotels and restaurants were still closed, including the hotel where we had reservations, so we were instead placed in a small, somewhat out-of-the-way little inn owned by the ex-chief of police. The place was surreal. The staff was friendly, but naively incapable of running a real hotel operation. The guy at the front desk was a total space cadet who, I am reasonably certain, carried a passport from Tralfamadore.

We were stuck in Leh for five nights. This initiated an iPhone relationship between Leonard and our tour guide that continued throughout the trip with the guide trying to make up for our less-than-ideal beginning. One of Leonard's tech-savvy employees had tuned up his phone so that it worked perfectly throughout our travels over the subcontinent, thankfully, because mine never worked at all, though my computer worked just fine.

There was no outdoor pool in our "hotel" in Leh, which would have been frozen solid anyway. So we would go our different ways each morning, walking the roads and trails of the village and the hills over and around it. Above it all rose the massive 16th century Leh Palace built by King Sengge Namgyal. It is modeled on the Potala Palace in Lhasa, Tibet, and is nine stories high.

We took scheduled tours of ancient Buddhist shrines, including the Hemmis Monastery, the largest monastic institution in Ladakh predating the 11th century. But most days involved long drives across the sere countryside. On one drive we passed over a beautiful emerald river and visited the Alchi Chhoskhop Temple, which was founded by Rinchen

Zangpo in the 11th century and featured some of the oldest Buddhist paintings in the Ladakh. Ladakh looked and felt to me as if we were in Nepal or Tibet, China rather than in India.

The last morning in Leh we had to catch a flight early in the morning. The power had gone off during the night, and it was pitch black when we got up. On top of that a heating pipe had broken in my room, and there was water all over the tile floor. Worst of all, though, I had diarrhea and shit my pants.

Our next stop, flying east southeast from Kashmir, was Varanasi, in Uttar Pradesh. Varanasi could not be more different than Leh. It is a religious hub of not only Hinduism and Jainism but also of Buddhism. It sits astride the Ganges River and could rightfully be known as the "City of Sensual Overload." Varanasi is the quintessential Indian experience. All the things you want most to experience in India and all the things you are most reluctant to experience are intertwined in intimate and unavoidable abundance there: the trash, the colors, the poverty, the beauty, the history, the odors, the sounds, the humanity--all uncensored, undisguised and up close.

Buddha is said to have begun Buddhism in Varanasi when he delivered his first speech there, "The Setting in Motion of the Wheel of Dharma," in 528 BCE. But even under Mughal rule, Varanasi remained a vital center of Hinduism. The Mughal emperor Akbar was a patron of the city and dedicated two temples to the worship of Shiva and Vishnu.

A ghat is a flight of steps leading down to a body of water. The most famous ghat in Varanasi is the Dashashwamedh Ghat. According to Hindu legend, Lord Brahma created the ghat to welcome Lord Shiva. Hindus and Sikhs who can afford it bring the bodies of their loved ones from far and wide to have their souls purified in funeral pyres of sandalwood on the steps of the ghat. The wood is expensive and there is a crematorium available for those who cannot afford a pyre.

Those who are very poor will wrap the body of a loved one in cloth, weigh it down, and just drop it into the Ganges River. Many people walk down the ghat to bathe in the holy water of the Ganges, wading through the ubiquitous garbage and filth. While we were in the city there was quite a controversy in the press about the trash problem, but no one seemed to know quite what to do about it. Picking it up would be a good start. Where is Shiva "the Destroyer" when you need him, I wondered.

There was also, in the press, the proud revelation of India's newly developed multi-head, nuclear-tipped, intercontinental missiles. I noted there was no mention of neighboring Pakistan in the articles—only China, the main takeaway being that the Indians considered the Chinese to be their primary existential threat.

Having been picked up and dropped off from the Taj Ganges Hotel by our guide, we wandered toward the ghat through a virtual maze, past vendors in cubbyholes in narrow alleyways where ancient pipul trees, a member of the fig or mulberry family, actually grew into and became a part of the walls and overhead structures.

The pipul tree is a sacred fig, reputed to serve as home to many deities. Gautama Buddha attained enlightenment while meditating under the branches of one. It is said that the pipul tree will bring prosperity to those who talk to it, but that it is unadvisable to sleep under it.

Interestingly, and unusual for a tree I guess, the pipul releases oxygen even during the night. It is the home of many Hindu deities, including Lord Vishnu, Goddess Lakshmi, Lord Shiva and Lord Brahma, so it is never to be cut and is one of the longest living trees on earth. Jaya Shri Maha Bodhi, a sacred fig tree in the Mahamewna Gardens, Anaradhapura, Sri Lanka, is said to be the southern branch from the historical Sri Maha Bodhi tree at Buddha Gaya in India, under which Lord Buddha attained Enlightenment. The Sri Maha Bodhi is said to be the oldest and longest-surviving tree in the world, planted in 288 BCE during the reign of King Devanampiyatissa and brought to India by Princess Sagamittda.

We squeezed past sacred cows grazing on garbage. They had the right of way, of course. The place was ripe for Chilkoot Charlie stickers and I took full advantage. I used to have a lot of fun spreading our logo far and wide.

Everyone we met was either friendly or self-absorbed in some incantation or other. In fact, I did not meet an unfriendly person on the entire subcontinent. Saddhus—religious mendicants with painted bodies and faces, perhaps long nails or outrageous hairdos, and sometimes with only the barest of clothing—were numerous on and near the ghat and willing to have their photos taken for a few rupees. Some, I suspect were real ascetics; others were in it for the rupees.

In the maze of alleyways we discovered a perfume shop where they concocted their own formulas from a wide variety of natural fragrances.

"This is Goldie Hawn's favorite!" we were told proudly.

We took a morning and an evening cruise on the Ganges River in a rowboat rowed by two men as we photographed people bathing, or being cremated, one click of the camera shutter apart. Looking over the river—away from the ghats—the golden sunset with the Ganges in the foreground, boats silhouetted against it and incongruous jet aircraft contrails arching across it high in the sky, we saw stunning beauty. As the sun sank below the horizon, we floated flower petals with little lighted candles in them across the water surface. Due to the combined efforts of many boats, the result was quite pleasing to the eye as well as the soul.

After two nights in Varanasi it was time to fly to Khajuraho, built by the Chandelas in AD 950-1050 and home to some of the world's most unique erotic art—the Kamasutra carvings. The Chandelas ruled this area of central India from the 9th to the 13th century. After settling into our rooms at the Taj Chandela, we visited the large temples dedicated to Jainism and Hinduism, some as big as multi-story apartment buildings. Most were in good condition considering their age. They were dotted around a large park-like area and left nothing to the imagination. They displayed every imaginable form of sexual activity, including bestiality. The damage that has been done to the carvings is reputedly by offended Muslims who do not approve of any kind of humanistic, representative art, much less XXX rated.

After a night in Khajuraho we were driven to Gwalior—a cross-country trip that took about three hours.

When we arrived, the entire staff of the Taj Usha Kiran Palace Hotel walked to our car to greet us with cold drinks and umbrellas to shade us from the bright sunshine. As we were being registered, they seated us in the lobby and offered tea and crumpets. Indians like to say "Our guests are our gods." It really was very impressive. We felt like potentates.

After a day of visiting the 1,000-year-plus old Gwalior fortress, we headed by chauffeured car to Agra, site of the Taj Mahal. Like an exotic mirage, at a distance it appears to be literally floating on the banks of the Yamuna River. It was created by the fifth Mogul emperor Shah Jahan in loving memory of his consort, Mumtaz Mahal. A colossal, perfectly proportioned marble monument to conjugal love, constructed by 20,000 craftsman and laborers over a period of seventeen years, it is alone more than enough reason to visit India. The shah's son, Aurangazeb, felt the empire's money could be better spent, so he took over power and installed his father in the Agra Fort, high above the river from where the old man could view his handiwork, but that's all he could do. Shah Jahan remained in the fort until his death at age 74 in 1666.

While in Agra we stayed in the beautiful, world-class Oberoi Amarvilas in spacious rooms overlooking the breath-taking pool and hotel grounds, and the unparalleled Taj Mahal in the distance. No fan of Bill Clinton's, I would have to grudgingly agree with his comment that "there are two kinds of people in the world: those who have seen the Taj Mahal and those who have not," though I paid for my visit and we all paid for his.

After two days of touring the Taj Mahal and then the Agra Fort where Shah Jahan spent the last eight years of his life, we traveled five hours by chauffeured car to Ranthambore to try our luck at spotting some Bengal tigers.

In short, we had no luck spotting tigers, though we did drive in an open four-wheel drive vehicle through the park, which appeared badly in need of rain. We ventured out twice—once in the morning and once in the evening—and saw peacocks and several varieties of deer, some alligators, but no tigers.

Tigers or no tigers, spending two nights at the Oberoi Vanyavilas in what were understatedly described as "luxury tents" was a grand experience. The perfectly maintained grounds and impeccable service at this hotel are unmatched in my experience. There is a main building with the restaurant and bar and adjacent pool; the luxury tents are scattered, clustered and connected by trails throughout a beautifully landscaped wood. The tents themselves are as nicely furnished and decorated as anything you might possibly imagine. The staff anticipates your every need without being intrusive or presumptive. It is an absolutely amazing resort experience.

Next we drove cross-country to Jaipur, passing through small communities, photographing a kaleidoscope of activities along the route and sharing the road with everything from wedding groups dancing in the trail of colorfully decorated trucks festooned with loudspeakers blaring music, to herds of camels, some hauling building materials on carts specifically constructed to accommodate their gangly embodiments. We saw men who were having their faces shaved in open-air barber shacks along the road, next to a sounder of swine wallowing in putrid, free-standing water.

Jaipur is also known as the "Pink City." The entire city was painted pink during the reign of Sawai Ram Singh I as a welcoming gesture to H.R.H. Albert Edward, Prince of Wales, who was later to become King Edward VII, Emperor of India. If you ever begin to feel you are important, think about that. Much of the city remains pink to this day.

We were to spend two nights in Jaipur in another Oberoi hotel, the stunning Rajvilas, again with lovely spacious grounds, beautifully appointed rooms and a grand outdoor swimming pool. We were able to take close-up images of a gorgeous peacock as he fanned his majestic tail wide to mesmerize two drab-looking peahens, right on the front lawn. The show was awesome. One had to wish him well.

Jaipur has urban sprawl and the feel of a real cultural and commercial hub. It is a proud city. On the first day we visited the Jantar Mantar monument, which was completed in 1743 by Rajput king Swai Jai Singh II and features the world's largest stone sundial. With the instruments here, one can observe astronomical positions with the naked eye. Featured instruments operate in all three of the classical celestial coordinate systems. These are the horizon-zenith local system, the ecliptic system, and the equatorial system. I am not making this up. Ask me about them though and I'll have to get back to you. I'm a liberal arts major.

Our driver in Jaipur was a Hindu gentleman with a doctorate in archeology, but he drove tourists around all day because he could make more money doing that than by practicing his profession or teaching. The next morning he drove us to the University of Rajasthan area, stopping by his home briefly where he gently hand-washed his Hindu idols and replaced them on a mantel, then outside the city to visit Amer Fort and the palaces within it. Many of the medieval structures of the Meenas, the ruling tribe of the Rajasthan area, have been destroyed or replaced, but the Amer Fort and palace, built by the Rajput Maharajas, are well preserved.

Leonard and I, along with a train of others, were carried on platforms atop a banner-bedecked and colorfully-painted elephant whose trainer, in white pajamas and an orange turban, perched in front of us, riding just behind the beast's head. Once inside the fort we were met by our guide, an urbane young man with a leather satchel over one shoulder, who showed us around the interior and explained its history. The architecture and artistry were splendid, though of typically restrictive Islamic patterns and style.

On our last day in Jaipur we visited an antique store where we both got caught up in some spirited bargaining with the proprietors. It is also the day we were surprised to glimpse a totally naked gentleman of the Jain religious persuasion walking right down the sidewalk in the middle of the city.

Leonard bought some heavy masonry statues of some Hindu gods for a remodeling job he was doing on the entrance of his home. I bought a mixed-medium painting of a young man serenading a young lady with a long-necked guitar-style instrument; both are adorned in fashionable Indian clothing. He is sitting under an umbrella in the stern as he plays his instrument while she relaxes, stretched out in the bow of a small boat on a river, suitably entertained. I bought the piece as a gift for Shelli to distract her from the much larger painting I was compelled to buy, as is my nature—a beautiful copy of an original painting by celebrated Indian Malayali painter, Raja Ravi Varma (1848-1906), of Sir T. Madhava Rao, Diwan of Baroda. It is in my garage in Anchorage because I have absolutely nowhere else to put it. Perhaps I was thinking of another addition to Koot's. The Indian Room?

During our journey, Leonard was on a strict vegetarian diet and I had been a pescatarian for over twenty years. I ate then, and still eat now, seafood but no meat or fowl. Despite that, neither of us had any trouble at all finding good food during our travels. Both of us like our wines, and we were able to identify a local red and a white that were acceptable and affordable. Imported wines from Europe, America and Australia tended to be in questionable condition, as well as pricey.

Our next stop was the city of Mumbai, with a population of 24 million. It is the largest city in India and home to the thriving Bollywood film industry. We arrived by airplane for a three-night stay at the Oberoi Hotel, a tall, modern five-star hotel situated along the waterfront. The scenery outside my high hotel room window was spectacular. I was able to see from left to right the total expanse of Mumbai Bay.

Only four years before, in an incident that captured the attention of the entire world, the Oberoi hotel was one of the targets of brazen, widespread, brutal and systematic terrorist attacks against innocent civilians.

The terrorists rampaged around the city for two whole days. They attacked a railway station, a Jewish center, and the Leopold Café, a popular hangout for backpackers. The Oberoi is right up the street along the oceanfront boulevard from the Taj Mahal Palace Hotel, scene of the worst of the outrages that got most of the coverage, where the terrorists took over the entire building, slaughtering residents and staff with hand grenades and machine guns in front of international news cameras.

In the hotel attacks, the terrorists set their sights specifically upon British and American guests. The killers were young Pakistani Islamist extremists who had sailed out of Karachi. Of course there were the inevitable violent acts of retribution by Hindu extremists in the aftermath.

Shiv Sena, the right-wing Hindu political party, forced the name change from Bombay to Mumbai in 1995, though some buildings and institutions still use the English appellation—an anglicized Portuguese name taken from Bom Bahia, or good bay. The new name is a tribute to the goddess Mumbadevi, protector of fishermen, the area's original inhabitants.

Maranthi is the dominant ethnic group and language of the State of Maharashtra, of which Mumbai is the capital, and the Maranthi had always called the city Mumbai. Other cities in India have recently changed their names as well. Madras has become Chennai, and Calcutta has become Kolkata.

I had recently read the autobiography of Mohandas Karamchand Gandhi, *The Story of My Experiments with Truth*, and I read the *Bhagavad Gita* and the *Upanishads* as we crisscrossed the country. The Indians loved it when they saw me reading the *Bhagavad Gita* or the *Upanishads*. They would express their pleasure and inquire as to whether I was enjoying them.

With Gandhi fresh on my mind after visiting his pyre in New Dehli, it was especially gratifying to be able to visit Mani Bhavan, his home in Mumbai. It has been turned into a museum exhibiting lots of photos, artifacts and furnishings including the great man's treadle sewing machine, in such a way that you could witness how austerely he lived—this man who single-handedly brought the British Empire to its knees by the use of peaceful protestation. That home was the focal point of Gandhi's political activities between 1917 and 1934 and where his association with the charka, a domestic spinning wheel, began in 1917.

I should mention, and what better time, that the most important thing and perhaps the only favor, albeit unwittingly, that the British gave the Indians was a map. When the British, French and Portuguese were colonizing different parts of the sub-continent, there was no local concept of "India." Different areas were ruled by different tribes, the Mughals and/or local potentates. The colonizers logically played one group or ruler against the other.

The five-decades-long Trigonometrical Survey (1802-1852) was completed under Survey General Lt. George Everest. As part of this a renowned mathematician and surveyor, Radhanath Sikdar measured Mount Everest in 1852 with a height of 29,002 feet. Recent measurements indicate a height of 29,037 feet, but all agree the mountain is still ascending, so that must account for at least part of the difference.

We visited an open-air construction of the subcontinent made of stone, topographically correct, and to scale, that you could actually walk over and visually contemplate. I don't remember where it was—probably in New Delhi?—but I recall that I was really impressed with how abruptly the Himalayan mountain range protrudes upward from the northern portion of the landmass, visually dramatizing the enormous force of those tectonic plates colliding.

One day in Mumbai we took a ferry to Elephanta Island out in Mumbai Harbor, home to the ancient Elephanta Caves that are dedicated to the Hindu god, Shiva, and overrun with monkeys. It is like an enormous underground shrine built into the caves, featuring large, intricately carved stone representations of Shiva in various forms and manifestations.

We spent an afternoon walking through the Hanging Gardens of Mumbai featuring hedges carved in the shape of various animals. I was not very impressed with the hanging gardens, but it was a lovely day. We came across an older Indian gentleman sitting on a park bench in shorts, an orange golf shirt, and a navy blue ball cap with red stitching of the Big Dipper and "Alaska" underneath it. Turns out the guy had been in the U.S. Coast Guard in Kodiak. Small world.

On the way out of the park we passed an enclosed hilltop area with vultures lazily circling over it and a sign explaining that it was the site of a Zoroastrian "sky burial" cemetery. This religious group places deceased human bodies in an exposed location so animals and the elements will hasten decomposition. They believe a body becomes impure upon death and contaminated by evil spirits. Sky burial prevents putrefaction since birds and other animals can reduce a body to a skeleton in a very short time. It seemed to be pretty efficient land-use planning at the very least.

Driving with our guide through a heavily populated part of the city we stopped at an over-ramp with a vista which included an outdoor laundry operation in the foreground. It was the size of a full square block, at least, with rows of washing bins and racks of colorful clothes drying in the air. Skyscrapers loomed in the background as an army of workers carried out their chores in silence. We visited the huge, gothic Chhatrapati Shivaji Maharaj Terminus, formerly Victoria Terminus which serves as the headquarters of the Central Railways. It also contains the Rajabai Clock Tower which, inspired by the Big Ben and designed by an English architect, rises to a height of 85 meters or almost 280 feet.

We had a couple of very expensive cocktails at the Taj Mahal Palace Hotel, just to check it out and went out to dinner in a local eatery where we met an Australian couple on vacation. I said to Leonard after we departed, "They thought we were a couple." We both had a good laugh.

On our way to the airport to fly to Goa, we crossed over the expansive eight-lane, cable-stayed Bondra-Worli Sea Link Bridge, which was completed in 2009 after nine years of construction. It is proudly reputed to weigh the equivalent of 50,000 African elephants, and its breadth and twin spires are indeed impressive.

Goa is far different from the rest of India. Situated on the western Konkan coast, it is the smallest Indian state by area and an ancient ocean-trading center. Goa has been ruled by many different dynasties over the millennia, but most recently by the Portuguese. In the late fifteenth century, Vasco da Gama broke the Arab monopoly on trade and in 1510, Afonso de Albuquerque defeated the Muslim King of Bijapur, Ismail Adil Shah and his Ottoman allies. Albuquerque gained the support of the Hindu populace, and it was Portuguese rule from then until Indian armed forces captured it with little resistance from the Portuguese inhabitants in 1961.

After Albuquerque, the Jesuits soon arrived and established Goa Medical College. St. Francis Xavier of Goa founded Saint Paul's College—a seminary—and the first Jesuit headquarters in Asia, to train Jesuit missionaries. From Goa the Jesuit order spread to other parts of India and all over Asia, establishing Roman Catholic colleges, universities and educational facilities.

Goa had its own inquisition. Between 1561 and 1774, 16,202 people were brought to trial. A few were executed, some were burned in effigy; others suffered lesser penalties. The purpose of the inquisition was to punish relapsed New Christians, Jews and Muslims who had converted to Catholicism but were suspected of practicing their old religions in secret.

We toured the 400-year-old Basilica of Bom Jesus, which holds the remains of St. Francis Xavier. Before being interred here, his body had been buried in three different countries. We also toured the Church of Our Lady of Rosary, the Rachol Seminary, the Church of St. Francis of Assisi, and the Se Cathedral, constituting entirely too much Catholicism for one day.

In spite of the Goa Inquisition, the Portuguese influence upon Goa has left a sort of freewheeling, openly hospitable and nonjudgmental atmosphere. Add beautiful beaches and sunny weather to the tolerant locals, and it is no wonder Goa has been a magnet for adventuresome American and European young people.

We were taken from the airport to the Zuri White Sands Hotel, a sprawling resort, which was nice enough but to our dismay about an hour-and-a-half drive from the beaches of Goa where all the activity was. So we ended up doing a lot of driving. We wandered the streets of the small town near the beaches, taking pictures of the colorful houses and shops with a feeling almost of the Caribbean.

We had dinner in an open-air restaurant right on the beach, and somewhere along the way spent quite a lot of time with a young man polishing and repairing shoes on a street corner. He was charming, and very good; he practically rebuilt my shoes, top to bottom, and they are still good to this day. By the time we left him, he and his surroundings were nicely decorated with Chilkoot Charlie paraphernalia.

The next stop Cochin, in the state of Kerala, much farther south along the west coast—almost to the very bottom of the subcontinent, was one of my favorite locations. We remained three nights in the quaint, compact but comfortable two-story colonial Old Harbour Hotel with its lush grounds and my favorite swimming pool of the trip tucked into the lily pool-festooned back yard. It was laid-back and casual, like being in someone's village abode. I think we both felt more comfortable in Cochin than anywhere else on the trip, though we did not feel uncomfortable anywhere.

Seafood was abundant, and the food in the hotel and restaurants was excellent. We walked through the parks sucking fresh coconut juice through plastic straws right from the coconuts, which had been freshly opened for us with a machete. As we strolled we watched the fishermen harvest their overhead fishing nets, selling their catches of fresh crabs, shrimp and fish on ice from tables directly behind the nets along the shoreline.

Kochi was under the rule of a number of foreign powers throughout its history, with the Raja of Kochi its last titular head. It was the location of the first European settlement in 1500 when the Portuguese period began, lasting until 1663. Next came a hundred years of Dutch rule. They established Fort Kochi as the first municipality of the Indian subcontinent in 1664. In 1773 came the Mysore invasion, and in 1814, by the terms of the Anglo-Dutch Treaty, the islands of Koch—Including the Fort of Kochi and its territory—were ceded to the British for the island of Bangka off the east coast of Sumatra. India gained independence from British rule in 1947.

During our sojourn in Cochin we visited the St. Francis Church of Fort Kochi, originally built by the Portuguese Franciscan friars in 1503, and the original burial location of Vasco da Gama. His body was returned to Portugal fourteen years later, but the original location in the Church of Fort Kochi is still clearly marked. For the record, I never adorned churches or museums with Chilkoot Charlie stickers.

Cochin is at sea level. Munnar, our next stop, is at 6,500 feet. The Blackberry Hills Retreat and Spa in Munnar, a collection of colonial-style, individual cottages with one central facility, is built right into a hillside with a stunning view of the high tea-growing country. The cottages are connected by rather steep cobblestone trails lined with manicured hedges and flower gardens and shaded by tall trees.

During our two-day stay in Munnar, we drove high into the hills and took a short hike in the uplands where we were able to view and photograph our fill of Nilgiri tahrs, a small goat variety, male and female, both of which have curved horns, the male being somewhat larger and darker, and which live between 3,900 feet and 8,500 feet elevation in open grasslands interspersed with pockets of stunted trees.

On another day we drove down to the valley below, visiting an open-air market on the way, to the tea plantation. The plantations themselves are some of the most beautiful landscapes I have ever seen, frequently surpassing in beauty even the elevated, mountainous Napa Valley wine vineyards. The country is lush and green and misty with here and there small groups of pickers in colorful clothing standing out in contrast to the verdant green geometric patterns surrounding them. Outcroppings, occasional trees, or clusters of trees appear naturally within the patterns. Sometimes you drive through large patches of trees that appear to be poplars standing straight up like soldiers at attention in the morning mist.

The tea trees are kept clipped to waist-height of an average-size woman of the region, so they don't have to bend over to clip the young leaves from the tops of the trees. The best tea is crafted from those young leaves. Pickers are among the lowest-paid workers in Kerala, making a little over $10 per day. In 2015, 6,000 female pickers went on strike claiming collusion between the union and management.

There is one notable exception to this scenario. Tata, the car maker and one of the biggest conglomerates in the country, decided to exit the business in 2005 and handed over management to their employees. Today, 98% of the company's 13,000 workers together own about 68% of the company. Each employee has a minimum of 300 shares. Production has increased 58%, the company is profitable, the employees get fatter bonuses and dividends, and Tata still owns 14% of the company. When it owned 100%, it was losing money.

After a roughly three-hour drive, mostly downhill from Munnar, through a greenish blur of tea plantations, spice gardens, and exotic flowering vegetation, we arrived at Aanavilasam Plantation House, near Thekkady. The Plantation House is remote, in the middle of a breadfruit, papaya and coriander orchard. The guest villas are a short distance from the main house and reached by walking on a rough, raised, jungle trail of un-lumbered, unfinished wood. There is, however, nothing rustic about the guest villas—architecturally modern interconnected stucco struc-tures, and each with its own little private pool.

The lady of the house was an attractive widow whose husband had been an architect. She was not Indian. I believe she was either Australian or British. Breakfast and dinner were provided in her home, the main building on the estate.

From Aanavilasam Plantation House we drove to Periyar Wildlife Sanctuary for a ride on a boat—one of several—that you might expect to read about when it capsized and most of the tourists on board drowned. It was a waste of a day. The water level was low and dead trees protrud-ed from the waterline everywhere, making for an ugly vista. The only wildlife we saw were some water birds and a herd of some kind of large deer. The guy with the microphone tried to make it sound exciting, but it was not.

After two pleasant nights at Aanavilasam Plantation House, we drove to the Kumarakom boat jetty for transfer to the houseboat, *Spice Pepper* for an overnight cruise of the backwaters. We each had a luxury suite. In a way the cruise reminded me of being on the Thai khlongs because people lived facing the water, and we were slowly cruising along look-ing into their homes, watching them eating, washing, brushing their teeth, combing their hair, shaving—you name it. We saw people wash-ing dishes, reading a paper in a dugout canoe, traveling from one place to another for commerce or socialization. For a guy with a telescopic lens-equipped camera, it was a target-rich environment. Don't get me wrong. All of what was captured was what appeared to an outsider to be an insouciant, bucolic lifestyle, indifferent to our passage.

We motored out beyond the canals, with people living on both sides, to relatively deep open water and a rustic little marina on stilts where we purchased some enormous blue shrimp. Then we cruised back to the jet-ty for dinner and a good night's sleep in our air-conditioned suites. Early the next morning we took another cruise, caught a lot of people bathing and brushing their teeth, and returned again to the jetty to head for our final destination of the trip, Kovalam, approximately a three-hour drive.

I must mention that Leonard and I had a driver on the last part of our sub-continental journey who drove both of us crazy. He could have personally provided half of the material for Peter Sellers' hilarious por-trayals of Indians in his movies. I wish I could remember his name. No I don't. Let's just call him Reyansh, meaning ray of light, because he was compelled to shed a ray of light on and about everything, no matter how minute, mundane, meaningless or—especially—obvious.

He was a virtual fountain of unnecessary, unwanted and unrequested information about which he would babble incessantly as Leonard and I rode along in the back seat. Reyansh was supposed to be a driver, not a tour guide. Unfortunately for us, he saw himself as a tour guide. I asked Leonard to stop saying "Uhhuh" and "Yeah" over and over because he was inspiring Reyansh to continue with his babbling by implying that he had an audience.

We thought we had seen the last of Reyansh when we boarded the *Spice Pepper*. I was so annoyed with him that Leonard dealt with the tipping. I couldn't bear to face the man. Nonetheless, when we finished our canal cruising, there he was, ready for duty, the "Tour Guide from Naraka"—Hindu for Hell. My heart sank.

The distance from the boat landing to Kovalam was about 135 kilometers or 84 miles and lasted three agonizing hours. At one point well into the drive, Reyansh pointed to and described a more-than-obvious fish market for me.

Leonard, grinning, looked at me out of the corner of his eye and said, "Aren't you glad he told you what that was?"

I had never been closer to committing "tour guide homicide."

We were now almost at the very bottom of the subcontinent, deep in present-day Muslim country, with minarets, covered women, and limited alcoholic selections. A lot of Indians in southern India work in Arab countries and send their money home, so the area is visibly more prosperous and the Islamic influence can be readily seen and felt.

Regent Maharani Sethu Lakshmi Bayi of Travancore built Halcyon Castle as a beach resort in Kovalam around the end of the 1920s. It became an elite tourist destination in the 1930s. In the early 1970s the area really took off when it was overrun with hippies on their way to Ceylon and the Hippie Trail. From a small fishing village on the beach in Kerala, the area has become one of the major tourist destinations in all of India. With 17 kilometers of coastline encompassing three sandy beaches, separated by rock outcroppings, lapped by the warm, emerald waters of the Arabian Sea, it is no wonder. It was a perfect place for Leonard and me to recuperate from extended confinement with Reyansh.

We stayed in the five-star Turtle on the Beach Resort for two nights where we relaxed, dined and prepared for our flight from Trivandrum back to the States, via New Delhi. It had been quite a journey-the vacation of a lifetime. Leonard and I had never had a cross moment the entire five weeks. I had stickered the greater part of a subcontinent with my Chilkoot Charlie's logo. I had a shorter bucket list, a ton of photos and visual memories, and a very large copy of a painting by an Indian master with absolutely nowhere to hang it.

It has been just short of seven years since my Indian adventure with Leonard, and I am only now getting around to writing about it. Why is that? I have given it a lot of thought and it's quite simple really. The trip was manifestly overwhelming. The cultures of the various peoples, the history, the art, the architecture, the religions, the geography, the vastness; the sights and sounds and colors and smells, the contradictions: the poverty, the wealth, the humanity, the diversity, the functionality of such a mish-mash of everything; the fact that everyone could vie for and drive in the middle of the road and not crash into one another or even lose their temper; that every Indian is a philosopher; that the courtesies and the genuine hospitalities extended—all amounted to more than I could absorb and comprehend over a lesser period of time. In India, people use their car horns to alert and inform, not to alarm and condemn. This extraordinarily complex mass of humanity gets along with itself because it knows how, inherently. Certainly there are underlying crosscurrents, but they rarely overflow their banks. When they do, religion is usually at the bottom of it.

Lastly, in the "Conversations Emeritus" article, Ruben is quoted as saying *"When a guy has invested quite a number of years in a place, if you have any presence, you get spoiled. To go Outside and become anonymous looks bleak. But, the fact is, a journey across the kitchen is rough. 'Ten days ago that very journey nearly became his last.'"*

"But I never thought I'd make 81 years, so everything is bonus now. I'm happy to have lived in a time when I was friends with Bill Egan, Ernest Gruening, Cap Lathrop, Anthony Dimond. You younger generation didn't experience it. And that's too bad."

"Granted. But some of us experienced something just as precious to us. And for winters to come, when we hear 'Clair de Lune,' we will unconsciously glance toward the mountains, half expecting Gaines' voice to follow and say something that will stick with us forever."

"Those who indulge the old Alaska belief that the landscape has feelings and opinions may well suspect that the Chugach itself is a little jealous and lonely when it realizes that Ruben is warming his joints so far from their view."

The characters Ruben created will live forever as our treasured heritage: Chilkoot Charlie, Six-Toed Mordecai, Susy Floe, Mrs. Maloney and Clarence, the sassy seagull. Even crusty old Pop, after annoying Ruben by enunciating the "P" in the Pfeifer Insurance ad, would have to say, "He was a pretty good kid after all, dagnabit!"

Becoming a Rotarian

Even a tangential tale about me would be incomplete without mentioning Rotary.

I had been a Rotarian for many years when I journeyed to India with Leonard. Knowing full well how vibrant Rotary was in that country, I would have thoroughly enjoyed attending one or more club meetings. But our schedule was so crowded with tours and travel, with so little spare time, I was unable to do so even once.

When my friend, Walter John, the statewide manager of Alaska Distributors, a liquor wholesaler based in Seattle—since absorbed by The Odom Corporation—asked me to join Rotary, I hesitated.

People had told me that it took only one member objecting to the entry of a prospective new member of Rotary for the application to be denied. In 1995, my niece was going through an ugly divorce with the son of a professional man I knew to be a member of Anchorage Downtown Rotary. There were three children involved in the dispute and there was no love lost between the families.

The father of the husband had recently told me, "It's too bad. I've always been fond of you, Mike."

I don't think I said anything, but I thought, "What have I ever done to your family besides get your son a job as an attorney in the municipality's legal office when he really needed it?"

In addition to that aforementioned issue with a longstanding member of the club, I was also the owner of a controversial watering hole in Spenard and not at all sure the rest of the membership, made up of what I supposed to be the "Who's Who" of downtown business interests, would approve of me joining their prestigious club.

Walter's then-fiancée and later wife, Sharon Richards, who started the YWCA in Anchorage, was also a member of the club. Between the two of them, they convinced me that I would not be rejected. So I applied and, as they had assured me, I was accepted. It was reminiscent to me of the old Groucho Marx remark about not wanting to belong to a club that would have someone like him as a member, but I did want to be a member and I was pleased to have been accepted.

The Rotary Club of Chicago, formed on February 23, 1905 by attorney Paul Harris and three friends, was one of the first service clubs in America. The Rotary wheel was adopted because of the group's habit of rotating their meeting places. Today there are more than 1.2 million business and professional men and women in more than 30,000 Rotary clubs worldwide. Rotary is open to all faiths and is non-partisan politically. Its motto is "Service Above Self."

The members of any particular club will generally pursue a combination of local, national and international goodwill projects—from stamping out polio around the world to upgrading the garden at the local library or putting on an annual local health fair.

Rotary International also operates the largest private student exchange program in the world as a means of fostering world peace and understanding. Boys and girls in their junior year of high school travel to and from countries the world over for a year of education in another country living with Rotary families while learning the languages and cultures of the countries to which they are posted.

It is a life-changing experience for the children lucky enough to be chosen, as well as for the families. Exchange students and their exchange parents are generally families for life.

Polio Plus is Rotary's commitment to ending polio. It is Rotary's biggest and longest-lasting international effort. Along with its partners, including the United Nations and the Gates Foundation, Rotary has immunized 2.5 billion children in 122 countries and has reduced the incidence of the disease by 99.9 percent. There remain a few countries, namely Pakistan, Afghanistan and Nigeria, where the disease stubbornly hangs on because poor sanitation and civil strife create an unhealthy setting along with an inability to immunize. But Rotary is committed to completely eradicating the disease.

Anchorage Downtown Rotary, formed in 1941, is the oldest club in Anchorage and the largest, with around 300 members, and meets each Tuesday at noon. For those who prefer smaller clubs or need to meet at another time, there are numerous clubs in the city to choose from. They meet on different days for breakfast, lunch or dinner. All clubs operate similarly, but each has its own personality.

Other cities of any size around the world usually have a variety of clubs to choose from as well and most small and medium-size cities have at least one club. Rotary requires its members to have a sixty percent attendance record and you are allowed to make up at any club in the world, including the on-line club known as eClub One, the first online club chartered in 2002. I had perfect attendance for twenty-one years before I retired, moved full time to Halibut Cove, and could no longer get to meetings with regularity.

I was accepted into Anchorage Downtown Rotary in 1995. It was only a couple of years after I had made my third attempt on Mt. Everest. I had received a lot of local publicity, so my mountain climbing activities were well known. My club sponsor, Walter John, was the program chairman for a month and asked me to make a presentation to the club. I agreed. The date set was months away, so I did not feel much pressure initially, but as the time drew nearer and nearer I became more and more anxious.

I didn't want to mount the stage and just present a slide show on climbing. My intention from the beginning of the commitment had been to say something important; to express something worthwhile. On the other hand, as I progressed with the formulation of the presentation, I worried about getting up in front of the "Who's Who" of Anchorage and making a fool of myself.

My presentation was heartfelt. It was about my personal struggles and how I had used mountain climbing to overcome them. I was essentially going to bare my soul and I was terrified. I slept hardly a wink the night before the presentation.

Our meeting that Tuesday at noon was at the iconic 4th Avenue Theatre, the lingering landmark of the golden days of downtown Anchorage where I had once been required to eat popcorn out of a Kotex box. I used a slide projector and depicted successive photos of my Denali climb as the story of my life and my ascent of the mountain progressed. It was a full house, but you could have heard a pin drop. When I had finished there was a moment of silence and I thought, "Oh, my God, I've ruined my reputation."

Then there was a thundering applause, followed by the most sustained standing ovation I have ever witnessed at an Anchorage Rotary event. I stood there on the stage with tears running down my cheeks as the clapping went on and on and on. It seemed like everyone in the room came up to me afterwards to hug me or shake my hand and congratulate me. And it was in that extended moment that I became a Rotarian.

There are people who attend Rotary—some for lifetimes—and never actually become Rotarians. They are called "Knife and Fork Rotarians" or "Rinos." But there are many others who are real Rotarians, and they can all tell you of that moment when they became a Rotarian. Perhaps it was a trip to India to immunize children. Maybe it was hosting an exchange student. They will know exactly the moment.

I was accepted. I was embraced. And for all the good Rotary does in places large and small to make the world a better place, it has always been the fellowship that is most dear to me. The fellowship is what sealed the deal.

I so wish I had been a member of Rotary when I was globe-trotting, climbing the highest mountain on each of the seven continents. I cannot help thinking of all the clubs in all the different places I might have attended and made friends because you are immediately accepted by fellow Rotarians no matter the location. I have, however, made up in a variety of locations. I have attended meetings of all the Anchorage clubs as well as in Homer, Alaska, where I am an honorary member; Washington state; three clubs in New Mexico; San Antonio, Texas, where I attended the International Conference while president of the Anchorage Downtown Rotary Club; several clubs in Nevada; Oregon; Whitehorse, Yukon Territory, Canada; Argentina; Thailand; Nepal; England; Hungary; Italy; Barcelona, Spain and Portugal.

On May 4, 1987, thirty-seven years after the first proposal to allow women to join Rotary, the US Supreme Court ruled that Rotary Clubs could no longer exclude women from membership on the basis of gender.

Rotary was slow in accepting women as members, and in my experience there are still some clubs in the world that manage not to accept them. The Bangkok club I visited was an all-male club. One of the members told me with a wink, "We've never turned down a female member; it's just that no one has ever sponsored one."

He acknowledged, however, that their new District Governor was a female and that someone was probably going to sponsor one soon. The club I attended in Barcelona was also an all-male club—but the vast majority of clubs accept women. Clubs are more vibrant and get more done with women in them. The exclusive, all-male club is an outdated model that will disappear completely over time.

Attending my first district conference in Whitehorse, I viewed with interest a presentation by the Juneau Glacier Valley Club of a program called Pillars of America. The program provided presentations by notable speakers with outsized accomplishments or who had overcome significant obstacles—they were the pillars of America. Speakers were astronauts, ex-POWs, and other kinds of inspirational people presented in a patriotic way to middle and high school students. The Juneau club presented three speakers each year and the program had been carried on successfully for a dozen or more years.

I asked the president of the club, "How come this wonderful program hasn't spread beyond Juneau? It should go at least nationwide."

I then asked, "Would you object to extending the program to Anchorage Rotary?"

He said, "We'd be happy to help you get it started in Anchorage."

I grabbed samples of all the materials on hand, including posters, brochures and stickers, then headed home after the conference, intent upon establishing Pillars of America in Anchorage.

What I envisioned was a program in Anchorage that would involve all the clubs in town. I put together a small group of fellow Rotarians from different clubs and delegated responsibilities for promotion, organization of the venue, coordination with the Anchorage School District, and acquisition of the speakers.

The operation was mostly funded by the Mountain Mike Upward Quest, in which I sponsored some employees, then a fireman and a policeman on alternating years, to a guided climb of Denali. My staff and I, along with participating Rotarians and the climbers, raised money by getting people to pledge one dollar per foot of altitude gained by the climber from base camp to summit. Alaska Mountaineering and Hiking sold clothing and gear for the climb at their cost and all three major liquor distributors—K & L Distributors, Inc., Alaska Distributors Co., and The Odom Corporation contributed generously to the expenses. Every dollar raised went to the Pillars of America program.

Our first speaker was Viktor Belenko who had previously spoken in Juneau. On September 6, 1976, Viktor had defected from the Soviet Air Defense Forces by flying his super-secret MiG-25 "Foxbat" aircraft from Vladivostok, U.S.S.R. to Hokkaido, Japan. For those who are interested, Viktor has penned an interesting memoir titled *Mig Pilot*.

Viktor and I became friends. He wanted to visit another friend, retired Homer police chief, Michael Daugherty, so I drove him to Homer. I remember we watched a heavy-weight boxing match at Mike's house together, and Viktor helped me work on my hillside driveway that had turned into a monumental erosion problem at the time.

I also brought Viktor over to Halibut Cove. When he passed around the corner of the walkway and saw our house he said, "Dacha!" A dacha in Russia is a second home, usually in the country.

I liked Viktor. He was brash, hardworking, outspoken, obviously brave and principled, and had a good sense of humor. He lived in Texas, had married an American woman, and had a couple of teenage boys. We have gradually lost contact over the years, but his message to the kids of Anchorage comparing America and the U.S.S.R. was interesting, compelling and important for them to hear.

The Pillars of America program in Anchorage lasted about fifteen years. We would fill the Egan Convention Center with students who were allowed time off from classes and provided with transportation by the school district. I loved seeing the kids flock around the speakers after the presentations, asking questions and seeking autographs. By all accounts it was a successful multi-club program; however, when the Great Recession hit the state in 2008, sponsorship money dried up and we had to shut down the program. That last year I wrote a rather large company check to break even on the event, and I could not afford to do that at the time any more than others could afford to make donations like they had previously.

In addition to Viktor, we brought to the stage a couple of astronauts; the Native American actor, Wes Studi; a woman who had been kidnapped in Yemen; a pilot who survived being shot down over Kosovo; an Olympic wrestler born with no legs; a couple of Alaskan Olympic female cross country skiing champions; a woman who went from living on the streets to graduating from Harvard; high school basketball's controversial Coach Carter and more, including another pilot who, while flying as a passenger, assisted in landing a big commercial plane that had lost its hydraulics. I have to believe some young lives were inspired and changed for the better because of those speakers.

Over the years, Shelli and I have hosted dozens of Rotarians who have come to Halibut Cove in groups as large as eight, staying with us for two nights with all food and wine included. We offered the trips to the Rotary Foundation through the annual Rotary Foundation event, and Rotarians have donated rather large amounts of money to join in the weekend of camaraderie. It was fun getting to know fellow club members better and to simultaneously raise significant amounts of money for the foundation.

Additionally, we held our twentieth Labor Day weekend barbecue in 2019 for our friends in the Homer/Kachemak Bay Rotary Club. A group of thirty to forty Rotarians and their friends and families come over to Halibut Cove for the event, which lasts most of the afternoon. We provide hamburgers, hot dogs, and beverages, and the Rotarians bring desserts and side dishes with them. The Covid-19 pandemic cancelled the 2020 annual event.

During earlier years of the event, I made the burgers or tacos. Later, Dr. Bob Warren and his friend David would visit us for a few days and help set things up and man the barbecue, so I could spend more time socializing. After Dr. Bob died, Nate and Colleen Baer—a couple whose wedding I officiated in our backyard in the Cove—stepped in to do the same, usually with help from a few other friends. The last two years there have not been as many boat owners in the club as previously, so the Thurstons, owners of Still Point Lodge, have graciously provided one of their boats to haul people back and forth from Homer.

Whether it's picking up trash along the highways, promoting Pillars of America, attending a district or international conference, making a motivational presentation, putting on a barbecue, or making up meetings at another club, I have often told people that my only regret about Rotary is that I was not asked to join earlier in life.

I owe a debt of gratitude to Walter John for sponsoring me into Rotary. Thank you, Walter. I have personally sponsored a number of new Rotarians, and I am sure those who have stuck with it feel as I do.

It has been my honor to serve as club president and to receive the club's Merit Award, after a runoff election by the entire membership of the Anchorage Rotary Club. It hangs above my desk in Halibut Cove today.

And to think I had worried they would not even have me as a member. Receiving that award was simultaneously the proudest and humblest moment of my life.

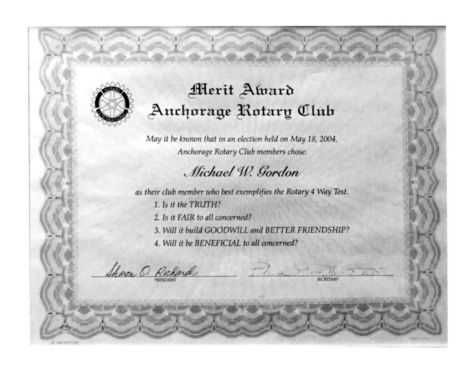

"First Bear Track"

His mark of record

    in the sun-warmed patch

    of clay is more than

    just the symbol of a

    passage through here

    recently; he left a

    promissory message

    with it, and the

    nature of the country,

    looking dead and icebound

    to the far horizon

    where the tundra curves

    away, is in an instant

    animated, eagerly

    responding to the

    statement made by

    him, the signatory,

witnessed with his

seal: abundant life,

not far behind, is

on the way.

A Chugach Album and On Youth ©1979 Ruben Gaines

"Hattie Boy"

Towhead can have a couple of different meanings. It can refer to a low alluvial shoal or sandbar in a river, or the "tow" in towhead can refer to the light-colored flax, hemp, or jute used in spinning. Thus people with light-colored and/or unruly hair are often referred to as towheads—especially children. My father was one such. His name was Harry, but his nickname and the name he was known by his entire life was Whitey.

Early in his life my dad had another nickname. The youngest surviving of eleven children, his older sisters referred to him as "Hattie Boy." The name Hattie is English for the French name Henriette which became the female diminutive of the French Henri, or in English Henry or Harry. The name Henry is derived from the German words "haim" meaning "home" and "ric" meaning "ruler or power." Hattie became a popular nickname toward the end of the 19th century.

When the girls returned home from school and everything was neat and tidy and in its proper place in their bedrooms they would announce, "'Hattie Boy' was here!" Dad had an alacritous compulsion for orderliness. I remember he had a shop in the garage of the house on Cambridge Way in Anchorage that he and mom moved into after the Great Alaskan Earthquake of 1964 destroyed their home on Mckenzie Drive. Using a pencil, he had outlined the shape of his carpentry tools—like hammers, saws, levels and pliers—on the wall of the shop. And that is where you would always find those tools: right where they belonged.

Here's where the story gets a little interesting. During the second semester of my sophomore year at the University of San Francisco, I lived off-campus on nearby Grove Street with Jim Braun, a Californian, and Marty Bell, who had graduated a year later than me from Anchorage West High School.

I remember one photo taken at the time particularly well, although I don't know where it is now or who took it. I was standing in front of the cupboards in the kitchen with Jim and Marty, showcasing rows of canned food in the background. The labels of each can were facing precisely in the same direction, outward and evenly. My roommates had never seen anything like that, so they assigned me the nickname "Mother Goose" and memorialized it with that photo.

I don't know if my dad had an angle issue. He probably did. I do. I like forty-fives, nineties, one-eighties and even divisions of same. I do not like odd angles. I don't like clutter and I cannot abide a crooked painting. Rocky Fuller—nephew of my mentor Skip Fuller, and the bartender at Chilkoot Charlie's who noticed that Shelli had gotten a desk— knew of this quirk of mine. If I arrived at my office and all the paintings and photos on the walls were crooked, I knew there had either been an earthquake or Rocky had been there.

I drove to California planning on a return to school at the University of San Francisco just before the 1964 quake. I ended up going to work to support my wife, Lilla, and young daughter, Michele. Bob Shepardson was the guy who at that time recruited me to go to work for New York Life as an insurance salesman. Years after Bob's death his widow Marion came to visit me in Alaska. Ours was a very caring but strictly platonic relationship.

Marion spent a few nights in Anchorage with me in the late '70s. I recall it was during the winter. Of course we spent some time in Chilkoot Charlie's. During Marion's last night in town I asked her what she wanted to do and she said without hesitation, "I'd like to spend another evening at your bar."

Marion and I were seated at the Show Bar being entertained by one of my bartenders, Tom Biss, who was reciting *The Spell of the Yukon*, by Robert Service. Tom was in great form. He was also the person with whom I was later to drive down the Alcan Highway in the middle of the night, destination Belize, to become an expatriate dive shop operator.

Marion laughed at Tom's antics and said to me, "This place is fucking crazy, but it's so YOU! It's so neat and organized!"

Now here's where things get even more interesting.

I recently flew to New Mexico to see my youngest grandson, Joseph, graduate from New Mexico State with a bachelor's degree in creative media. Next I traveled to Bellingham, Washington to visit my son, Michael.

As mentioned previously Michael is schizophrenic and had just resurfaced from a serious mental breakdown. He had been hospitalized for months and was finally getting settled into his own apartment. It was his fifty-second birthday. Michael loves sushi so his mother, Lilla, and I took him to a sushi bar. After sushi we took him shopping at a Michaels Arts and Crafts store for some posters for his apartment walls and to another store for some food and supplies.

Though the posters weren't put up until that night and then unveiled to us the next day—perfectly aligned with each other and their surroundings—the food went directly into Michael's kitchen cupboard. Each can was precisely lined up, the labels all facing outward. We celebrated with a birthday cake, but I interrupted the festivities by taking a photo of Michael in front of his properly organized food cache.

Talk about a testament to the awesome power of genetics. Michael's mother and I were divorced early in his life. He has spent most of his time in Washington State. He has, of course, spent time around me but he has never, as far as I know, seen me put the canned food away. He is simply an authentic third generation "Hattie Boy"—at least.

Though this tidiness is a trait that has been passed from father to son for at least three generations, it likely will end with Michael. Growing up I was always told by my parents that I had to be prolific in order to keep the Gordon name alive because my father was the only male in his family to father a boy. It was probably more important to keep "Hattie Boy" alive than the family name. I did my job fathering Michael, but Michael, being schizophrenic, will probably not father any children at all. And who knows how far that trait goes back in time and exactly how it got passed along from generation to generation.

I imagine a guy who looks sort of like me but hairier, stooped over, organizing similarly-sized smooth, rounded river rocks into a fire pit in front of a cave opening, while the rest of the clan looks on, mesmerized...

Afterword

My maternal grandfather, Michael Boisch, (1888-1978) was a second generation American whose father had emigrated from Slovakia via Germany and found work in the coal mines of western Pennsylvania. Michael worked as an equipment operator for the city of Pittsburgh and during prohibition he also operated a hotel with a speakeasy.

Michael had an affair with his second wife's sister. His wife brought morals charges against him and he was forced to leave the state of Pennsylvania for Florida. There he settled in Daytona Beach and opened a gambling and horse booking operation that he ran very successfully for many years until a forced retirement.

Vacationers from New York and New Jersey, on their way to and from Miami, stopped in Daytona Beach to gamble and party at granddad's club. It was the main attraction. Granddad was the big guy in town. After World War II concluded, Florida elected a new attorney general dedicated to cleaning things up. He told Michael he needed to retire and if he didn't he was going to sic the Internal Revenue Service on him. Michael did retire, fishing almost every day for the rest of his life, while his junior partner in the business, Manny, moved on to Las Vegas.

So I guess it's no surprise considering my genetic history that I ended up in the nightclub business. What is surprising is how things just sort of fell into place as if predestined.

Mel Rokeberg loans $8,000 to his son, Norman, me and Johnny Tegstrom and we purchase the Bird House Bar. There I meet Bill Jacobs whose mother loans us $20,000 to purchase the Alibi Club in Spenard. And, finally, I meet Ruben Gaines in a totally unrelated search for a new career opportunity and he not only allows me exclusive use of the name of his notorious, titanic character, Chilkoot Charlie, he draws the logo for me. The rest, as they say, is history.

Which event was most important in shaping the rest of my life? It's hard to say. There is no doubt, however, which one had the most profound effect upon me personally. Everything else might have come together, but my life without Ruben's friendship would be greatly diminished. I am who I am to a large degree because of Ruben's influence. When Shelli reads my writing she tells me how proud of me Ruben would be if he were still alive.

I hope you have been entertained by my musings and, though Ruben would always have been a part of my life, I have done my best to help bring him into yours, dagnabit!